CHOICES

UPPER INTERMEDIATE STUDENTS' BOOK

MICHAEL HARRIS • ANNA SIKORZYŃSKA

CONTENTS

CONTENTS

MODULE 1

RELATIONSHIPS

Objectives: **Listen**, **read** and **talk about** personal relationships; **give a presentation about** trends; **learn more about** present and past tenses and quantifiers; **write** a personal email with news.

TOPIC TALK

1 Look at the network and make guesses about the relationships in the photos (a-c).

2 1.2 1.3 Listen to Fiona, Toby and Sally. Match them with the descriptions (a-i).

Fiona: a, ...

a has a very close family
b has a difficult family life
c has a complicated family
d has lots of virtual friends
e has a few good friends
f has a boyfriend
g loves talking on the phone
h keeps in touch with his/her best friend online
i talks on Skype

3 1.4 1.5 Listen again to Fiona. Complete the information in the network below.

4 1.6 Pronunciation Listen to compound words. Underline the main stress. Which part of the word is stressed?

girlfriend boyfriend classmate grandfather great-grandmother half-brother stepmother

LANGUAGE CHOICE 1: PAGE 3

5 Work in pairs. Use the network to talk about the most important relationships in *your* life.

a

b

c

My relationships

I've got a [1]*big/small* family with [2]*lots of/a few* [3]______.
We [4]______. I get on especially well with my aunt Julie and we [5]______.
My [6]*best friend/girlfriend/boyfriend* is called Alice.
We [7]*got to know/met* each other when we were [8]*classmates/teammates/schoolmates*.
I suppose we get on well together because we [9]______.
We [10] ______ at least once a [11]*day/week*.

Relations
aunts, uncles, (first/second/third) cousins, (great-)grandfather/mother, half-brothers/sisters, stepmother/father/brothers/sisters

Relationships
all get on brilliantly, always have a real laugh together, are (not) very close as a family, don't really get on, get on well together, (don't) often get together, have rows, always put family first, hardly ever see each other

have a lot in common, similar interests and tastes, a similar sense of humour

are very close, are fond of each other, are in love, are loyal to each other, do things together, help each other out when we've got problems, like each other's company, trust each other

Communication
go out together, meet up, see each other, talk on the phone, talk on Skype, text each other, use a social network (e.g. Facebook) to keep in touch

LESSON 1

SKILLS

COMMUNICATION

Warm Up

1 **Work in pairs. What are the advantages of modern communication technology, like smartphones?**

You can easily keep in touch with people who live a long way away.

Reading

2 **Read the article quickly. What is its main argument?**

a Communication technology makes our relationships with other people better.
b Communication technology can be bad for us and we need to learn how to use it better.
c We should stop using communication technology because it is bad for us.

3 **Read the article again. Which of these reasons supporting the main argument can you find in the text?**

a Communication technology can be addictive.
b Communication technology is bad for relationships between people.
c Because of it, people waste time that could be used for other things (e.g. sport or study).
d People don't pay attention to what they're doing because of communication technology.
e People give away too much personal information online.
f People are losing their social skills because of communication technology.

4 SKILLS BUILDER 10 **Use the strategies to 'map' the reasons given in the text. Then evaluate the argument.**

I think the article is well-argued/not well-argued because it mentions ...

5 **Do you agree with Professor Turkle? Why/Why not?**

I agree with her because I think that we use communication technology too much.

Real Lives 1.7

Alone Together

Professor Sherry Turkle thinks communication technology has such an important impact that we need to start taking into account its effects on our lives. Professor Turkle talks about her new book.

Over the past fifteen years, my research has documented that, for many, online life and smartphone connections have got in the way of things that people feel are important. We're so busy communicating that we don't have time to think, we don't have time to sit down and have a conversation. We'd rather text than talk. It makes us feel more in control.

A young woman Skypes her grandmother in another city but does her email during these conversations. She tells me that she hardly pays attention to what her grandmother is saying. The young woman does not feel good about these conversations, although her grandmother seems pleased. A mother explains that she cannot resist the 'little red light' telling her that she has a new message on her BlackBerry, even when she is driving on the motorway with her children in the car. The unread message, that red light, has come to stand for our feelings of hope. That someone wants us, that something new is coming into our lives.

A woman explains that when she was in hospital, her husband worked from her bedside but was so busy with his device that he didn't talk to her.

6 Vocabulary Look at the Word Builder. Match the verbs in bold with the paraphrases below.

- is our responsibility to
- thinking about
- listens to
- contact
- established
- negatively affected

Word Builder Multi-part verbs (1)

1. We need to start **taking into account** its effects on our lives.
2. Smartphone connections have **got in the way of** things that people feel are important.
3. She hardly **pays attention to** what her grandmother is saying.
4. If you really need to **get in touch with** me, just shoot me a text.
5. We have **put in place** a powerful technology.
6. It **is up to us to** make and shape it.

LANGUAGE CHOICE 2: PAGE 3

Children complain about parents texting at breakfast and dinner. Parents at the playground push a swing with one hand and scroll through their messages with the other. I go to a funeral and people are texting, hiding their phones under their hymn books.

I remember, not so long ago, when a student remarked on the first time a friend interrupted a conversation to take a call. 'It made me feel like he was putting me on pause,' he said. Now, we all treat each other as 'pausables'.

An impatient high-school student says to me, 'If you really need to get in touch with me, just shoot me a text.' He sounds just like my university colleagues who tell me they would rather avoid face-to-face meetings and would prefer to communicate with 'real-time texts'.

I do not want to condemn technology but think that we have put in place a powerful technology and have not yet learned to use it in the best way. But these are early days for the internet. It is up to us to make and shape it. I wrote my new book to mark a time of opportunity. We need to form a more empowering partnership with technology. Our job is to shape it to our human purposes.

7 Look at the Sentence Builder. What comes after *so* and what after *such*: a noun or an adjective?

Sentence Builder Result linkers (1)

1. He is **so** busy with his device **that** he doesn't talk to her.
2. Communication technology has **such an** (important) impact **that** we need to start taking into account its effects on our lives.

LANGUAGE CHOICE 3: PAGE 3

8 Join the sentences using *so* or *such*.

1. I was very busy. I forgot to call my grandmother.
   I was so busy that I forgot to call my grandmother.
2. I spent a long time on the computer. I didn't get to bed until 3 a.m.
3. My internet connection is very slow. I can't watch video or TV on my computer.
4. I have got a very old phone. It hasn't got an internet connection or a camera.
5. She is a real Facebook addict. She updates her wall ten times a day.
6. Some people have good fun online. They hardly ever go out and meet people.

Your Choice

9 Work in pairs. Choose two of the options (a-c) to discuss.

a **Social media use (e.g. Twitter/Facebook)**
How often do you use social media? How many hours do you spend online every week? Has your use ever affected your studies or your sleep?

b **Online friendship**
How many friends have you got on social networks? How many of them are real and how many are virtual? Have you ever met any of your new virtual friends?

c **Dangers of social media**
Have you ever seen cyberbullying online? Have you ever given away personal information? Has a stranger ever approached you online?

10 Tell the class some of your experiences and opinions.

We've seen quite a few examples of cyberbullying. We think that ...

No Comment

'Twitter is a great place to tell the world what you're thinking before you've had a chance to think about it.' Chris Pirillo

LESSON 2

GRAMMAR

LOVE RESEARCH

Warm Up

1 Look at the photos of couples (a-c). Read the sentences. Which of them do you think are true about romantic relationships?

1 People usually think that their partners are more attractive than they really are.
2 In relationships, people find differences attractive.
3 Men like women who are more intelligent than they are.
4 You should boast about your achievements when you're trying to chat up a girl.

2 Read the text and check your guesses from Exercise 1.

3 What would your ideal girlfriend/boyfriend be like? What, in your opinion, is the recipe for an ideal relationship?

Present and past tenses

4 Read the sentences (1-9) in red in the text. Match them with the names of tenses. There is more than one example of some of the tenses.

- Present Simple
- Present Continuous
- Present Perfect
- Present Perfect Continuous *1*
- Past Simple
- Past Continuous
- Past Perfect

5 Match the present tenses with the uses (a-f) and the past tenses with the uses (g-i). Look again at the sentences (1-9) from the text for help.

- Present Simple *a, c*
- Present Continuous
- Present Perfect
- Present Perfect Continuous
- Past Simple
- Past Continuous
- Past Perfect

a it happens regularly
b this state or situation started in the past and is still true
c it is a permanent situation
d it is happening now or around now
e it happened in the past but it doesn't matter when
f this activity started in the past and is going on now
g it happened at a specific time in the past
h it happened earlier than other events in the past
i this activity formed the background to some past events

1.8

Q: For a few weeks now [1]I've been going out with a man who is much better looking than me. [2]We were dancing in a club last night and a dozen women tried to chat him up. Is our relationship going to survive?

A: [3]People usually go for someone as good-looking or plain as they are (though this rule excludes rich people, who are all gorgeous ☺). Those who are less similar are more likely to split up. A study found that the husbands who were more attractive than their wives were less supportive of them. Interestingly, we usually overestimate how attractive our partners really are.

Q: My girlfriend loves opera and [4]I have always hated it. Do opposites attract?

A: [5]We're not dealing with magnetic poles here, where opposites really attract. In relationships, couples usually share religious and political beliefs, are about the same age and similar in their education and intelligence.

Q: [6]My last boyfriend dumped me because [7]I had won the scholarship for the best student in our college. Should I act stupid because men don't like intelligent women?

A: Both men and women rate the importance of intelligence equally. Interestingly, [8]men prefer women who are almost as smart as them but it's usually not intelligence but being opinionated or uninterested that will put men off. So play nice rather than dumb. Interestingly, there is no evidence suggesting men want someone less attractive than them.

Q: [9]I've never managed to chat up a girl. Are there chat-up lines that work?

A: A chat-up line works if it makes you look interesting, humorous, athletic or rich. Questions work better than statements. In three-minute speed dates, men who had started the conversation with 'What is your favourite pizza topping?' were voted the most popular. The worst lines were 'I have a PhD in computing' and 'My best friend is a helicopter pilot'.

Practice

6 Choose the correct thing to say in each situation.

1 You are explaining why Peter is not at home.
   a He's gone out with Kate.
   b He'd gone out with Kate.
   c He's going out with Kate.

2 You want to say that Kate loved Peter.
   a She's been in love with Peter for weeks.
   b She's in love with Peter.
   c She was in love with Peter.

3 You want to say that first Peter and Kate divorced and then their dog Digger died.
   a They had divorced when Digger died.
   b They divorced when Digger died.
   c They were divorcing when Digger died.

7 Use the cues to write sentences. There may be more than one correct answer in some cases.

1 You're into speed-dating. (I / love speed dates)
   I love speed dates.
2 You're talking about your last date. (We / go to a concert)
3 You meet a friend you haven't seen for some time. (What / you do / recently?)
4 You're unhappy. (My girlfriend / dump me)
5 You're interested in your friend's current boyfriend. (Who / you go out with?)
6 You're explaining why you broke up with your boyfriend. (I / break up with him / because / he / cheat on me)
7 Your friend looks very sad. (What / happen?)
8 You're describing the first date with your girlfriend. (She / wear a red dress)

8 Complete the dialogue with the correct form of the verbs in brackets.

A: Hi, Paula. I [1]________ (not see) you for ages. What [2]________ (you / do) here so early in the morning?
B: Hi, Julie. I [3]________ (go) to work. I [4]________ (work) for a student dating website for two weeks.
A: What [5]________ (be) your job?
B: I [6]________ (improve) people's profiles. Many people [7]________ (not know) what to write about themselves and [8]________ (send) very boring profiles.
A: How [9]________ (you / get) this job?
B: I [10]________ (surf) the Net when I [11]________ (find) an advertisement. I [12]________ (apply) but they [13]________ (say) they [14]________ (hire) someone else. But, after two days, they [15]________ (call) me with a job offer.

Grammar Alive
Sharing personal information

9 1.9 Listen to the dialogue. Use the cues and the correct name (Joe, Steve or Lucy) to write sentences. Use correct tenses.

1 study for exams
   Joe has been studying for exams.
2 meet a lovely girl
3 study photography
4 take photos for a project
5 meet Lucy in the park
6 take a photo of Lucy
7 break up with her boyfriend
8 wait for Steve's call

10 Work in pairs. Use the questions below to interview your partner about his/her love life. You don't have to tell the truth!

- Are you seeing anyone?
- What does your boyfriend/girlfriend do?
- How long have you been going out with him/her?
- Have you met his/her family?
- What do you know about his/her family?
- Where do you usually go together?
- How did you meet?
- Who did you go out with before him/her?
- Why did you break up?

A: *Are you seeing anyone?*
B: *Yes, I'm seeing someone famous.*
A: *What does she do?*
B: *She is a rock singer.*

LESSON 3 SKILLS

FAMILIES

Families in the UK

Warm Up

1 Look at the chart. Which of these kinds of households are shown in it? Match them with the numbers on the chart.

a unmarried couples with their own children

2 Cohabiting (birth parents)

b unmarried couples with stepchildren
c married childless couples
d single parents with children
e married parents with their own children
f extended families (three generations living together)
g remarried parents with stepchildren
h unmarried couples without children
i single people living on their own (e.g. unmarried, separated, divorced, widows, widowers)

2 Your Culture **What do you think are the most and least common types of families and households in your country now?**

Listening

3 1.10 1.11 **Listen to a radio interview. What are some of the important trends in British family life?**

There are more households.

4 1.10 1.11 **Listen again and choose the best answers to the questions.**

1 The number of households has gone up by:
a 17 million. b a million. c 16 million.

2 The proportion of households with people living on their own is now:
a 3%. b 25%. c 33%.

3 The number of people marrying:
a has gone down a little.
b has stayed the same.
c has gone down a lot

4 The number of unmarried couples has gone up by:
a over two million. b under two million. c nearly two million.

5 The proportion of British children living with one parent is about:
a 25%. b 33%. c 50%.

6 Out of young adult children who live at home there are:
a more women than men.
b more men than women.
c the same number of men as women.

7 The number of extended families is:
a going down. b staying the same. c increasing.

8 About a third of households have:
a childless couples.
b extended families.
c families with children.

DVD Choice

5 DVD 1 **Watch the documentary without sound. Are the sentences true (T) or false (F)? Watch the documentary again with sound and check your guesses.**

1 It is about an extended family in India.
2 Sukhvinder is the father of four young children.
3 Sukhvinder's parents live with him.
4 The family are close and all help each other.
5 The family are happy living together.

6 DVD 1 **Watch again. Match the comments with the people: journalist (J), Sukhvinder (S), Anmol (A) and Tsher Preet (TP).**

1 People with Indian roots are more likely to live in extended families than other British people.
2 You should look after your parents because they have done so much for you.
3 I enjoy helping my granddad use the internet.
4 We believe that if you look after your parents, you will be looked after yourself.
5 This is how our people have always lived and I would never change it.

7 **Would you like to live in the same way as the Bamrah family? Why/Why not?**

Speaking Workshop

8 1.12 1.13 **Listen to the presentation. Complete the sentences.**

1 _________ of 19-year-olds are now qualified to go to college or university.
2 Unemployment is at nearly twenty-two percent for _________ -year-olds.
3 The number of obese boys in the UK _________ between 1995 and 2009.
4 Only _________ of 11 to 16-year-old British boys do an hour's exercise every day.
5 98.7% of the UK's young people are _________ .
6 Over ninety percent of British young people use _________ regularly.
7 British 12 to 16-year-olds spend nearly as much time online as they do _________ .

9 **Look at the Talk Builder. Match the words or expressions in bold with the meanings (a-g).**

a the way that a situation is changing *trend*
b number
c to increase
d to decrease
e quantity
f conclude
g to talk about (x 2)

Talk Builder
A presentation: describing trends

1 In this talk we're going to **look at** ...
2 The first interesting **trend** to point out is that ...
3 That **figure** is up by ... percent from last year.
4 Another area to **comment on** is ...
5 The proportion of ... **has gone up** to ... percent.
6 The percentage of ... went up from ... percent to ... percent between 1995 and 2009.
7 The **amount** of ... **has gone down**, too.
8 Only one in three ... and a quarter of ... do ...
9 One of the main reasons for young people being more ... is ...
10 So to **summarise**, ...

SKILLS BUILDER 32

10 1.14 Pronunciation **Listen and repeat the sentences describing trends.**

11 **Complete the sentences with words from the Talk Builder.**

1 The *proportion* of young people without work has gone _________ to over a fifth.
2 One worrying _________ to point out is that nearly one _________ five boys are obese.
3 The _________ of time spent watching TV has gone _________ to 17 hours from 20 hours two years ago.
4 The _________ of young people using the Net went up _________ 60% _________ 98% _________ 2004 and 2011.

12 **Work in pairs. Give a presentation about trends.**

1 **Look at the statistics and tables on page 105 and write notes.**
2 SKILLS BUILDER 33 **Use the strategies to prepare your presentation.**
3 **Give your presentation to another pair. Take turns to give information. Afterwards, ask questions about the other pair's talk.**

13 **What was the most interesting or surprising information in your partners' talk? Tell the class.**

I was surprised that only 37% of American young people sent messages every day on social networks.

LESSON 4

GRAMMAR

MODERN PARENTS

Warm Up

1 **Look at the photo. What do you argue about with your parents?**

2 **Read the text. What should/shouldn't parents of teenagers do to gain their children's respect?**

(1.15)

The concept of parental authority has changed. Today, no parent can take their children's respect for granted: authority has to be earned. Several studies have shown the following problems.

1 Trust

A lot of young people say their parents don't trust them. Some of them have no privacy: their parents read all their emails and enter their rooms without knocking. All of these actions demonstrate lack of respect. Consequently, these teenagers have little respect for their parents.

2 Communication

Hardly any teens discuss their problems with their parents. That's because very few teens feel their parents really listen to them. Instead, most parents tend to fire off an immediate response to their kids' first sentence.

3 Freedom

Interestingly, most rebels come from very authoritarian homes where kids have very little freedom. Teens need fewer rules but they have to be clear and unchangeable. Also, if the mother and father don't agree about discipline, teens have less respect for both parents. They also need a lot of support and a little freedom to take their own decisions. None of them enjoys just listening to adults.

4 Role models

Teens don't have much respect for their parents if neither of them actually does things they expect their children to do. Like everybody, teens appreciate people who practise what they preach.

3 **Do you agree with the opinions expressed in the article? Why/Why not?**

Quantity

4 **Look at the phrases in red in the text. Find:**

a four that are <u>only</u> used with uncountable nouns. *little*
b two that are <u>only</u> used when we talk about <u>two</u> people or things.
c synonyms of *not much* and *not many.*
d comparative forms of *little* and *few.*

5 **Put the words on the scale.**

some few hardly any no many much most

100% — 0%

all ¹_____ a lot of ²_____ ³_____ several ⁴_____ little ⁵_____ ⁶_____ none ⁷_____

6 **Use the text to answer the questions with the words from Exercise 5.**

1 How many parents have to earn their children's respect?
2 How many teenagers feel their parents pay attention to what they say?
3 How much freedom do teenagers need?
4 How many teenagers like following adults' orders?

7 **Complete the sentences with *both, neither, few, little, fewer* or *less.***

1 I think ________ my parents understand me really well. I've had a ________ conflicts with them but ________ of them has ever shouted at me. They have very ________ time for me during the week but they have________ work at the weekend and we spend a lot of time together.
2 ________ my grandmothers are amazing. They have very ________ money but ________ of them complains about her life and ________ of them always have presents for their grandchildren.
3 It's horrible. I've got ________ friends now than in primary school and I think I've got ________ time for them because I have to study all the time. I really need a ________ time off.

LANGUAGE CHOICE 6: PAGE 4

8 **Use the expressions to make true sentences about your class.**

None of us Hardly any of us Some of us
Many of us Most of us All of us

Hardly any of us spend weekends with our parents.

Writing Workshop 1

1 Read the email. Which two of these adjectives would you not use to describe Karen?

active sociable sporty lazy
independent materialistic

From: Karen
Subject: How are things?
To: Lucy

Hi there Lucy!

1 How are things? I'm sorry for not writing back sooner but I've been really busy – actually I haven't had time for anything.

2 As you know, I'm in the town volleyball team and we've been training three nights a week. It's fun but EXHAUSTING!!!!! And I've got lots of school work too, especially for history ☹. How are you getting on at school?

3 I'm also trying to decide what to study at university. My parents want me to do law but I'd like to study journalism, though it pays less. To be honest, after my work experience in that lawyer's office, I don't think I'd ever be a good lawyer. It's so DULL!! How are your plans getting on?

4 Anyway, I also wanted to tell you about Alan - things aren't great ☹. He's becoming a control freak! He always wants to know what I'm doing and he's always complaining about my volleyball. What do you think I should do?

5 By the way, I met Jamie Wilson at a party last week. Do you remember him? He was that funny little guy with red hair in Year 7 but he's quite good-looking now and he's got a great sense of humour. In fact, I haven't laughed so much for ages ☺!!! Would you like to meet up with him when you come over in the holidays?

6 I hope all's well with your family and with Tony ☺.

Love,

Karen xxxxxxxxxx

2 Read the email again. Answer the questions.

1 What is the relationship between Karen and Lucy?
2 Who do you think Alan and Tony are?
3 What news does Karen want to know about Lucy's life?
4 What opinions and advice does she want Lucy to give her?
5 What do you think is going to happen between Karen and Alan?

Text Builder

3 Match the parts of the email (1-6) with the topics (a-f).

a news about my everyday life
b problems with a relationship
c finishing the letter
d introduction - apologies for not writing before
e meeting an old friend
f my plans for the future

4 SKILLS BUILDER 11 **Use the strategies to find examples of informal style in the email.**

5 Look at the words in blue in the email. Match them with the uses (1-6).

1 to say something that you have just remembered
2 to change the subject
3 to say what you really think
4 to add information to emphasise or explain what you said before (x 2)
5 to emphasise one example of something
6 to mention something the other person knows

6 Choose the correct words to complete the email.

How are things? I'm REALLY busy. [1]*In fact/As you know*, I'm at university and we've got exams. [2]*To be honest/Anyway*, I'm really worried about them – [3]*by the way/in fact*, I'm having problems sleeping.
[4]*To be honest/By the way*, how's your mum? My dad's not very well – [5]*actually/anyway*, he's in hospital. [6]*Anyway/By the way*, I should stop now. I'm busy this week, [7]*actually/especially* on Tuesday.

7 Write a reply to Karen's email.

SKILLS BUILDER 22

1 **Write notes with answers to Karen's questions. Include one piece of false information about yourself.**
2 **Use your notes to write your email.**
3 **Check your email for mistakes.**

8 Give your email to your partner to read. Can they find the piece of false information?

Language Review Module 1

1 Talking about relationships **Complete the text with one word in each gap. The first letter of each word is given.**

My best friend and I are very [1]c________ . We do everything [2]t________ and help each other out when we have problems. We can tell each other everything because we [3]t________ each other and know that the other person won't give away our secrets. We spend a lot of time together because we like each other's [4]c________ and we always have a [5]l________ together because we share the same sense of humour. I get on well with a lot of people and I'm [6]f________ of them all but no one else is such a good friend. /6

2 Multi-part verbs (1) **Complete the sentences with one word in each gap.**

7 How can I get ________ touch with my old school friends?
8 It's ________ to you what information you make public on your website.
9 ________ attention to the rules of the website before you use it.
10 It's not too expensive when you take ________ account all the things they offer.
11 Don't let your social networking page get in the ________ of your studies.
12 Everything you need has been put ________ place and is ready for you to use. /6

3 Result linkers (1) **Choose the correct word to complete the sentences.**

13 I've had *so/such* many comments on my blog that I haven't read them all yet.
14 Lisa's *so/such* a good friend that I don't know what I'd do without her.
15 I was *so/such* upset that I didn't go out for a week.
16 I've got *so/such* a big family that I have never met some of my cousins. /4

4 Present and past tenses **Complete the sentences with the correct form of the verbs in brackets.**

17 I ________ (not get) on very well with my brother.
18 Sorry I'm late. I ________ (chat) to a friend online earlier and I forgot the time.
19 I went to the shops yesterday but I ________ (not buy) anything.
20 Before I met Melanie, I ________ (never / have) a proper girlfriend.
21 My parents ________ (not meet) my new boyfriend yet.
22 **A:** How long ________ (your mum / work) at the hospital?
B: About three months. She loves it there.
23 What ________ (you / do) at the moment?
24 I agreed to meet my friends at 8 p.m. but I was late and, by the time I got there, they ________ (all / go) home.
25 Hi, Steve, how are you? I ________ (not see) you for ages.
26 ________ (your sister / like) computers? /10

5 A presentation: describing trends **Complete the text with one word in each gap.**

Ten years ago, the average person had only one or two friends that they had never met. Now that figure is [27]________ by a huge amount. We have many virtual friends, in fact the [28]________ of people with virtual friends has increased from eight percent just a few years ago to about eighty percent now. In our class, only one [29]________ four people don't have any Facebook friends that they have never met and over a quarter [30]________ the people we asked had virtual friends from internet forums and blogs. [31]________ of the main reasons for this change in how we make friends is that communication is much easier now. So, [32]________ summarise, changes in communication have affected our friendships to some extent but not completely. /6

6 Quantity **Choose the correct words to complete the sentences.**

33 There are hardly *any/many* people here.
34 Why do I earn *less/fewer* money than everyone else here?
35 I've got *few/little* very close friends.
36 There are ten people here but *any/none* of them are from my class.
37 Two boys in my class have got Italian parents but *both/neither* of them speak much Italian.
38 There's *several/a little* time left before the film starts.
39 I've never met *some/any* famous people.
40 *All/All of* us like meeting friends at the weekend. /8

Self Assessment

1.16 **Listen and check your answers. Write down the scores. Use the table to find practice exercises.**

Exercise	If you need practice, go to
1	Language Choice 1
2	Language Choice 2
3	Language Choice 3
4	Language Choice 4 and 5
5	Students' Book p.11 ex.11
6	Language Choice 6

LEARNING LINKS: 1 Check Your Progress 1 → MyLab / Workbook page 11. Complete the Module Diary.
2 Sound Choice 1 → MyLab / Workbook page 12. Choose three pronunciation activities to do.

MODULE 2

CAMPAIGNS

Objectives: **Read, listen** and **talk about** different sorts of campaigns; **discuss** issues and **write** a 'for and against' essay; **learn about** the Past Perfect Continuous; **learn more about** linking prepositions.

TOPIC TALK

1 **Describe what is happening in the photos (a-c).**

2 1.17 1.18 **Listen to the conversation. Match the people, Dan (D), Carol (C) or both of them (B), with these opinions.**

1 is against nuclear power
2 is worried about global warming
3 is in favour of wildlife conservation
4 belongs to an NGO (non-governmental organisation)
5 wants to go on a demonstration

a A demonstration

b Volunteering

3 1.17 1.18 **Listen again. Complete the information in the network for Dan and Carol.**

Big issues

There are [1]*some/a lot* of issues that I care about. I support campaigns [2]________ but I don't really approve of those [3]________ . I think other issues are more important, like [4]________ . We should really do something about [5]________ . I [6]*belong to Greenpeace/am not in any NGOs.* I've [7]________ but I've never [8]________ .

Campaigns

for better education, disabled people's rights, the environment, freedom (of speech), healthcare, human rights, peace, public transport, wildlife conservation, women's rights

against animal testing, bullying, child poverty, corruption, cruelty to animals, drugs, global warming, homelessness, nuclear power/weapons, pollution, public spending cuts, racism, street crime, vandalism, whale hunting

Activities

attended meetings, been on a demonstration/protest march, donated money, signed a petition, taken part in fundraising activities, worked as a volunteer

4 1.19 Pronunciation **Listen to the expressions. Which of the sounds 'disappear' in rapid speech?**

1 going to
2 don't know
3 last night
4 not that simple
5 last big one
6 against hunting
7 want to
8 get back

LANGUAGE CHOICE 11: PAGE 8

5 **Work in pairs. Use the network to talk about issues *you* care about.**

c A fundraising run

GRAMMAR

KINDNESS

Warm Up

1 Look at the photos (a–c). Are such acts of kindness common where you live? Why is kindness important in everyday life?

2 Read about random acts of kindness. Which of the people, Wendy (W) or Brian (B):

a was in a hurry?
b was doing shopping?
c helped someone confused?
d experienced someone's empathy?

3 What acts of kindness have you seen or done yourself?

Talking about the past

4 Read sentences (a–e). Use the text to put the actions in chronological order. Two of the actions happened at the same time.

a He **was looking** for cat food.
b He **had left** his glasses at home.
c I **found** the packet he wanted.
d I **used to have** cats.
e I **would buy** loads of cat food.

5 Match the verb forms in the sentences (a–e) from Exercise 4 with their uses (1–5).

1 a single event in the past
2 an action that was repeated regularly in the past
3 an event that happened before other past events
4 a past activity that formed the background to past events
5 a state that lasted for some time in the past

1.20

The RAK (Random Acts of Kindness) campaign is supported by a lot of non-profit organisations and social networking websites. They encourage us to do small things that can make other people's lives easier or happier. The impact of such acts can be enormous. Kindness is contagious – when you smile and say hello to a stranger, you make them smile and feel happier, which makes you happy in turn. Read some stories from people who have experienced or performed random acts of kindness.

Wendy

One day in a supermarket, I saw an old man in front of the cat food shelf. He had been standing there for some time and looked lost. I used to have cats and I would buy loads of cat food so I offered to help. He was looking for canned food for his neighbour's cat but he had left his glasses at home and he couldn't read the labels. I found the can he wanted and he was so grateful. It was a simple thing but made me feel so much better about myself.

Brian

When I was a student I used to go home every weekend. One Friday I was queuing to buy my train ticket. I had left the library a bit late and now my train was already on the platform and there were still two people in front of me. Suddenly, the woman in front of me turned and said that I could go in front of her. She had probably sensed my tension because I had been fidgeting so much. Anyway, she saved my weekend as I managed to get home in time for dinner.

Past Perfect Continuous

6 Match the verb forms in the sentences (a-d) with the uses (1-2).

a I saw an old man in front of the cat food shelf. He **had been standing** there for some time.
b He **had left** his glasses at home and he couldn't read the labels.
c I **had left** the library a bit late and now my train was already on the platform.
d She had probably sensed my tension because I **had been fidgeting** so much.

1 an event that happened before other events in the past
2 a longer or repeated activity that happened before other events in the past

7 Match the uses (1-2) from Exercise 6 with the timelines (a-b).

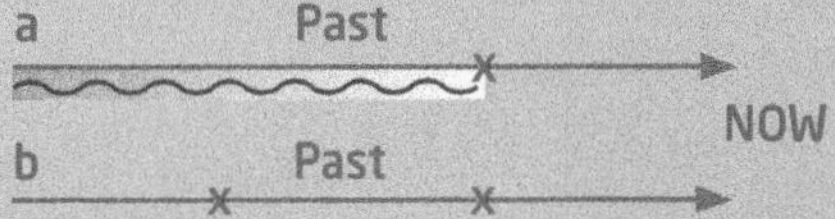

Practice

8 Use the cues in brackets and the Past Perfect Continuous to explain the situations.

1 I sent a 'thank you' letter to a friend. (look after my cats)
I sent a 'thank you' letter to a friend. He had been looking after my cats.
2 The man was desperate. (try to start his car for half an hour)
3 I was tired. (help my neighbour in her garden)
4 The shop assistant offered to help me. (look for free-range eggs in the supermarket)
5 Mary was unhappy. (argue with her boyfriend for weeks)
6 We sang a few songs at a charity concert. (practise for weeks)

LANGUAGE CHOICE 7: PAGE 6

9 Use the cues in brackets to write two explanations for each situation: one in the Past Perfect and one in the Past Perfect Continuous.

1 The girl started to cry. (lose her money, look for her lost toy for hours)
The girl started to cry because she had lost her money.
The girl started to cry because she had been looking for her lost toy for hours.
2 Heather was chosen as the most popular person at her school. (represent her school at some song contests, help other students with maths)
3 Mike felt excited. (someone buy him a lottery ticket, get mysterious love letters)
4 The homeless man was shocked. (someone give him $50, someone bring him fresh coffee every morning for a week)

LANGUAGE CHOICE 8: PAGE 6

10 Complete the text with the correct past tense of the verbs in brackets.

When I was a child, we [1] *spent* (spend) our holidays in the mountains. One year, we [2]________ (travel) there when the car [3]________ (break down) in the middle of nowhere. We [4]________ (drive) for over six hours and we [5]________ (be) really tired. To make things worse, our mobiles [6]________ (be) dead – we [7]________ (forget) to charge them! We [8]________ (wonder) what to do when an elderly man [9]________ (pull up) next to us. He [10]________ (fix) our car with my father's help and then [11]________ (invite) us to his home. He [12]________ (live) in an old house which [13]________ (be) a shepherds' cabin. He [14]________ (work) as a forest ranger all his life and he [15]________ (have) a lot of incredible adventures. We [16]________ (spend) a lovely evening with him.

Grammar Alive Telling stories

11 1.21 Listen to the girl's story and answer the questions.

1 What happened?
2 Why was she tired?
3 Why was she scared?
4 Why was it strange that she didn't know the man?

12 Use the cues to tell stories. Use the Past Simple, Past Continuous, Past Perfect and Past Perfect Continuous in each story.

1 walk home – see an old man – drop his walking stick – try to pick it up for some time – be desperate – pick it up for him – accompany him home
2 wait at the bus stop – a jogger stop – look very tired – run too long – ask me to call him a taxi – leave his mobile at home
3 travel on a train – meet an old friend – not see him since school – be very happy to see me – try to get in touch with me for a long time – want to invite me to his wedding

LESSON 6 SKILLS

RESISTANCE

Warm Up

1 **Look at the photos and read the headlines. What do you think the protests were about?**

Reading

2 **Read the book extracts and check your guesses from Exercise 1.**

3 **Read the extracts again. Are the sentences true (T), false (F) or is no information given (NI)?**

1 African Americans had the same rights as the whites in the 1950s.
2 A white woman told Claudette to give up her seat.
3 She started her protest because she knew about politics and history.
4 She appeared in court with Luther King.
5 She was braver than the adults around her.
6 The British had the full support of the people of India.
7 British soldiers stopped people from leaving the public garden.
8 Gandhi organised non-violent protests.
9 Gandhi campaigned for women's rights.
10 People around the world were interested in Gandhi's campaign.

4 SKILLS BUILDER 12 **Read the extracts again. Use the strategies in the Skills Builder and the words below to describe the writer's opinions about the things (a-d).**

arrogant brave clever cruel determined idealistic imaginative peaceful proud of ... (e.g. your country) rebellious undemocratic unfair untrue violent well-educated

a the situation of African Americans in 1955
The author thinks it was unfair and undemocratic.
b Claudette Colvin
c British rule in India
d Gandhi

Teenage Defiance

In the 1950s, African Americans were second-class citizens. In the South, they had to sit at the back of buses and give up their seats for whites. A courageous schoolgirl called Claudette Colvin challenged this unjust discrimination.

On March 2 1955, while riding a bus in Montgomery, Alabama, Colvin refused to give up her seat and was thrown off the bus and arrested for her peaceful protest. Decades later, Colvin looked back on the incident: 'We had been studying the Constitution in class. I knew I had rights. I was thinking "Why should I have to get up just because someone tells me to or just because I'm black?".' Colvin was also inspired by strong women who had fought against slavery a century earlier. 'My head was just too full of black history. I couldn't stand up,' she later said. Colvin became a key witness in a court case that went to the Federal District Court of Alabama and then the US Supreme Court. It finally outlawed segregation on the buses forever. Martin Luther King Jr declared Colvin a 'brave young lady' for her defiance.

Fifty years later, she described her feelings. 'As a teenager, I kept thinking, "Why don't the adults around here speak out about this?"' she said. 'You have to take a stand and say, "This is not right."'

5 Vocabulary **Look at the Word Builder. Match the verbs in bold with the meanings (a-f).**

a remember
b say something publicly in protest
c force to leave a vehicle
d make something happen at an earlier time
e give to someone else
f stop something by force

Word Builder Multi-part verbs (2)

1 Colvin refused to **give up** her seat and was **thrown off** the bus.
2 Colvin **looked back on** the incident.
3 Why don't the adults around here **speak out** about this?
4 British rulers in India decided to **put down** protests in the city of Amritsar.
5 ... this **brought forward** the end of the empire.

LANGUAGE CHOICE 12: PAGE 8

END OF EMPIRE

In April 1919, the British rulers in India decided to put down protests in the city of Amritsar. As people gathered in the public garden during the festival of Vaisakhi, a British general ordered his soldiers to block the exits and shoot into the crowd. As well as thousands of injuries, there were hundreds of deaths.

Despite the violence and anger that followed, Mohandas Gandhi was able to organise non-violent protests such as a boycott of British goods. But how could peaceful resistance force the British to leave India?

Gandhi began a campaign of non-cooperation with the British authorities. Parents stopped sending their children to British schools, people refused to go to British law courts and others walked out of their jobs for the government.

The British tax on salt also became a concern for Gandhi. In a hot country like India, salt was important to everyone and the tax represented an enormous amount of money for the British. So Gandhi began a new campaign with a march across the country to collect salt without paying tax. Thousands of people joined him but the authorities could do nothing about it as going for a walk was not a crime.

Gandhi finally reached the end of his journey at the town of Dandi, where he broke the law by producing salt. The British arrested him as soon as they could but now millions of people had joined his campaign and the world was watching. Civil disobedience spread across India and this brought forward the end of the empire.

6 Look at the Sentence Builder. Match the words in bold (1-6) with their uses (a-f). How do you say the words in bold in your language?

a to describe something happening at the same time
b to give a reason
c to compare something
d to describe someone's role or job
e to give an example
f to add information

Sentence Builder *as*

1 **As well as** thousands of injuries, there were hundreds of deaths.
2 Gandhi was able to organise non-violent protests **such as** a boycott of British goods.
3 **As** people gathered in the public garden, a British general ordered his soldiers to block the exits.
4 The authorities could do nothing about it **as** going for a walk was not a crime.
5 The British arrested him **as** soon **as** they could.
6 **As** a teenager, I kept thinking, 'Why don't the adults speak out about it?'.

LANGUAGE CHOICE 13: PAGE 8

7 Use the cues to make sentences with *as*.

1 at university / he worked / volunteer / for an NGO
At university he worked as a volunteer for an NGO.
2 he did / different jobs / fundraising and writing letters
3 after university / he got / a job with a charity / he had experience working for NGOs
4 he visited / Africa / several times / going to the USA and Australia
5 one day / he was going to work / he had an idea for a new NGO
6 his new group / is not big / other NGOs but he is happy

Your Choice

8 Your Culture Choose a story from your country's history. Answer the questions and write notes.

1 What was the situation?
2 Who was involved? What did he/she/they do?
3 What happened next? What problems were there?
4 What happened in the end?

9 Work in groups. Tell your partners your story.

My country was invaded by the French in 1066 ...

No Comment

'You can cage the singer but not the song.'

Harry Belafonte

LESSON 7 ANIMAL RIGHTS

Warm Up

1 Your Culture **Work in pairs. Look at the photos (a-c). Ask and answer the questions.**

1 Do you think cruelty to animals is a problem in your country? Why/Why not?
2 How strict are the laws about animal cruelty in your country?
3 How strong are animal rights groups or animal welfare groups (e.g. the RSPCA: the Royal Society for the Prevention of Cruelty to Animals in the UK)?

Listening

2 1.23 1.24 **Listen to the radio programme. Match the opinions (a-f) with the speakers (1-5). There is one extra opinion.**

a We should live without exploiting animals.
b It's disgraceful that people abandon pet animals.
c Hunting is natural and good for the environment.
d It is cruel to have animals performing for people's amusement.
e Animals should have the same rights as humans.
f The government should ban all types of hunting.

3 1.23 1.24 SKILLS BUILDER 1 **Listen again. Use the strategies to list three facts and three opinions that the speakers mention.**

4 **Look at the Sentence Builder. How do you say the sentences without emphasis?**

1 *I dislike people who kill animals for fun.*

Sentence Builder Emphasis (1)

1 **The people I dislike are those who** kill animals for fun.
2 **The people I disagree with are the ones who** organise all this anti-hunting stuff.
3 **An organisation I admire is** the RSPCA.
4 **The thing I hate is** the use of animals in circuses.

LANGUAGE CHOICE 9: PAGE 6

5 **Rewrite the sentences starting with the words in brackets.**

1 I dislike the use of animals for sport. (The thing ...)
The thing I dislike is the use of animals for sport.
2 I really admire people who speak out for animals. (The people ...)
The people I really admire are those who speak out for animals.
3 I really love Alsatians. (The dogs ...)
4 I am in favour of campaigns against animal testing. (The campaigns ...)
5 I am afraid of insects that bite. (The insects ...)
6 I love going to the local zoo. (The place ...)

6 **Work in pairs. What are your opinions about animal rights? Tell your partner.**

A: *The thing I really hate is the use of animals in circuses.*
B: *The thing I dislike is people abandoning their dogs and cats.*

Speaking Workshop

7 Read sentences 1-5. Do you think they are probably true (T) or false (F)?

1 A lot of medical research involves the use of animals.
2 Animal testing for cosmetics is still legal everywhere in the world.
3 Animal testing has helped to develop drugs that have saved millions of lives.
4 It is easier to see the long-term effects of drugs by testing on humans rather than on animals.
5 The numbers of larger animals used for testing have gone down in the last few years.

8 1.25 DVD 2 **Listen to or watch the discussion and check your answers from Exercise 7.**

9 Look at the Talk Builder. Match the expressions in bold with the uses (a-e).

a to say something is certain
b to add new information (x 2)
c to show agreement (x 2)
d to show you are being direct and honest
e to show you'd be surprised if someone did not think something

Talk Builder Discussions

	Opinions	Reactions
1	There's no doubt that ...	I'm afraid I don't agree with that at all. **Actually**, ...
2	In my opinion, we should ...	That's a valid point.
3	It's clear that ...	**Absolutely**. I completely agree that ...
4	It's **definitely** true that ...	**Exactly**, ... But what about ... ?
5	**Frankly**, I think ...	I don't think so. **In fact**, ...
6	Personally, I think it's disgraceful that ...	I'm sorry but that's just not true.
7	**Surely** that's a good thing? Don't you think so?	I'm afraid I'm not convinced.
8	It's obvious that ...	No, I wouldn't say that.

SKILLS BUILDER 34

10 1.26 Pronunciation **Listen and write down the word that is most emphasised. Then listen again and repeat the words.**

1 *Actually*

11 Choose the correct expressions to complete the dialogue.

A: 1*In my opinion/Definitely*, we should ban animal testing now.
B: 2*Absolutely/Personally*, I don't agree. 3*Actually/Exactly*, I think it can be useful.
A: But 4*definitely/surely* too many animals die and suffer every year?
B: 5*Frankly/Surely*, I think that human lives are worth more than those of animals.
A: 6*Absolutely/Actually*. But animals don't need to suffer. 7*Personally/In fact*, there are other good ways of doing experiments. Computer models are useful.
B: 8*Frankly/Exactly*. They're useful but they can't replace animal testing.

12 Work in groups. Have a discussion about animal rights.

1 **Choose one of the statements to discuss. Choose two people to be in favour of the statement and two people to be against it.**
- All hunting should be banned.
- Animal testing is okay if it saves people's lives.
- We should all be vegans or vegetarians.

2 SKILLS BUILDER 35 **Use the strategies to prepare for the discussion.**

3 **Have your discussion. Take turns to give your opinions and react to other people's.**

13 Tell the class about your discussion. Which of the arguments do you think were stronger?

We discussed animal testing. I think the strongest argument was that animal testing saves lives.

LESSON 8

GRAMMAR

NATURAL BEAUTY

Warm Up

1 Look at the photo. In what ways do you think fashion models are different from most people?

2 Read the text. What did the 'Be Natural' campaign aim to achieve?

PHOTOSHOPPED

1.27

The beauty and fashion industry all over the world promotes a distorted idea of beauty. Young women's self-esteem is systematically challenged because of computer-manipulated photos of unnaturally thin and heavily made-up models in the media. As a result of the pressure of glossy magazines, young women, except for confident individuals with really strong personalities, try to conform to 'ideal body standards'. In spite of looking absolutely normal, fifty-three percent of women in the UK say that they often worry about looking short and fat. In addition to constantly watching their diet, fifty percent of 16 to 21-year-old girls in the UK would consider having cosmetic surgery to alter the way they look. The aim of the 'BeNatural' campaign was to make teenage girls and women aware that lots of images in the media are artificially manipulated and that women should accept their looks as they are, instead of trying to look like the models in the photos. Apart from raising awareness, the organisers wanted fashion and beauty companies to display a special sign on photos that have been airbrushed. The campaign was a huge success. It gained support from models, designers and celebrities and was promoted during a huge event at a London shopping centre.

3 Do you think photos of people should be computer-manipulated? Why/Why not?

Linking prepositions

4 Match the linking prepositions (1-5) in red in the text with the meanings a-e.

1 because of, as a result of
2 in addition to, apart from
3 instead of
4 except for
5 in spite of

a although
b not including
c as a consequence of
d as well as
e rather than

5 Which two of the forms below can follow the linking prepositions in Exercise 4?

- a noun
- the *-ing* form of a verb
- an infinitive

LANGUAGE CHOICE 10: PAGE 6

6 Complete the text with the linkers below.

except for   instead of   because of
in spite of   in addition to

My friend Michael started a 'Beautiful Streets' campaign in our town. All schools took part in it, [1]__________ very young children. We collected litter from the streets and cleaned graffiti. [2]__________ cleaning, we did talks in schools and tried to convince people that, [3]__________ dropping wrappings and empty cans on the streets, they could put them in the bins. We could only run the campaign in the afternoons and at weekends [4]__________ our school duties. [5]__________ the limited time, our campaign was a real success and the streets of our town are much cleaner now.

7 Rewrite the sentences starting with the words given.

1 We gave up the idea of a protest march and organised a rally.
Instead ______________
2 We carried banners as well as photos of homeless animals.
Apart ______________
3 Everybody helped in the preparation but not my brother.
Except ______________
4 The rally went on for three hours although the weather was horrible.
In spite ______________
5 After we organised the demonstration, the government promised to change the law.
As a result ______________

Writing Workshop 2

1 **Look at the photo. What do you know about factory farming? Tell the class.**

2 SKILLS BUILDER 13 **Read the essay. Use the strategies to decide if the statements (1-6) underlined in the essay are facts or opinions.**

1 *Factory farming involves keeping farm animals inside buildings to increase the production of meat or eggs. According to the Worldwatch Institute, [1]seventy-four percent of the world's poultry, forty-three percent of its beef and sixty-eight percent of its eggs are produced in this way.*

2 *The main argument for factory farming is that, apart from being a lot cheaper than traditional or organic farming, it provides more food for [2]a world population that has already reached seven billion, according to the United Nations. As factory farms do not use a lot of workers, the costs are low and production is high. Moreover, the animals suffer from fewer diseases than those living outside.*

3 *On the other hand, critics of factory farming say that [3]it is cruel to the animals. For instance, many farm animals are kept in small spaces where they can hardly move. Animal rights activists claim that [4]these animals suffer terrible stress. Furthermore, factory farming has a negative impact on the environment because [5]it creates a lot of waste products and uses a lot of pesticides and antibiotics as well (UK 'Farming Today' 2013).*

4 *To sum up, despite producing cheap food, factory farming is bad for the planet and for the animals themselves. In my opinion, [6]we should try to reduce this kind of farming although we would have to pay more for our eggs and meat.*

Text Builder

3 **Read the essay again. Match the topics (a-d) with the paragraphs (1-4).**

a conclusion (your opinion)
b arguments against something
c introduction to the topic
d arguments for something

4 **Which of the linking expressions in red in the text do the following?**

1 summarise
2 add new information (x 4)
3 give examples
4 mention sources of information
5 contrast statements (x 3)

5 **Choose the correct linkers to complete the sentences.**

1 *According to/Furthermore* Greenpeace, factory farming is bad for the environment.
2 *Although/Apart from* it produces cheap food, factory farming does not create jobs.
3 *Despite/Apart from* producing most of our meat, factory farms produce ninety percent of our eggs.
4 Factory farms produce cheap meat. *Furthermore/On the other hand*, the conditions are cruel to the animals.
5 Factory farm animals are uncomfortable. *On the other hand/Moreover*, they only live a few months.

6 **Write a 'for and against' essay.**

SKILLS BUILDER 23

1 **Choose one of the essay titles (a-c) or choose another topic from the module.**
   a We should only have organic farming.
   b Performing animals should be banned in circuses.
   c We should not use animal products (e.g. leather and fur) in clothes.
2 **Brainstorm ideas for and against the statement you have chosen.**
3 **Then write notes for your introduction and conclusion.**
4 **Use your notes to write your essay. Use linking expressions.**

7 **Work in groups. Tell your partners your opinions about the issue you wrote about. Have a discussion and then report to the class what you agree and disagree about.**

We agree that organic farming is better but we don't think it should be the only sort.

Language Review Module 2

1 Talking about big issues **Complete the sentences with the words below.**

conservation cuts power rights speech

1 More should be done about human ________ .
2 Our campaign group is against nuclear ________ .
3 We believe it is wrong to have spending ________ now.
4 The government is trying to stop our freedom of ________ .
5 We must do more about wildlife ________ before some animals die out. /5

2 Past Perfect Continuous **Use the cues to write questions and answers.**

6 **Tom:** How long / you / drive / when the accident happened?
7 **Kate:** We / drive / for eight hours.
8 **David:** Simon looked tired when he arrived. What / he / do / ?
9 **Jack:** He / jog / .
10 **Mum:** Your shirt was dirty when you came home. What / you / eat / ?
11 **Paul:** I / eat / spaghetti bolognaise – very quickly! /6

3 Past Perfect or Past Perfect Continuous **Complete the sentences with the correct form of the verbs in brackets.**

I was lucky on Saturday. It [12]________ (rain) all morning but the sun came out at lunchtime so I decided to walk into town. I [13]________ (walk) for about fifteen minutes when it started raining again. I [14]________ (not take) my umbrella and I was getting really wet. Suddenly, Luke and his dad stopped for me in their car. They [15]________ (see) me from the other side of the road and they turned round to get me. They're so kind. /4

4 Multi-part verbs (2) **Complete the sentences with a verb.**

16 You should ________ out about this issue because it affects us all.
17 Don't ________ up your place in the dinner queue even if the bullies from Year 12 try to get in front of you.
18 When you ________ back on the campaigns you fought for in the 1990s, are you proud of what you achieved?
19 The organisers want to ________ forward the time of the march to midday.
20 You can't ________ me off the train. I've got a ticket. /5

5 *as* **Complete the sentences with the phrases below.**

as important as such as as well as as a

21 Animal rights are ________ human rights.
22 ________ student, my father joined the Labour Party.
23 I belong to several protest groups, ________ Greenpeace and CND.
24 We want freedom of the internet ________ freedom of speech. /4

6 Emphasis (1) **Rewrite the sentences using the words in brackets.**

25 I disagree with people who want to cut spending. (The people / ones)
26 We agree with the Green Party. (The party)
27 I don't like people who are cruel to animals. (The people / those)
28 I don't understand why some people are so greedy. (The thing) /4

7 Discussions **Complete the sentences with one word in each gap.**

29 There's no d________ that our campaign is working.
30 I'm s ________ but that's just not true.
31 S________ that's a good thing, isn't it?
32 I'm a________ I'm not convinced.
33 In my o________ , governments don't care. /5

8 Linking prepositions **Complete the text with one word in each gap.**

No one in my family is interested in politics except [34]________ me. I've joined a campaign against poverty [35]________ a result of a television documentary that I saw. Instead [36]________ sitting at home, I'm going to be more active. Apart [37]________ recycling, I've never done anything political but next week, in spite [38]________ my parents' worries, I'm going on a protest march. Because [39]________ our actions, we may convince other people to join our campaign and, [40]________ addition, we may even force the government to change its decisions. /7

Self Assessment

1.28 **Listen and check your answers. Write down the scores. Use the table to find practice exercises.**

Exercise	If you need practice, go to
1	Language Choice 11
2	Language Choice 7
3	Language Choice 8
4	Language Choice 12
5	Language Choice 13
6	Language Choice 9
7	Students' Book p.21 ex.11
8	Language Choice 10

LEARNING LINKS: 1 Read and listen to a poem by Langston Hughes in Culture Choice 1 on page 106. Then do a project about your country's history.
2 Check Your Progress 2 → MyLab / Workbook page 21.
3 Exam Choice 1 → MyLab / Workbook pages 22-24. Complete the Module Diary.

MODULE 3 # THE MEDIA

Objectives: **Read, listen** and **talk about** different types of media; **describe** a scene; **learn more about** verb patterns and negation; **write** a review of a TV programme.

a

TOPIC TALK

1 **Look at the photos (a-e) and the network. What types of media can you see?**

a *local radio*

2 2.1 2.2 **Listen and match the extracts (1-4) with the types of broadcasts (a-e). There is one extra type.**

a national news report
b an opinion podcast
c report in online music magazine
d local news report
e interview in online film magazine

3 2.3 2.4 **Listen to Simon. Complete the information in the network.**

My media use

To get information about my interests, I often check out [1]__________.
Whenever I want to keep up with the latest news, I [2]*read/watch/listen to* [3]__________.
To chill out, I [4]*read/watch/listen to* [5]__________.
My favourite TV programmes are [6]__________.
When I want to express my own opinions, I post comments on [7]__________.
When I'm doing research for school work, I use [8]__________ and [9]__________.
To catch up with my friends' news and give my own, I use [10]__________.

4 2.5 Pronunciation **Listen to the sentences. Use the context to identify the word you hear.**

1 whether/weather	5 weak/week
2 where/wear	6 no/know
3 our/hour	7 site/sight
4 write/right	8 two/too

LANGUAGE CHOICE 14: PAGE 9

5 **Work in groups. Use the network to talk about *your* media use.**

Print media
- fashion, film, men's, music, news/current affairs, sport, women's **magazines**
- daily/weekly, local/national, tabloid/quality **newspapers**

Broadcast media
- **TV programmes:** chat shows, comedy programmes, discussions, documentaries, drama series, films, game shows, reality shows, sitcoms, soap operas, the news, the weather forecast
- **Radio programmes (local/national):** discussions, documentaries, music, news, phone-ins, plays

Online media
- **Blogs:** fashion, personal, sport, travel
- **Websites:** celebrity, file-sharing, health, news, online magazines (e.g. film/music/sport), online radio, online shopping, reference (e.g. online dictionaries), school, science, social networking, video-sharing (e.g. YouTube), wikis (encyclopedias)
- podcasts, search engines

BREAKING NEWS

Warm Up

1 Your Culture **Work in pairs. Ask and answer these questions.**

1 What are the main national newspapers and current affairs magazines in your country?
2 Where do *you* get news about films, music, sport and technology?
3 How do you find out about what is going on locally?

Reading

2 **Read the three texts. Match the summaries (1-4) with the texts (a-c). There is one extra summary.**

1 Hurricane Irene was caused by global warming.
2 Hurricane Irene affected millions of people and caused severe damage in twelve states.
3 Hurricane Irene did not affect New York City as badly as predicted.
4 The US media exaggerated the dangers of Hurricane Irene.

3 **Read the texts again. Match the sentences (a-h) with the gaps in the text 1-7. There is one extra sentence.**

a All airports in the area are now closed.
b We now have final figures for the hurricane.
c The hurricane was not caused by global warming.
d 'But sometimes New Yorkers lose their heads.'
e Okay, there was flooding and wind damage.
f 'We all hope for the best and prepare for the worst,' he had said.
g Then he jumped into the sea for a swim. *1*
h At least nineteen people were killed on Saturday as Hurricane Irene moved up the east coast.

4 **Use the strategies to classify the three texts.**

- unreliable and biased
- reasonably objective, fair and reliable

5 Vocabulary **Look at the Word Builder. Match the expressions (1-6) in bold with the meanings (a-f).**

a an event whose importance is exaggerated
b panic
c was lucky to escape
d not so bad after all
e losing strength
f is no longer worried

USA NEWS

a

New York breathes a sigh of relief

(2.6)

New York 'dodged the bullet' on Sunday as Hurricane Irene weakened into a tropical storm.

By Jon Swaine, New York, Sunday August 28

Gary Atlas had jogged along Coney Island seafront on each of the past 1435 mornings – and he was not about to give up the 1436th because his mayor and president had ordered him to stay inside. 'I'm not going to miss a day, hurricane or no hurricane,' said Mr Atlas, 59, as the eye of Irene entered New York City directly above him. 1________

As his fellow New Yorkers awoke to streets covered with leaves and puddles rather than the smashed skyscraper windows they were warned to expect, his decision seemed reasonable. But many elsewhere were not so fortunate. 2________

By the time it reached New York, however, Irene had been downgraded to a tropical storm. Some local residents thought that the authorities had overreacted. 'It's not as bad as they said it would be,' said John Harris, 37. 'Where I'm from, we're used to strong hurricanes,' said Miss Sweatt from South Carolina. 3________

As they glanced southwards at what might have been, however, many New Yorkers were glad to have followed Barack Obama's advice. 4________

Word Builder Idiomatic language (1)

1 New York **breathes a sigh of relief.**
2 New York **dodged the bullet.**
3 Sometimes New Yorkers **lose their heads.**
4 It was **not the end of the world.**
5 It was more like **a storm in a teacup.**
6 The hurricane is **running out of steam.**

→ LANGUAGE CHOICE 15: PAGE 9

This week

b

STORM IN A TEACUP
DOC KEMP TALKS

In the old days, Americans used to just get ready for hurricanes and think no more about it. Nowadays, the media turn every hurricane into a catastrophe 'caused' by global warming. For example, last weekend we were waiting for Hurricane Irene to hit the USA and the TV and newspapers were in a panic. What happened in the end? 5_______ Unfortunately, a few people were killed. But it was not the end of the world – it was more like a storm in a teacup. This came as a surprise to a lot of people but not to me. It is clear that this government and its media friends have got used to exaggerating weather events to get more money for the criminal lie that is global warming.

c

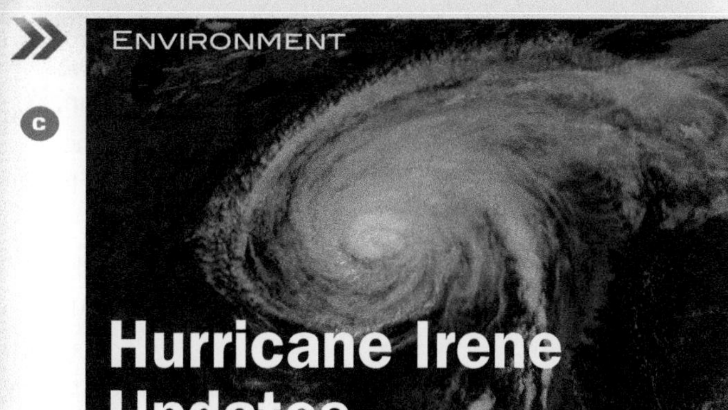

24/7 Weather USA

Saturday 11.00 p.m.
Operators finished shutting down the Oyster Creek nuclear reactor at 5.00 p.m. 6_______ 2.3 million people have been evacuated from their homes.

Sunday 03.30 a.m.
The hurricane has hit New Jersey with 75 mph winds. Severe flooding is being reported in Philadelphia. Many homes are without power.

Sunday 07.00 a.m.
Strong winds and heavy rain are affecting New York City but the hurricane here has been downgraded to a tropical storm. It looks like Irene is running out of steam.

Monday 06.00 p.m.
7_______ Forty people have been killed, with 55 million people affected in twelve states. It will make history as the most expensive natural catastrophe in American history and could cost $37 million.

6 Look at the Sentence Builder. Match the expressions (1-3) in bold with the meanings (a-c).

a be familiar with something
b did something regularly in the past
c become familiar with something

Sentence Builder *used to*

1 In the old days, Americans **used to** just *get ready* for hurricanes and think no more about it.
2 Where I'm from, **we're used to** *strong hurricanes*.
3 This government and its media friends have **got used to** *exaggerating* weather events.

LANGUAGE CHOICE 16

7 Work in pairs. Ask and answer the questions.

1 What did you use to enjoy at school when you were about ten or eleven?
When I was ten or eleven, I used to enjoy art classes a lot.
2 Are you used to spending time on your own? When are you usually alone?
3 Would you get used to living in the USA? What things would you not get used to?
4 How did you use to get to school when you were five or six?
5 When you first came to your present school, what things weren't you used to?
6 What will be difficult (and easy) to get used to when you leave school?

Your Choice

8 Imagine you work for a local newspaper. Choose an important event (real or imaginary) and write notes about:

- what the event was
- when the event happened
- where it happened
- what the consequences were
- your conclusion

9 Work in groups. Find out about your partners' news stories.

A: *What happened?*
B: *There was a very bad storm on 10 March.*

No Comment

'It's amazing that the amount of news that happens in the world every day always exactly fits the newspaper.'

LESSON **10** GRAMMAR

24/7 NEWS

Obama's Historic Speech

Ryan Gosling voted the hottest star!

Neil Armstrong walks on the Moon

Warm Up

1 **Look at the photos and the headlines. Which of the news events do you consider important? Which will be remembered in twenty years' time? Why?**

2 2.7 **Listen to the three people talking about the media. Which of them (1-3):**

a likes the radio?
b thinks that the news on 24/7 TV is not presented in an effective way?
c says that we don't have in-depth knowledge of current affairs?

3 **Read the text. What would be the best title for it?**

a No news is good news!
b Think before you read (or watch)!
c Gossip rules the media!

4 **Work in pairs. Discuss the news below. Which will matter in the future? Why/Why not?**

a Water has been found on the moon.
b Bill Gates has spent a billion dollars on agricultural research.
c Scientists have used a tiny robot to treat a tumour in a mouse.
d A British tourist has been killed by a shark.

Verb patterns

5 **Read the three extracts from Exercise 2 on page 105. Put the verbs and expressions below in the correct place in the table.**

can't stand want require be worth ~~avoid~~ enjoy prefer manage give up start not mind used to decide finish be used to learn

verb + infinitive	
verb + *-ing* form	*avoid*

US|NET NEWS
REVIEWS NEWS HOW TO DOWNLOAD MARKET PLACE

FEATURED POSTS 2.8

We are literally drowning in news. Have you ever tried reading the whole newspaper, including the financial and sports pages? Or have you followed every piece of news on the front page of a news website? It's practically impossible. Reuters alone puts out 3.5 million news stories a year. And that's just one source. And how many of these stories are actually going to matter twenty years from now? You probably remember following the news about Michael Jackson's death or Prince William's wedding but will these stories make any difference for the future? Will they change our lives? We're probably going to forget watching the last Olympics sooner than we think. Maybe we should stop to think about which news is really important so that in the future we don't regret wasting our time on trivial things.

But the amount of news is not the only problem. Unfortunately, the view of the world we get from the media is seriously distorted. Most of the news we get is local – the accident of a minor celebrity or a local society scandal is covered more extensively than important international news. Try to find out what's going on in other parts of the world – it's not easy. English-speaking networks often 'forget' to report news related to other parts of the world than their own. In the USA, the coverage of Russia, China and India together is one percent of the total news. The main reason for this is that covering your local Britney Spears or Paris Hilton is cheaper. And also, people love trashy gossip. I regret to say I'm a fan myself!

Dr John Adams, a media psychologist, suggests that 'We should stop watching or reading whatever is on. Next time you go online, turn on the TV or pick up a newspaper, remember to select something worthwhile. If there's nothing really worth watching, try turning the TV off. You can spend this time in a much more useful way.'

6 **Some verbs can be followed by both *-ing* forms and infinitives. Match the sentences (1-10) with each pair of meanings (a-b).**

1 **Try to find** current news. *a*	a make an effort to see if you can do something difficult
2 **Try turning** the TV off. *b*	b do something and see the results
3 You **remember watching** the Oscars.	a recall a past experience
4 **Remember to select** the news that is worth your time.	b not forget an obligation
5 We should **stop to think** which news is worth watching.	a give up an activity
6 **Stop watching** whatever is on.	b pause in an activity in order to do something else
7 I **regret to say** I'm a fan myself!	a feel sorry about something you did before
8 We don't **regret wasting** our time.	b feel sorry about something you are going to do or say
9 News networks **'forget' to report** the news related to other parts of the world.	a not do something because you forgot about it
10 We're going to **forget watching** the 2010 World Cup final sooner than we think.	b do something and later forget that you did it

Practice

7 **Complete the sentences with the infinitive or the *-ing* form of the verbs in brackets.**

1 I have stopped __________ (watch) news channels: there's too much violence. I'm going to try __________ just (read) my daily newspaper from now on.
2 I hated the film. My sister said it was worth __________ (watch) but she forgot __________ (tell) me it was a horror film.
3 I haven't managed __________ (read) the newspaper yet. Usually I don't mind __________ (read) on the bus but there was too much noise this morning.
4 Tom, did you remember __________ (buy) my newspaper? I can't stand __________ (read) the news online.
5 On the way home, I stopped __________ (talk) to a neighbour who used to __________ (work) for the local radio station.

LANGUAGE CHOICE 17: PAGE 10

8 **Use the cues in brackets to continue the situations.**

1 I've been to one football game in my life. (remember / be bored to death)
I've been to one football game in my life. I remember being bored to death.
2 My brother spends hours in front of his computer. (not stop / play computer games)
3 You think television is horrible these days. (try / listen to the radio)
4 There was no one interesting at the party. (regret / go there)
5 Peter and Ann are at home! (forget / invite them to dinner)

9 **Use these expressions to give your views about television, newspapers and other media.**

It's not worth I enjoy I can't stand I am used to
I don't mind I used to I have given up I avoid

I enjoy listening to music on the radio but I have given up listening to political debates.

LANGUAGE CHOICE [illegible]

Grammar Alive
Telling people what to do

10 2.9 **Listen to the dialogues (1-5) between two sisters, Jane and Bev. Complete the sentences.**

1 Jane wants Bev to stop __________ rubbish.
2 Bev should remember __________ Jane's laptop.
3 Bev should try __________ something more ambitious.
4 Bev should try __________ in politics.
5 Bev needs to remember __________ the windows.

11 **Work in pairs. Use the cues to complete the dialogues.**

1 I'm going out. → Okay. (remember / be back at ten)
A: I'm going out.
B: Okay. But remember to be back at ten.
2 I love vampire stories. → They are horrible. (stop / read them)
3 It was a great match. → Sport is so boring. (try / watch something different)
4 I'm cooking pasta. → Great! (remember / add salt to the water)
5 I'm going for a walk. → Okay. (Don't forget / take the dog with you)
6 I can't sleep. → You go to bed too late. (stop / watch those late-night horror films)
7 I'm watching the news. → It's all about crime and disasters. (try / find a good book instead)

LESSON 11 SPOOFS

A spoof is a deception like the BBC documentary about flying penguins or a parody like the comedy series *The Office*. The first famous spoof was a programme on Halloween in 1938. Orson Welles, the famous director and actor, adapted H.G. Wells's story *The War of the Worlds* for the radio. He introduced the play first but the rest of it sounded like real live radio with interruptions for news bulletins about the Martian invasion of the Earth. Thousands of listeners were tricked and frightened because they thought it was real.

Warm Up

1 Your Culture **Work in pairs. Read the information about spoofs and answer the questions below.**

1 In the UK, 1 April is April Fools' Day (a time for jokes and tricks) and, in the USA, 31 October is Halloween (a time for tricks and scaring people). What similar day is there in your country? Are spoof programmes ever shown on that day? Do people believe them?

2 Are there any spoof comedy programmes on TV in your country? What programmes do they make fun of (e.g. documentaries, news programmes)? How funny are they?

Listening

2 2.10 2.11 **Listen to three extracts from a modern spoof radio play. Order the events (a-f).**

a A journalist and a professor go to the crater where the objects landed.
b Unusual activity was observed on planet Kepler-22b.
c Suddenly, one of the objects opens and a horrible creature comes out.
d They hear a strange sound coming from the round, metal objects.
e Five or six objects land in the desert outside the town of Alice Springs.
f A group of large objects move rapidly towards the Earth.

3 2.10 2.11 SKILLS BUILDER 2 **Listen again. Use the strategies to match the words (1-8) with the meanings (a-h).**

1 spokesperson *g*	5 red alert
2 to monitor	6 flash
3 update	7 impact
4 meteorite	8 to hum

a the most recent information about something
b a bright light that shines for a short time and then stops shining
c to make a low continuous sound
d to carefully watch and check a situation in order to see how it changes over a period of time
e a piece of rock or metal from space that has landed on Earth
f a warning that there is very great danger
g a person who has been chosen to speak officially for a group, organisation or government
h the force of one object hitting another

4 **Work in pairs. Ask and answer these questions.**

1 Why do you think so many people believed that Orson Welles's adaptation of *The War of the Worlds* was real?
2 Would people nowadays believe a spoof about an alien invasion like the radio play in Exercises 2 and 3? Why/Why not?
3 What films have you seen about alien invasions? What is your favourite?

DVD Choice

5 DVD 3 **Watch the spoof and the documentary. Order the things the BBC did (a–e).**

a They used computer animation to make the penguins fly.
b They looked for good film of penguins in the BBC archives.
c They combined all the film and animation to make the spoof.
d They showed the spoof on April Fool's Day on national TV.
e They filmed the presenter speaking in the studio.

6 DVD 3 **Watch again and answer these questions.**

1 What advantages would flying penguins have?
2 How long has the BBC been making spoofs on April Fool's Day?
3 What movements did the animators copy to get the penguins flying?
4 What special effects did they use when filming Terry Jones?
5 Why did they use a green screen when filming him?

7 **What spoof would you like to make? What techniques would you use to make it?**

Speaking Workshop

8 2.12 2.13 **Listen to the dialogue. Which of these things does Colin find funny about the scene?**

1 the introduction about the check-in assistants
2 Melody's first comment to the woman
3 the story of the man and his shoe
4 Melody and Keeley phoning each other
5 passing over the boarding pass
6 Melody telling the woman that everybody's got speedy boarding

9 **Look at the Talk Builder. Match the linkers in bold with the meanings (a–e).**

a the last thing to happen/after a long time (x 3)
b initially/in the beginning
c the first thing to happen in a series of events
d just at the moment that
e then

Talk Builder Describing scenes

1 The scene starts off with ...
2 **First of all**, she ... . Then ...
3 **At first**, the woman ...
4 It's just hilarious because ...
5 Anyway, **eventually** she persuades her to ...
6 Unfortunately, ... so she immediately ...
7 It's so funny because ...
8 **The next thing that happens is that** ...
9 It's ridiculous because **as soon as** she gets it she ...
10 **In the end**, the woman doesn't look very happy at all and **finally** ...

➔ SKILLS BUILDER 36

10 2.14 Pronunciation **Listen to and repeat Colin's reactions.**

11 **Choose the correct linker to complete the sentences.**

1 Last year, I started playing squash. *First of all/At first* it was difficult but I'm good at it now.
2 I went to the gym after school. *At first/First of all*, I got changed and warmed up.
3 I started laughing *as soon as/while* that comedy programme started.

12 **Describe a scene from a comedy programme or film.**

1 **Choose a scene.**
2 **Write notes about what happens in it.**
- Where are the characters?
- Who is there?
- What happens first?
- What are people's reactions?
- What happens next?
- What happens in the end?

3 ➔ SKILLS BUILDER 37 **Read the strategies for describing scenes. Practise saying things about your comedy scene.**
4 **Work in pairs. Tell your partner about the scene.**

13 **What was the funniest part of your partner's scene? Tell the class.**

The best bit was when she asked the woman to ...

LESSON **12**

BAD SCIENCE

1 **Do you follow the news about science? What recent news reports do you remember?**

2 **Read the book description. According to the book's author, are the statements true (T) or false (F)?**

The UK media report scientific studies:

a without providing clear evidence (figures, methodology).
b objectively.
c as something sensational.
d in an over-simplified way.

BAD SCIENCE (2.15)
by Ben Goldacre

In this fascinating book, Goldacre tries to explain why science in the media often seems pointless, simplistic or just wrong.
Science is done by scientists but it is often written about by journalists without any science education. So people who understand nothing about science try to convey difficult new ideas to a broad audience. Goldacre classifies science stories in the media into three categories. Wacky stories, like 'Infidelity is genetic', show scientific research as pointless and absurd. Scare stories, like anti-vaccine scares, based on very little evidence, present light risk as immense danger. Breakthrough stories, like 'Pomegranate juice protects us against wrinkles', report unconfirmed and unreliable experiment results. According to Goldacre, very few science stories contain any evidence and science journalists hardly ever provide useful scientific information. There is never any crucial data: no description of experiments, no relevant facts and figures. Why? Because they think no one will understand the 'science bit' so all stories involving science must be dumbed down. They don't quote any sources but use empty phrases like 'scientists revealed' or 'scientists warn'.
Goldacre's claim is that in this way the media create a parody of science. Journalists, who are usually humanities graduates with hardly any understanding of science, create an impression that science is wacky, contradictory and hard to understand. In this way, the media effectively reinforce the idea that science hardly makes sense.

3 **Do you agree that the media present scientific research in a wrong way? Why/Why not?**

Negation

4 **Look at the negative sentences. Which of the words (1-5) in bold:**

a are used with *not* and other negative words?
b mean 'almost no'?

1 They don't quote **any** sources.
2 There are people without **any** science education.
3 They give **no** description of experiments.
4 Very **few** science stories contain any evidence.
5 Scare stories are based on very **little** evidence.

5 **Read the pairs of sentences. Underline the phrase in the second sentence which means the same as the underlined phrase in the first.**

1 They think no one will understand it.
They think people won't understand it.
2 They understand nothing about it.
They don't understand anything about it.
3 There is never any crucial data.
There isn't ever any crucial data.

6 **Change the words in *italics* and use the words in brackets to paraphrase the sentences.**

1 There *isn't anything* interesting in them. (nothing)
2 We *haven't* got *much* time to finish. (little)
3 You can't understand science *without any* science education. (no)
4 Journalists *shouldn't ever* write about things they don't understand. (never)
5 I *don't* think *anyone* believes tabloids. (no one)
6 There *aren't many* facts in this book. (few)

7 **Read the Sentence Builder. Translate the sentences into your language.**

Sentence Builder *hardly*

Science journalists **hardly ever** (= almost never) provide useful scientific information.
Science **hardly** (= almost doesn't) makes sense.
Journalists are humanities graduates with **hardly any** (= almost no) understanding of science.

8 **Use *hardly* to paraphrase the sentences.**

1 He almost doesn't give any scientific facts.
2 I almost never read science articles.
3 Almost no journalists have science degrees.
4 We almost didn't understand the lecture.

Writing Workshop 3

Come Fly With Me **BBC 1**

1 With their TV series *Little Britain* (2003–2007), David Walliams and Matt Lucas became the most famous British comedians of the 2000s. Now the comedy duo has just finished a new series, *Come Fly With Me*, a spoof documentary set in a fictional British airport. Walliams and Lucas play a cast of thirty-six different characters of airport staff and cabin crew.

2 The concept is definitely a good one as modern air travel is such a good target for satire. There is some good acting and great characters, too, like the rude check-in girls, Melody and Keeley, the snobbish airline stewardess, Penny, and the xenophobic immigration official, Ian Foot. There is a real 'mockumentary' feel, too, with the voiceovers and characters talking directly to camera.

3 However, there are so many characters that you lose the sense of the story. As with *Little Britain*, there is so much repetition that you get bored with the same jokes and lines. Worst of all though are the crude racial and sexual stereotypes like the lazy West Indian coffee lady, Precious. Some of the humour is cruel and laughs at people with real problems, like the McDonald's worker who is mentally disabled.

4 To sum up, this show has some very funny bits but it does not really get off the ground and there are such a lot of bad jokes that it becomes dull. Let's hope that the second series, starting in a couple of months, is a lot better than the first one.

1 **Quickly read the review of the spoof documentary *Come Fly With Me*. Is it positive or negative?**

2 **Work in pairs. Make a list of the good and bad things mentioned in the review of the TV series.**

Text Builder

3 **Read the review about the TV series again. Match the paragraphs (1-4) with the topics (a-d).**

a good things
b conclusion
c bad things
d basic information

4 **Look at the Sentence Builder. Which of the linkers can be used with:**

a countable nouns? b uncountable nouns? c both?

Sentence Builder Result linkers (2)

1 There are **such a lot of** bad jokes **that** it becomes dull.
2 There are **so many** bad jokes **that** it becomes dull.
3 There is **so much** repetition **that** you get bored.
4 There is **such a lot of** repetition **that** you get bored.

5 **Join the sentences using linkers from Exercise 4.**

1 In the programme, there are thirty or forty characters. You cannot remember their names.
There are so many characters in the programme that you cannot remember their names.
2 The film cost a lot of money to make. The production company went out of business.
3 Most of the dialogues were bad. I turned off the TV.
4 There was a lot of traffic in the town centre. We got to the cinema late and missed the film.
5 There was a lot of noise in the cinema. I made a complaint to the management.

6 **Write a review of a TV series that you have seen recently.**

SKILLS BUILDER 24

1 **Choose a TV series. Write notes about:**
- basic information (subject/TV channel/main actors/when it started)
- good things about it
- bad things about it
- your personal conclusions

2 **Write your review in four paragraphs.**

3 **Check your review for mistakes of grammar, vocabulary and punctuation.**

7 **Work in groups. Read each other's reviews. Choose the most interesting one and tell the class about it.**

Language Review Module 3

1 Talking about media **Complete the sentences with one word in each gap.**

1 How often do you check ________ what your friends are posting online?
2 I find it difficult to keep ________ with all the celebrity gossip.
3 Facebook is a great way to catch ________ with everyone's news.
4 I spend too much time on my ________ networking site.
5 I never watch reality shows or soap ________ . /5

2 Idiomatic language (1) **Complete the sentences with the words below.**

head sigh steam teacup world

6 The runners started quickly but soon ran out of ________ .
7 Everyone breathed a ________ of relief when the storm passed.
8 Marie lost her ________ when she heard the news and started screaming.
9 Don't get so upset about losing your phone. It's not the end of the ________ .
10 Don't worry. It's only a storm in a ________ . Tomorrow, someone else will be on the front page of the newspapers. /5

3 *used to* **Use the cues to write sentences.**

11 I / used / wake up at 7 a.m. but now I have to get up at 6 a.m.
12 I'm slowly / get / used / be / a celebrity
13 The British / not / used / snow
14 I / not use / like / documentaries but now I love them
15 I'm in Year 12 at school so / I / used / study /5

4 Verb patterns **Complete the sentences with the correct form the verbs in brackets.**

16 I tried ________ (translate) the article but it was too difficult.
17 Do you regret ________ (spend) all day on the internet?
18 Did you remember ________ (buy) an umbrella when you were in the town centre?
19 I stopped ________ (write) a blog because I got bored with it.
20 I'll never forget ________ (get) my first Facebook friend.
21 I spent all morning reading the news online but I had to stop ________ (give) my eyes a rest. /6

5 Describing scenes **Choose the correct words to complete the text.**

The scene starts [22]*up/off* with a company boss performing a dance for charity. The office manager is jealous and, at [23]*first/firstly* he tries to convince everyone that the dance is no good. That doesn't work and it's just [24]*hilarious/at that moment* because he does his own dance which is awful. Everyone watching is embarrassed and, as [25]*fast/soon* as the office manager has finished, they leave. In the [26]*last/end,* he says that the boss was only better because he had practised his dance. /5

6 Negation **Rewrite the sentences using the words in brackets.**

27 There is nothing to do here. (anything)
28 There was no one to talk to. (anyone)
29 I never want to see you again. (don't)
30 There are no great journalists anymore. (any)
31 I didn't see anyone famous. (no one)
32 We don't ever publish gossip. (never) /6

7 *hardly* **Rewrite the sentences starting with the words in brackets.**

33 I don't know him very well at all. (I hardly)
34 I very rarely use my home phone. (I hardly)
35 Almost none of my friends has a blog. (Hardly)
36 There is almost no useful information on this website. (There is hardly) /4

8 Result linkers (2) **Use the cues to write sentences.**

37 There / such / lot / magazines / in this shop that I don't know which one to buy
38 There / so / adverts / in this newspaper that it isn't worth buying
39 I've got / so / work / to do that I haven't got time to watch television
40 There / such / lot / traffic / on the roads that it is quicker to walk to school than to go by car /4

Self Assessment

2.16 **Listen and check your answers. Write down the scores. Use the table to find practice exercises.**

Exercise	If you need practice, go to
1	Language Choice 14
2	Language Choice 15
3	Language Choice 16
4	Language Choice 17 and 18
5	Students' Book p.31 ex.11
6	Language Choice 19
7	Students' Book p.32 ex.8
8	Students' Book p.33 ex.5

LEARNING LINKS: 1 Check Your Progress 3 → MyLab / Workbook page 33. Complete the Module Diary.
2 Sound Choice 2 → MyLab / Workbook page 34. Choose three pronunciation activities to do.

MODULE

4 ADVERTISING

Objectives: **Talk about** advertising and shopping; **read** and **listen to** adverts and **about** advertising techniques; **ask for help with** a problem; **write** a letter of complaint; **learn more about** passives and nouns.

TOPIC TALK

1 Look at the adverts (a-c). What do you think they are for? Check your guesses on page 105. Which of them do you like the most? Why?

2 2.17 2.18 Listen to three adverts. Guess which of the products in the network they are for. Which advert do you think is the most effective? Why?

3 2.19 2.20 Listen to someone talking about advertising and complete the information in the network.

Advertising

I [1]*think/don't think* that advertising affects everyone.
The adverts I like most are [2]________ .
The ones that annoy me most are [3]________ .
For me, the best adverts are those that are [4]________ . I can't stand ads that are [5]________ .
My least favourite ones are those for [6]________ but I like ads for [7]________ .
Whenever I buy something important, I always shop around and [8]________ .

billboards, celebrity endorsements, covert adverts (e.g. in films/ on TV), direct mail (junk mail), email (spam), magazine/newspaper ads, radio/TV commercials, sponsoring of events (e.g. sport), text messages, website ads (e.g. pop-ups)

amusing, attractive, clever, dramatic, dull, emotional, funny, humorous, sexist, shocking, silly, tasteless, unusual, weird

clothes and accessories (e.g. gloves, jewellery, trainers)
electronic goods (e.g. hi-fi system, sat-nav, tablet computer, phone)
health and beauty (e.g. aftershave, cosmetics, perfume)
household products (e.g. washing powder)
snacks (e.g. crisps, drinks, sweets)

check out prices online, go window shopping, look for bargains, read product reviews, talk to friends and family, watch TV commercials

4 2.21 Pronunciation Listen to the sentences. Use the context to identify which of the unstressed function words are used.

1 a/(are)/or 3 a/are/or 5 and/an 7 the/there
2 a/are/or 4 and/an 6 the/there

LANGUAGE CHOICE 23: PAGE 14

5 Work in groups. Use the network to express *your* opinions about advertising.

LESSON 13 ADVERTISING TRICKS

Warm Up

1 Look at the photos (a-c). What products are being advertised? Which advert would encourage you to buy the product? Why?

2 Read the article. Which tricks (1-5) do advertisers use with children (C) and with teenagers (T)?

1 using celebrities
2 using cartoon animals
3 presenting the product as difficult to get
4 circulating news about a product by word of mouth
5 suggesting that not having a product will make you lonely

3 Do you think you and your friends are influenced by adverts? Why/Why not?

Streetcorner opinion

2.22

We are being bombarded with advertisements all the time and a lot of them are targeted at young people.

Smaller children, apart from spending their own pocket money, can also influence what their parents buy, so many TV ads are created with kids in mind. For example, adverts for drinks feature cartoon animals. Then, as two-year-olds are being pushed around the shop by their parents in a trolley, they recognise the drink from the advert and ask the adults to buy it.

As children grow older, some products are marketed to them as 'must-have' items, implying that children won't be liked by their friends if they don't get them. As a result, kids are desperate to get the product and parents can be made to feel guilty if they don't buy it for their child.

Teenagers are incredibly critical of adverts, so products aimed at them have to be advertised much more cleverly. As teens are driven by the desire to be part of the 'coolest' group in their school, products need to be given a cool feel. For example, advertisers give away stickers which direct teens to a difficult-to-find website with more information about a product. In this way, naturally rebellious teens feel that they have been invited to an exclusive club and can be sold expensive products.

As teens hate being influenced by adults, marketers let them persuade each other that a certain product is cool. Since the late nineties, 'street teams' of teenagers have been employed by clothing and record companies to spread the word about a product among young people. Because teens look up to celebrities, pop stars are often sent free clothes in order to be seen wearing them. Some celebrities also admit to being paid to say nice things about particular brands in interviews.

So how is the next cool gadget going to be advertised? Its profile may be set up on your social networking site so that the producer gets direct access to you and your friends. So, watch out and try not to be fooled!

The Passive

4 Complete the table with examples of the Passive in red in the text.

Present Simple	
Present Continuous	
Present Perfect	
Past Simple	*The ad **was shown** last week.*
Past Continuous	*The trick **was being used** by all car producers.*
Past Perfect	*It **hadn't been advertised** before.*
be going to + infinitive	
will + infinitive	
modal + infinitive	

5 **Match the verb forms (1-2) in bold with the names (a-b). Find one more example of each form in the text.**

1 As teens hate **being influenced** by adults ...
2 Pop stars are often sent free clothes in order **to be seen** wearing them.

a Passive infinitive
b Passive *-ing* form

6 **Match the sentences (1-2) with the reasons for using the Passive (a-b). Find more examples using a '*by* phrase' in the text.**

1 Some products are marketed to [children] as 'must-have' items ...
2 Children won't be liked **by their friends** ...

a to focus on the action when we don't know or it's not important who does it
b to put emphasis on who does the action

Practice

7 **Complete the sentences with the correct Passive form of the verbs in brackets.**

1 Most TV commercials ________ (show) between 6 and 10 p.m.
2 Radio commercials ________ (produce) since the beginning of the radio.
3 At this moment, thousands of ads ________ (read) on the internet.
4 A new jeans ad ________ (broadcast) tomorrow.
5 The first advertisements ________ (create) in ancient times.
6 I bought this watch because it ________ (advertise) by Brad Pitt.

LANGUAGE CHOICE 20: PAGE 12

8 **Complete the sentences with the correct Passive form of the verbs in brackets.**

1 Advertisements ________ (shouldn't / show) on public television.
2 I hate ________ (treat) like a child by advertisers.
3 Advertising ________ (should / ban) from children's programmes.
4 Children want ________ (accept) by their friends so parents ________ (force) to buy fashionable toys.
5 Word-of-mouth advertising ________ (use) with teens because they don't like ________ (tell) what to wear by adults.
6 It's easy ________ (cheat) by ads where new products ________ (praise) by celebrities.
7 Some products ________ (not have to / advertise) at all.
8 Adverts ________ (can't trust) because they ________ (create) to make us buy something.

LANGUAGE CHOICE 21: PAGE 12

9 **Complete the advert with the correct Passive form of the verbs in brackets.**

Do you like [1] *being ignored* (ignore)? No one does. We all want [2]________ (notice). Our new sunglasses, Bay Runs, [3]________ (design) with you in mind. They [4]________ (can / wear) all year round. They [5]________ (make) of top quality materials and make you look gorgeous. You [6]________(will/admire) by all your friends. And, last but not least, your eyes [7]________ (will / protect) against UV radiation.

Grammar Alive
Giving product information

10 2.23 **Listen to the dialogue in a health food shop. What information does the customer get about the drink?**

a its effects
b its preparation
c its safety
d its taste

11 **Work in pairs. Use the cues to make dialogues.**

1 computer → can / buy with free software and apps

A: *I'd like to buy this computer. Would you recommend it?*
B: *Yes. It can be bought with free software and apps.*

2 dress → have to / dry-cleaned

A: *I'd like to buy this dress. Would you recommend it?*
B: *Not really. It has to be dry-cleaned.*

3 pie → can / eat hot or cold
4 shoes → can't / wear in the rain
5 white trousers → have to / clean every day
6 cake → can / serve alone or with ice cream
7 cups → can't / wash in a dishwasher
8 watch → can / use underwater

12 **Think of something you often use. Use modals and the passive to give information about it.**

I love my jeans. They can be worn on all occasions. They don't have to be ironed after washing. The only problem is that they can't be washed in very hot water because they might shrink.

SKILLS BUY IT!

Warm Up

1 **Have you ever been disappointed with something that you bought because it looked good in an advert?**

I bought a digital camera because it looked great but it doesn't take very good photos.

Reading

2 **Read the texts (1-2). Match the messages (a-h) with them.**

a It'll make me look more attractive.
b It's great value for money.
c It will solve my problem.
d My friends will love it.
e It looks cool.
f It's a natural product.
g It'll be great fun.
h It's the only product of its type that works well.

1

ADVERTISEMENT

2.24

Natural Solution to Male Hair Loss

Cam Schinhan reports on new developments in the field of male baldness.

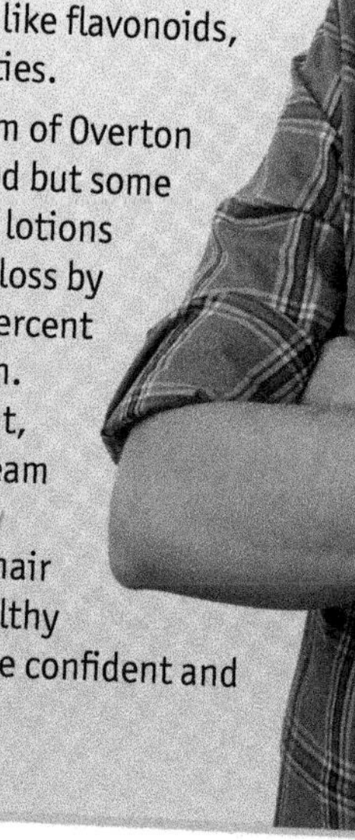

More and more men are suffering from baldness and the causes are, by and large, related to the male hormone dihydrotestosterone (DHT) which affects hair follicles and, bit by bit, stops new hair growth. The pharmaceutical industry has produced two products to delay and reverse hair loss: Finasteride tablets and Minoxidil lotion. However, both products need to be taken or applied daily, are extremely expensive and have low success rates so, sooner or later, most men get sick and tired of taking them and stop the treatment.

Natural Hair Technologies, a Cambridge-based company, has come up with an alternative solution using 100% natural plant ingredients from the ginkgo biloba tree. This has been used far and wide in traditional medicine and has been found to contain chemicals, like flavonoids, with powerful antioxidant properties.

According to Dr Herbert Puckham of Overton University, more research is needed but some clinical studies with ginkgo biloba lotions show they have reduced male hair loss by about ninety percent and in fifty percent of cases there has been new growth. Healthy Hair*, NHT's new treatment, is inexpensive and involves hair cream which only needs to be applied now and then to stop and reverse male hair loss once and for all. Thanks to Healthy Hair thousands of men will feel more confident and attractive than before.

* No guarantee of reversal of hair loss.

2

Life's for Sharing

Does your old computer need changing? The new cool-looking ZTAB2 tablet is the perfect solution for all your needs. You and your friends will have a lot to smile about with the latest version of our famous ZTAB – and it has the stunning reduced price tag of only €300.

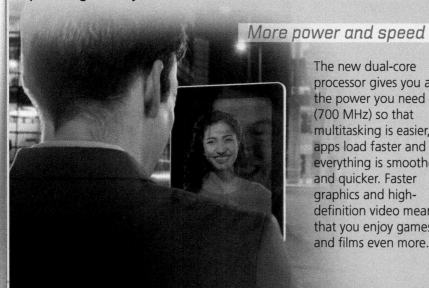

More power and speed

The new dual-core processor gives you all the power you need (700 MHz) so that multitasking is easier, apps load faster and everything is smoother and quicker. Faster graphics and high-definition video mean that you enjoy games and films even more.

Complete connectivity

With the new AYP wireless technology you can easily connect to wi-fi networks, and with 3G connectivity you can go online wher[e] you are out camping or away on holiday. At home, you can pick and choose what to connect your ZTAB2 to: your TV, projector, printer or bluetooth keyboard.

Two cameras

The ZTAB2 has two cameras, so you can talk face to face with a friend and film what is going on around you at the same time.

Stylish + easy to use

The ZTAB2 is twenty percent lighter, thirty percent thinner than the original ZTAB and the bigger 10-inch touch screen puts everything at your fingertips. The ZTAB2 has a longer 12-hour battery life (MMO7 tested) so you can watch films or listen to music with your friends all night!

3 Read the adverts again. Choose the best answers to these questions.

1 What is not true about the baldness products in the first paragraph?
a They need to be used regularly.
b They have excellent results.
c Users often do not finish the treatment.
d They are comparatively costly.

2 What is the main advantage of 'Healthy Hair'?
a It has been used in traditional medicine.
b It often starts hair growing again.
c It doesn't cost very much.
d It contains antioxidant chemicals.

3 Why does the latest ZTAB2 work faster than the previous version?
a It has better graphics.
b It has got new wireless technology.
c It has a more powerful processor.
d It has got greater connectivity.

4 Why has the ZTAB2 got two cameras?
a In case one doesn't work.
b To connect to the TV.
c To do two things at once.
d To film other people.

5 The new ZTAB2:
a needs its battery recharged after 12 hours' use.
b is fifty percent larger than the previous version.
c cannot be operated by using your fingers.
d can only be used for viewing films.

4 SKILLS BUILDER 15 **Use the strategies and the checklist to evaluate the advertisements. Which of the two adverts do you think is more informative, honest and reliable? Give your reasons.**

5 Vocabulary Look at the expressions in the Word Builder. Find the expressions in blue in the adverts and match them with the meanings below.

a gradually
b finally
c occasionally
d generally
e select
f an increasing number of
g in a lot of different places
h very tired of
i in front of each other
j certain to happen eventually

Word Builder Word pairs

Repeated words: more and more, bit by bit, face to face
Opposites: sooner or later, now and then
Synonyms: sick and tired, far and wide, pick and choose
Others: by and large, once and for all

LANGUAGE CHOICE 24: PAGE 14

6 Work in pairs. Say sentences about your plans, feelings and habits.

1 Sooner or later, I am going to ...
Sooner or later, I am going to start going to the gym every day.
2 Once and for all, I am going to ...
3 I am sick and tired of ...
4 Now and then, I ...
5 I spend more and more time ...
6 By and large, I think that ...

7 Look at the Sentence Builder. Which use of *need* (1 or 2) means that something should be done soon?

Sentence Builder *need*

1 Both products **need to be taken** or applied regularly.
2 Does your old computer **need changing**?

LANGUAGE CHOICE 25: PAGE 14

8 Complete the sentences with the words in brackets and *need* + *-ing* or *need to be* ... .

1 Someone should make that bed. That bed *needs making* . (make)
2 Those pills ________ every six hours. (take)
3 My shoes are broken. My shoes ________ . (repair)
4 Our dog ________ against rabies every year. (vaccinate)
5 Your hair is very long. Your hair ________ . (cut)
6 That face cream ________ every night. (apply)

Your Choice

9 Choose something that you would like to buy. Write notes about:

- name, price, company made by
- what it does
- its advantages over other products

10 Work in pairs. Ask and answer questions about your product.

A: *I'd like to buy a Zodiac Smartphone.*
B: *What's so good about it?*

No Comment

'Advertising is the art of convincing people to spend money they don't have for something they don't need.' Will Rogers

LESSON **15**

ONLINE ADS

a

COMPUTER DOCTORS
If we can't fix it, there's no fee
call 0207 73317890

b

You have won €1 million.
Click here to collect the money.

c

Delete | Junk | Reply | Reply All | Forward | Print

From: UBA <Majorbank@org.Ugh>
Subject: great discount ends at midnight – don't miss out!
Date: 8 July 2012 10:23:26 GMT+01:00
To: Mark Symonds <Mark@telesymonds.com>

Put your credit card number and your bank password here:

Warm Up

1 Look at the computer windows (a-c). Does online advertising bother you? What do you do to avoid it? Tell the class.

2 2.25 2.26 **Listen to three dialogues. Match the words (1-6) with the definitions (a-f).**

1 pop-under 3 phishing 5 open-source
2 reboot 4 targeted ads 6 spyware

a programs that track online movements
b an advert that appears after you've left a website
c to start a computer again
d tricking people into giving personal information, like bank account numbers
e free software that you can modify
f advertising directed at individuals

3 Listen to the dialogues again. Use the strategies to match the people (1-6) with their intentions (a-g). There is one extra intention.

1 Lisa 3 Tom 5 Keith
2 Lisa's dad 4 Katy 6 Sylvie

a wants to help the other person
b wants to know all about something
c wants to talk to the other person
d wants to go out with the other person
e wants to show off knowledge about something
f wants help with something
g wants to get on with doing something

4 Look at the Sentence Builder. Which expressions (1-4) express:

a what someone wants or doesn't want to do?
b what someone wants <u>someone else</u> to do or not to do?

Sentence Builder Preferences

1 **I'd prefer to** go on a nice holiday.
2 **I'd prefer you not to** get angry.
3 **I'd rather not** turn it off.
4 **I'd rather you didn't** interrupt me.

5 Use the cues to complete the dialogue.

A: Hey Monica. Why don't we go out tonight?
B: Well Lucy, I'd prefer [1]________ (doesn't want to go out). I'd rather [2]________ (wants Lucy to come to her house). We could watch a film.
A: Okay I'll come over but I'd prefer [3]________ (wants to talk). I'd rather [4]________ (doesn't want to watch film). It's a nice evening and I'd rather we [5]________ (wants them to sit outside in the garden). We could invite Tom and Fred.
B: Good idea but I'd prefer [6]________ (wants Lucy to ring them) because you know them better.

6 Work in pairs. Act out the dialogue in Exercise 5 and change the places, times, people and activities.

A: Hey Adam, I'd like to go to the cinema tonight.
B: Well, I'd prefer to go to ...

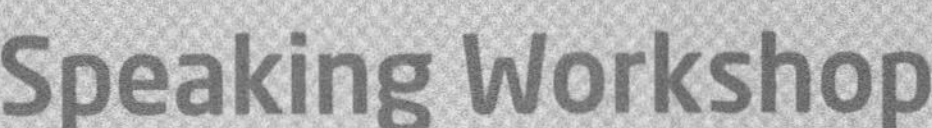

Speaking Workshop

7 Which of these computer problems have you ever had? Tell the class.

- it works very slowly
- the cursor freezes
- it fails to start
- overheating
- the screen goes blank
- you've spilt something on it
- it's got a virus
- problems with the power supply
- problems with the battery
- it makes a horrible noise

8 2.27 DVD 4 **Listen to or watch the conversation in the repair shop. Which of the problems from Exercise 7 has the woman had?**

9 Look at the Talk Builder. Can you leave out words in your language like this?

Talk Builder Leaving out words

1 Anybody there? (~~Is~~ anybody there?)
2 Anything I can do for you? (~~Is there~~ anything I can do for you?)
3 Of course, no problem. (Of course, ~~I can have a look at it. That's~~ no problem ~~for me~~.)
4 Since when? (Since when ~~has it been going slowly~~?)
5 Did it? (Did it ~~go blank~~?)
6 Yes, I have. (Yes, I have ~~checked the power supply~~.)
7 No, I haven't. (No, I haven't ~~dropped it recently~~.)
8 You didn't! (You didn't ~~drop it~~!)
9 Could be. (~~That~~ could be ~~the cause of the problem~~.)
10 Afraid not. (~~I'm~~ afraid ~~I cannot~~ ~~sort it out now~~.)
11 Don't think so. (~~I~~ don't think so.)

SKILLS BUILDER 38

10 2.28 Pronunciation **Listen and repeat the expressions.**

11 Which of the words in the dialogue can you leave out?

A: Good morning. ~~Is there~~ anything I can do to help?
B: Yes, there is ~~something you can do to help~~. My phone doesn't work. Do you think you could repair it now, please?
A: I'm afraid I cannot repair it now. Can you tell me what happened, please?
B: Yes, I can tell you what happened. I dropped it from my bike.
A: You didn't drop it!
B: But then it worked okay for a few days.
A: How long did it work for?
B: It worked for a couple of days. Then it started going funny.
A: Did it start to go funny?
B: Yes, it started making strange noises.

12 Work in pairs. Act out a situation in a repair shop.

1 **Choose two problems with your computer or mobile phone.**

- short battery life
- no connection
- works slowly
- blank screen
- a virus
- something does not work (camera/calculator/sound/games/keyboard)

2 **Write notes about the problems.**

Model: ZTAB2, tablet
Problems: doesn't start, ...

3 **Take turns to be the customer and the computer or phone expert. Act out the dialogues.**

13 How helpful and polite was your partner? Tell the class.

LESSON 16 GRAMMAR

YOU'RE WORTH IT!

Warm Up

1 **Look at the advert. What is being advertised? How do the advertisers make the product seem attractive?**

2 **Read the story of a famous advertising slogan. In what way did it differ from other advertisements in those days?**

(2.29)

Slogans in advertising have always been an important part of the marketing message. Companies spend large sums of money finding the right phrases to promote their brand. One of the longest-lasting phrases in the history of advertising was created in 1973 in response to sexist stereotyping.
Its author, Ilon Specht, was a rebellious and unconventional 23-year-old college dropout working at a New York advertising agency. She had written a famous television commercial for an NGO, where carefree people in California were shown in contrast with depressing facts and images of children from other parts of the world.
It wasn't easy to be a young woman in advertising in the seventies: the agency staff were mainly older men and young women were called girls. Ilon's intelligence and creativity were not appreciated.
On one project she worked with L'Oréal, a French cosmetics producer. The company was going to launch a campaign promoting a new hair colour, Preference. The advertising team were planning to do an ad with a beautiful woman sitting by a window, another in a series of the stereotypical ads of those days. The woman was treated like an object – she was not expected to say anything and only her looks were important. Ilon got so angry that she sat down and created a completely new advert that revolutionised advertising for women: a modern woman chooses an expensive product because she desires the best for her hair. The slogan is still used today.

3 Your Culture **What stereotypes can you see in current advertisements in your country?**

Nouns

4 **Complete the table with the words in red in the text. Then add the nouns below to the correct boxes.**

~~news~~ police media clothes stairs teeth trousers foot scissors time

uncountable nouns	history, *news*
nouns with regular plural	agency, facts
nouns with irregular plural	children
plural nouns with no singular form	people

5 **Read the pairs of sentences (1–2). Is the verb singular when we see the group of people as:**

- one body, an impersonal unit?
- a collection of individuals?

1 The agency **staff were** mainly older men.
Our **staff is** excellent.
2 The **company was** going to launch a campaign.
The **company are** trying to contact their customers.

6 **Rewrite the text making the nouns in *italics* plural if possible and making any other necessary changes.**

Those car commercials were quite original. ...

That car *commercial* was quite original. The *man* in the *advert* wasn't very attractive: his *hair* was dirty and his *clothes* were too small. His *child* was ugly and had a *tooth* missing. The *police* looked dumb: the *officer* was slow. In contrast, the *car* looked fantastic. A lot of *money* must have been spent on this campaign as this *ad* has been shown in all the *media,* including after the main TV *news.*

7 **Complete the sentences with the correct past form of the verb *be*, singular or plural.**

1 The news ________ rather pessimistic.
2 That last series of commercials ________ quite funny.
3 The ads she created ________ always original.
4 The police ________ involved in car adverts.
5 The money they spent on advertising ________ incredible.

8 **Choose the singular or plural verb form to complete the sentences.**

1 The commercial is good because the film crew *was/were* very experienced.
2 The average family in the UK *is/are* smaller now than a hundred years ago.
3 My family *is/are* great fans of funny adverts.
4 After the game, the team usually *take/takes* showers.
5 My favourite team *has won/have won* every game this season.

LANGUAGE CHOICE 22: PAGE 12

Writing Workshop 4

Sunrise Sound Station
The all-in-one charger, stereo, radio and alarm clock.
• crystal clear sound from top quality stereo speakers
• rapid charging for all MP3 players and mobiles
• digital radio and alarm clock with high quality LCD screen
• selection of 100 natural sounds to guarantee that you wake up
4:12

1 **Read the advertisement. Would you like to have a product like this? Why/Why not?**

2 **Read the letter of complaint. What false claims are there in the advertisement?**

Dear Sir or Madam,

1 I am writing to you about a series of problems that I have had with my new Sunrise Sound Station. I bought the sound station from your website for €120 on 30 January (product number Z49817Y) and it arrived five days later. I enclose copies of the guarantee and receipt.

2 In your advertising, you claim that the station has 'crystal clear' stereo sound. However, not only is the sound fuzzy but the volume is also extremely low. I have also had problems with the alarm clock which did not go off one morning so that I missed an important exam. Finally, three weeks ago the LCD screen went almost blank so that now you can hardly see the time and the machine is virtually useless.

3 When I phoned your customer service department, after waiting for twenty minutes I was put on to a Sunrise 'engineer'. I tried to explain the problems but the engineer told me rudely to read the instructions and hung up. Since then I have phoned your office three times but nobody has been able to sort out my problem.

4 Not only would I like you to refund my money but I would like an apology, too, for the rude behaviour of the engineer. Unless I receive a satisfactory reply within the next two weeks, I will have to take further action. I have already been in contact with my local consumer protection office and they have recommended that I take legal action if I do not get full satisfaction.

I look forward to hearing from you.

Yours faithfully,

Paul Davies (Mr)

Text Builder

3 **Read the letter again. Write the topics for the paragraphs (1-4).**

1 *reason for writing/product information*

4 SKILLS BUILDER 16 **Use the strategies to identify examples of formal language and think of the informal equivalents.**

5 **Look at the Sentence Builder. Look at the order of the subject and verb. Is it unusual in English?**

Sentence Builder Emphasis (2)

1 **Not only is the sound** fuzzy **but** the volume is **also** extremely low.

2 **Not only would I like you** to refund my money **but** I would like an apology, **too.**

6 **Rewrite the sentences starting with *Not only*.**

1 I would like a reduction in the price plus a formal apology.
Not only *would I like a reduction in the price but I would like a formal apology, too.*

2 The sound station is poor quality and one of the speakers is broken.

3 The charger works slowly and it uses a lot of energy.

4 I am going to contact my local consumer office and write to the newspapers.

7 **Write a letter of complaint.**

SKILLS BUILDER 25

1 **Choose one of these things. Think of things that could go wrong with them.**
- a mobile phone
- an MP3 player
- a computer
- a hi-fi system

2 **Write notes about these things.**
- the product
- what went wrong with it
- problems with customer service
- what you want

3 **Use your notes to write a letter of complaint.**

8 **Work in groups. Read each other's letters of complaint. Tell the class about them.**

Language Review Module 4

1 Talking about advertising **Complete the text with one word in each gap.**

I spend a lot of time looking [1]________ bargains. Even when the shops are shut, I like to walk through the shopping centre just [2]________ shopping. When I find something I like, I read product [3]________ to see what other people think and then I check [4]________ the prices. I always shop [5]________ until I know I'm getting the right thing at the right price. /5

2 The Passive **Complete the sentences with the correct form of the verbs in brackets.**

6 Unhealthy food shouldn't ________ (advertise) during children's programmes on TV.
7 I bought these trainers because they ________ (wear) by Cristiano Ronaldo in a TV commercial I saw.
8 I ________ (never / influence) by a TV commercial in my life.
9 Stars who appear in commercials ________ (usually / pay) a lot of money.
10 A new form of advertising ________ (plan) at the moment.
11 My boss was upset on Monday because he ________ (send) 150 emails over the weekend and 148 of them were spam.
12 New products have to ________ (advertise).
13 Our new product ________ (sell) all over the world when we have finished making it. /8

3 Word pairs **Complete the sentences with one word in each gap.**

14 The problem is that you can't pick and ________ which adverts your children watch.
15 Sooner or ________, adverts will appear during programmes.
16 Now and ________ I buy something because of an advert but not often.
17 I'm sick and ________ of all this junk mail.
18 Make up your mind once and for ________.
19 By and ________ I enjoy TV commercials. /6

4 *need* **Rewrite the sentences using the correct form of *need* and the verbs in brackets.**

20 Someone should control TV commercials. (controlled)
21 I should change my diet. (changing)
22 You should tidy your bedroom. (tidying)
23 Someone should organise the photos on this computer. (organising)
24 We have to finish this homework before tomorrow. (finished) /5

5 Preferences **Complete the sentences with the correct form of the verbs in brackets.**

25 I'd rather we ________ (talk) face to face.
26 I'd prefer ________ (wait) until we've read some reviews.
27 I'd rather you ________ (not send) me all those stupid email jokes.
28 I'd prefer ________ (not spend) too much money today.
29 I'd prefer us ________ (meet) in the shopping centre.
30 I'd rather ________ (not watch) adverts in the middle of a film. /6

6 Nouns **Complete the sentences with the correct form of the verbs below.**

be (x 3) cause not fit go

31 The news from Japan yesterday ________ very worrying.
32 The staff here ________ all very friendly.
33 These trousers ________ me.
34 Time ________ quickly when you're having fun.
35 The police ________ very helpful when I was robbed.
36 Money ________ more problems than anything else. /6

7 Emphasis (2) **Rewrite the sentences starting with *Not only*.**

37 It's really good and it's cheap.
38 I'd like to buy a new laptop and a new camera.
39 This shirt is dirty and it's the wrong size.
40 I would like you to stop sending me emails and also to remove me from your mailing list. /4

Self Assessment

2.30 **Listen and check your answers. Write down the scores. Use the table to find practice exercises.**

Exercise	If you need practice, go to
1	Language Choice 23
2	Language Choice 20 and 21
3	Language Choice 24
4	Language Choice 25
5	Language Choice 26
6	Language Choice 22
7	Students' Book p.43 ex.6

LEARNING LINKS: 1 Read and listen to an extract from *Pride and Prejudice* by Jane Austen in Culture Choice 2 on page 108. Then do a project about a best-seller from your country.
2 Check Your Progress 4 → MyLab / Workbook page 43.
3 Exam Choice 2 → MyLab / Workbook pages 44-46. Complete the Module Diary.

MODULE

5 WELL-BEING

Objectives: **Listen** and **read about** health, happiness and medicine; **discuss** health issues; **write** an opinion essay; **learn more about** future tenses and time references.

brain
jaw
collarbone
lung
heart
rib
liver
spine
kidney
wrist
ankle
heel
toe

TOPIC TALK

1 **Look at the picture. Which one of these statements about the human body is false?**

1 Twenty percent of the body's oxygen is used by the brain.
2 The heart beats 10,000 times a day.
3 Our kidneys filter 1 to 2 litres of blood every minute.
4 We breathe 25,000 times a day.

2 3.1 3.2 **Listen to a talk. Check your guess from Exercise 1. What other facts did you find interesting?**

The brain only uses 10 watts of electricity.

3 3.3 3.4 **Listen and complete the information in the network.**

Health

I've [1]________ but I've never [2]________.
I [3]*often/sometimes/never* have [4]________ but I've never had [5]________.
I never [6]________ but I do occasionally [7]________.
To keep healthy, I [8]*do regular exercise/have a good diet/get enough sleep.*
In my opinion, the most dangerous disease in my country is probably [9]________.

broken my ankle, arm, collarbone, finger, foot, hand, jaw, leg, nose, toe
broken a bone, rib
bruised, grazed, cut myself
pulled muscle, strained tendon, torn ligament
sprained my ankle, knee, wrist

a cold, constipation, a cough, diarrhoea, earache, flu, hay fever, headaches,
a high temperature, sinusitis, skin rashes, stomachache

asthma, chickenpox, hepatitis, measles, migraine, mumps, salmonella

feel anxious, depressed, down, irritable, on edge, over-tired, stressed out, under the weather
have no appetite, no energy, problems sleeping

AIDS, cancer (e.g. breast, lung), cholera, diabetes, heart attacks, kidney disease, liver disease, lung disease, malaria, meningitis, strokes, tuberculosis (TB), typhoid

4 3.5 Pronunciation **Listen and repeat the medical terms in blue in the network.**

LANGUAGE CHOICE 27: PAGE 15

5 **Work in pairs. Use the network to talk about *your* health.**

LESSON 17 SKILLS

SPEED

Warm Up

1 Look at the pictures. Which of these do you think are the two main factors limiting maximum human speed?

a lack of oxygen supplied to muscles
b lack of lung capacity to get oxygen
c lack of carbohydrates in food
d lack of energy to power muscles

Reading

2 Read the article. Check your guesses from Exercise 1.

3 Try to work out the meaning of these words (underlined in the text).

- physiology • rate • depleted
- to run out of (something)
- exhausted • breakdown
- tissues • performance-enhancing

4 Read the article again. Are the statements true (T) or false (F)?

1 When you do intense exercise, you breathe faster and your heart goes faster.
2 After a few minutes, acids like lactic acid build up in the muscles.
3 If you make too much effort, your body stops working properly.
4 During exercise, the breakdown of carbohydrate and fat produces a chemical that moves muscles.
5 When running fast, you cannot breathe quickly enough to get enough oxygen.
6 You need to eat a lot of meat and other proteins to prepare for exercise.
7 Drugs like anabolic steroids have long-term positive effects on your health.
8 Cheetahs can run more than three times as fast as humans.

5 What do you think are the two most interesting facts in the article? Tell the class.

I think it's interesting that humans are near their limits in terms of speed.

3.6

LIMITS TO PERFORMANCE

In 1998, the world-class Moroccan athlete, Hicham El Guerrouj, broke the 1500-metres world record with a time of three minutes, twenty-six seconds. Nearly fifteen years later, nobody has beaten that time. Have we got to the human speed limit? Dr Frances Ashcroft, Professor of Physiology at Oxford University, explains the limits of the human body during a race.

Hicham El Guerrouj

Crack!!! As the athlete moves forward, there is an immediate jump in the rate of breathing. The heart rate goes up rapidly to its maximum level and the haemoglobin in the red blood cells provides more oxygen to the muscles.

A few seconds into the race, immediate energy stores are depleted, lactic acid begins to accumulate in the muscles and the athlete starts to run out of oxygen. The athlete's body becomes exhausted because he is unable to supply fuel and oxygen quickly enough. If the runner does not slow down, the heart rhythm becomes less regular, the oxygen content in the blood may fall and the temperature rises. The athlete becomes uncoordinated and is close to collapse.

The key to performance is the rate at which energy – in the form of adenosine triphosphate (ATP) – can be generated to power muscle contraction. ATP must be replaced by the breakdown of carbohydrate or fat. Muscles contain a limited amount of carbohydrate which lasts for about an hour of exercise and oxygen is used to produce most of the ATP needed.

As everyone knows, you breathe faster and more deeply when you run and the harder you exercise the quicker your breathing gets. What is clear, however, is that breathing does not limit exercise.

6 Vocabulary Look at the Word Builder. Complete the lists with the words in blue in the text.

Word Builder Compounds

Nouns
Two words: *world record, ...*

Adjectives
Two words with hyphen: *world-class, ...*

LANGUAGE CHOICE 28: PAGE 15

ATHLETICS

In fact, most people tend to over-breathe during exercise. It may seem as if you are fighting for air but the problem is not that your lungs cannot get enough oxygen but that your heart cannot deliver it quickly enough to the tissues.

To improve performance, first-rate athletes need the right food. A top-level cyclist can burn almost 5900 calories a day. Many studies have shown that a high carbohydrate diet (for example potatoes and bread) helps prepare full-time athletes for intense exercise. Training is also vital and is the main reason why it seems much easier to cycle uphill after only a week or two of practice. The more you train the better the coordination of your muscles becomes and the stronger they get, too.

Unfortunately, some well-known athletes have also turned to performance-enhancing drugs despite the health-related dangers. The first victim was a British cyclist who died in 1896 and more recently the world-famous sprinter, Florence Griffith-Joyner, who died of a heart attack at the age of thirty-eight. She was a victim of anabolic steroids which improve speed and stamina but can have far-reaching, long-term effects on the heart, kidneys and liver.

Elite athletes, improved training, hi-tech shoes and better equipment all help improve performance but we are probably not far off the limits for humans. We certainly will never be able to compete with many animals. A top-ranking sprinter can run 200 metres at a rate of 35 kph but dogs can race at 56 kph, antelopes at 96 kph and cheetahs at an astonishing 112 kph!

Carmelita Jeter

7 Complete the sentences with the compound words below.

long-term heart rate full-time anabolic steroids world record performance-enhancing hi-tech ~~world-class~~ well-known

1 Hicham El Guerrouj was a _world-class_ athlete and still holds the ________ for the 1500 metres.
2 When you start doing exercise, your ________ goes up.
3 People who take ________ drugs like ________ often suffer ________ effects on their health.
4 I'd like to be a ________ professional tennis player.
5 Nowadays, athletes use ________ equipment from ________ brands like Nike.

8 Look at the Sentence Builder. When do we use the structures in bold?

- to show that one activity causes something else
- to compare two unrelated activities

Sentence Builder Comparatives

1 **The harder** you exercise **the quicker** your breathing gets.
2 **The more** you train **the better** the coordination of your muscles becomes.

LANGUAGE CHOICE 29: PAGE 15

9 Use the structure in the Sentence Builder to join the sentences with comparatives.

1 He runs fast. His face goes redder.
The faster he runs, the redder his face goes.
2 She practises tennis a lot. She gets better.
3 They eat a lot of pasta. They become stronger.
4 You work hard. You sleep less.
5 He talks loudly. It is difficult to understand him.
6 It became sunny. We spent time at the pool.

Your Choice

10 Work in groups. Write five questions about exercise, fitness and eating habits. Then ask your partners the questions.

A: *What do you think is the best way of motivating people to do more exercise?*
B: *I think the best way to motivate people is to make it more fun, like dancing.*

11 Tell the class some of the results of your survey.

Everybody in the group does some sport. Two out of three people ...

No Comment

'My favourite machine at the gym is the vending machine.'

Caroline Rhea

LESSON **18** GRAMMAR

TIME AND US

Warm Up

1 Look at the photos (a-c). Who do you think is the happiest? Which of the people:

1 thinks a lot about the past?
2 is living in the present?
3 is preoccupied with their future?

2 Read two students' descriptions of themselves. Which of them do you think:

1 is going to succeed in life?
2 will be happier?
3 is going to be healthier in 30 years' time?

3.7

Pete:

» I plan my time carefully. I always meet deadlines. I know precisely that at 9.30 tomorrow I will be working in the library and by the end of the week I will have read these two books. I have my annual medical check-up at 9 a.m. on Monday and in the afternoon I'm seeing my grandparents. When I've finished my studies, I'm going to work in a newspaper. I don't like thinking about the past: it reminds me of my failures.

Frances:

» I've got loads of friends and I love wild parties. I usually act on impulse. I don't think about my future, I have no idea what I will be doing tomorrow or next week. I don't have a lot of money but when I finally have some, I'll spend it immediately. I like meeting my old friends and remembering our happy childhood.

3 Read a psychologist's analysis of Pete's and Frances's descriptions of themselves on page 49. Were your answers the same? What is a recipe for a happy and successful life?

4 Who are you similar to: Pete or Frances? How often do you think about the future and the past? Are your thoughts positive or negative? Can you enjoy the present?

Future

5 Match the sentences (1-7) with the uses (a-g).

1 At 9.30 tomorrow I **will be working** in the library.
2 I **have** my annual medical check-up at 9 a.m. on Monday.
3 **I'm seeing** my grandparents in the afternoon.
4 He **may get** depressed.
5 **I'm going to work** in a newspaper.
6 He**'ll** probably **get married**.
7 He**'s going to be** a successful journalist.

a a weak prediction
b an intention or plan for the future
c a prediction based on the evidence in the present situation
d a prediction based on the speaker's opinion, knowledge or experience
e an activity going on at a certain time in the future
f a personal arrangement for the future
g a fixed event in the future that we can't move

6 Read the sentences (1-2). Underline the time expressions. Will the activities in bold:

a finish before that time?
b start but not finish before that time?

1 By the time she's fifty, she**'ll have** probably **developed** heart disease.
2 By the end of the week, I **will have read** these two books.

7 Which sentence below, 1 or 2, emphasises that the activity in bold must be finished before the other one? Find more examples like that in the texts.

1 When **your work has been done**, focus on the present.
2 When **I finally have** some money, I'll spend it immediately.

Dr Akerman comments: 3.8

Pete is a future-focused person – he's got clear goals and he's prepared to work hard to achieve them. He's definitely going to be a successful journalist. He'll probably get married and have a family. He also cares about his health. He probably exercises and eats carefully. This means that when he's reached old age, he's going to be fit and healthy. But he may be too busy to enjoy life now – meet his friends or listen to music. And if he thinks too much about unpleasant past experiences, he may get depressed.

Frances is a present-focused hedonist – she is really happy right now. Her memories from the past are pleasant and the future doesn't bother her. However, if she doesn't start thinking about the consequences of her reckless lifestyle, she may regret it. It's possible that she won't have a stable family and by the time she's fifty, she'll have probably developed heart disease. Statistically, her chances for professional success are low.

The happiest and most successful people are balanced – they plan for the future, enjoy the present and have happy memories from the past. So, when you have work to do, focus on the future. When your work has been done and it's time to relax, focus on the present. And find positive lessons in your past, too.

Practice

8 Complete the sentences with *will* + infinitive, *will have* + third form or *will be* + *-ing* form.

1 I think Pete *will have* (have) a large family.
2 By the time he's 35, Pete ________ (work) on five different newspapers.
3 At 8 a.m. on Saturday Frances ________ (sleep) and Pete ________ (jog) in the park.
4 By the end of this weekend, Frances ________ (go to) a few parties.
5 Pete ________ (probably / earn) a lot of money.
6 Pete ________ (publish) a book by the time he's 30.

LANGUAGE CHOICE 30: PAGE 16

9 Use the cues to write sentences. Use the Present Perfect and *will* + infinitive.

1 Pete feel good / after / he achieve his goals
Pete will feel good after he's achieved his goals.
2 As soon as / Frances pass her exams / she relax
3 Frances enjoy working / when / she find a job she really love
4 Pete find a job / as soon as / he graduate
5 Frances start treating life seriously / after / she run out of money
6 When / he do his morning jog / Pete take a shower

LANGUAGE CHOICE 31: PAGE 16

10 Complete the dialogue with correct future forms of the verbs in brackets.

F: Hi Pete. I [1] *'m going* (go) to a concert tonight. Would you like to come with me? It [2] ________ (start) at seven o'clock.
P: Sorry, Frances, at seven o'clock, I [3] ________ (prepare) a presentation.
F: Maybe we could meet after you [4] ________ (finish).
P: I [5] ________ (work) for two hours. I [6] ________ (be) free at 8.30.
F: Great! I [7] ________ (meet / you) at 9.30. The concert [8] ________ (finish) by that time.
P: Sorry, Frances, that is too late for me. At 9.30, I [9] ________ (lie) in bed with Steve Jobs's biography. You should read it too – it [10] ________ (change) your life.

Grammar Alive Planning

11 3.9 **Listen to the dialogue. Match the descriptions (a–d) with Lily and Fred.**

a irresponsible c relaxed
b future-focused d a good planner

12 Work in pairs. Use the cues to act out dialogues.

1 write that email all day? / go out in 10 minutes ➜ finish
A: *Will you be writing that email all day? We're going out in 10 minutes.*
B: *That's okay. I'll have finished by then.*
2 chat with your friends all night? / want to send an email before 10 p.m. ➜ finish
A: *Will you be chatting with your friends all night? I want to send an email before 10 p.m.*
B: *That's okay. I'll have finished by then.*
3 use the computer all evening? / have a meeting on Skype at eight o'clock ➜ do everything
4 watch TV all night? / want to watch a film at 10 p.m. ➜ match finish
5 sit here all night? / close the café in 5 minutes ➜ drink our coffees
6 look for that CD all night? / leave at six o'clock ➜ find it

13 Look at the times below. Write sentences about the things you will have done by then.

By 7 p.m., I will have written an essay.

- 7 p.m.
- the weekend
- the end of the month
- tomorrow
- the end of the school year
- the end of the lesson

LESSON 19 SKILLS WORLD HEALTH

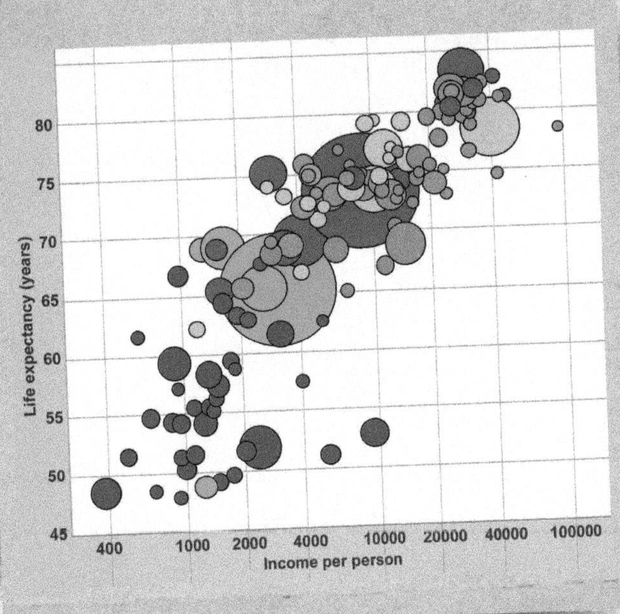

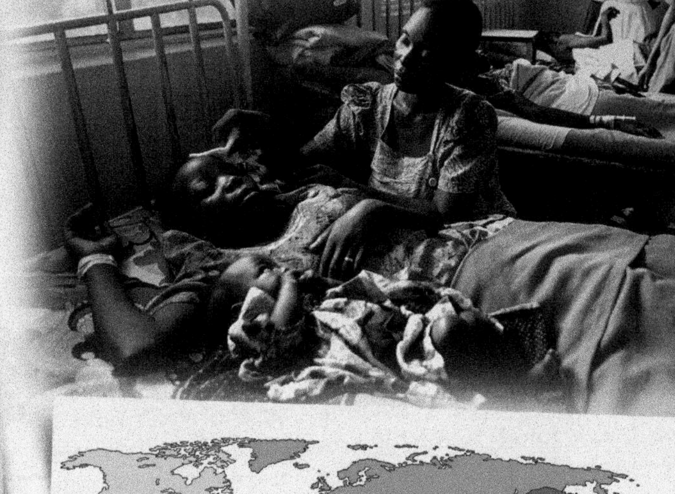

Warm Up

1 **Look at the graph showing different countries' life expectancy and income and the map of world regions. Are the statements true (T) or false (F)?**

1 Most of the poorest countries in the world are in sub-Saharan Africa.
2 The countries with the lowest life expectancy in the world are in sub-Saharan Africa.
3 Most mid-income countries have reasonable life expectancy.
4 The biggest country (China) has a low life expectancy.

Listening

2 3.10 3.11 **Listen to a talk about world health. Complete the notes.**

World health inequalities
Number of people living in poverty: [1] *over a billion*
(on around [2] $_______ a day)
Life expectancy: Lesotho [3] _______ Japan [4] _______
Infant mortality: death of children before [5] _______ birthday
Preventable/curable diseases
Most important diseases:
[6] _______ , tuberculosis and [7] _______
Number of new drugs a year for tropical diseases: [8] _______
Social inequalities
Life expectancy:
men in poor area of Glasgow [9] _______
men in rich area of Glasgow [10] _______
Action needed
- research into [11] _______
- better water supply and sanitation
- education, especially for [12] _______

3 3.10 3.11 **Listen again. Choose the best answers to the questions.**

1 Who is the speaker?
  a a businesswoman
  b an expert in world health
  c a teacher
2 Who is she speaking to?
  a a group of primary students
  b a group of Australian students
  c a group of British university students
3 Which institutions does she criticise most?
  a international drug companies
  b governments in developing countries
  c public healthcare in Africa
4 Which of these statements do you think she believes in?
  a women in the world should have more rights
  b all people in rich countries are lucky
  c it is impossible to stop inequality
5 What is her attitude to world health?
  a she is detached and objective
  b she feels strongly about it
  c she is depressed about it

4 Your Culture **Work in pairs. Discuss the questions about your country.**

1 Where do you think it is on the graph?
2 What health inequalities are there?
3 What diseases could be prevented? How?
4 What else could the government do to improve health?
5 What can people do to improve their health?

DVD Choice

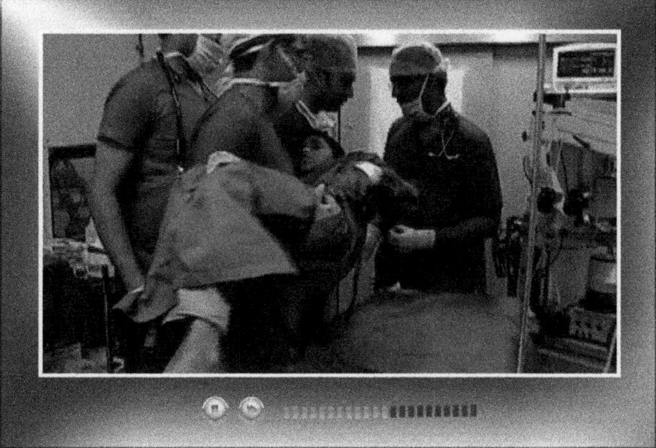

5 DVD 5 **Watch the documentary and complete the notes.**

Lifeline Express: world's [1]_________ hospital train
Distance it travels yearly: [2]_________ km
Patients: rural [3]_________
Number of people treated: [4]_________
Type of operations: [5]_________ , polio, cleft lips, [6]_________

6 DVD 5 **Watch again and answer these questions.**

1. What facilities are there on the train?
2. What does it provide for its patients?
3. Who enables the Lifeline Express to function?
4. What is Dashrath's problem?
5. What is the result of the operation?
6. What will happen when he is fourteen?

7 **What is your opinion of the volunteer doctors on the Lifeline Express? How do they change people's lives?**

Speaking Workshop

8 3.12 3.13 SKILLS BUILDER 4 **Listen to a classroom discussion about health and lifestyles. Use the strategies to match the opinions with the people: Isobel (I), Daniel (D) or both of them (B).**

1. I think we need to do something to reduce the number of cancer cases.
2. People should be able to choose their own lifestyle.
3. Advertising of junk food is a bad thing.
4. Taxing junk food is not a good idea.
5. The government should spend more money on sport.
6. People should live in a healthy way.
7. It's not up to the government to make people change their lifestyles.
8. The government should tell people how to live more healthy lifestyles.

9 **Look at the Talk Builder. Which of the two groups of expressions (1-4 or 5-8) are used after another sentence to:**

a express opinions based on facts?
b support opinions with facts?

Talk Builder Justifying opinions

In my opinion, we should do something about ...
1. **I think so because** lifestyle ...
2. **Actually**, regular exercise ...
3. **The fact is that** ...
4. **The reason for that is that** ...

40% of cancers could be prevented.
5. **So I think** the government should ...
6. **Therefore**, I think we should ...
7. **Because of that**, we need to ...
8. **That's why I think** we should ...

SKILLS BUILDER 39

10 3.14 Pronunciation **Listen and repeat the expressions.**

11 **Complete the opinions with words in bold from the Talk Builder.**

1. I think we should ban advertising of junk food. I think _________ because it kills millions.
2. We should do something about TB. The _________ for that is that it kills millions but can be cured.
3. Millions of people die from malaria. _________ , I think we should do something about it.
4. Junk food causes diabetes and heart disease. _________ of that, we should stop the sale of it.

12 **Work in pairs. Have a discussion about health and lifestyles.**

1. **Write notes about one of these topics.**
   - what the government should do to encourage physical exercise
   - how the government could improve people's diet
   - ways of reducing smoking, drinking and drug-taking
2. SKILLS BUILDER 40 **Look at the strategies. Which of them are most useful for you?**
3. **Have a discussion about the topics with your partner. Use the strategies and expressions from the Talk Builder.**

13 **What did you agree on? Tell the class.**

GRAMMAR

LESSON 20 COMMUNITY SPIRIT

Warm Up

1 Look at the photo. What do you think makes these old people happy and healthy?

- a healthy diet
- physical exercise
- family and friends

2 Read the text. What kept Rosetans healthy until the 1970s?

The Roseto effect

3.15

The small town of Roseto, in Pennsylvania, puzzled doctors in the 1950s: while heart attacks were an epidemic in the USA, there was hardly a Rosetan below 65 suffering from heart disease. At that time, heart disease prevention didn't exist – cholesterol-lowering drugs were to appear many years later. Additionally, there was no suicide, no alcoholism and very little crime in Roseto. People were dying of old age.

Researchers concluded that the secret was the community itself. The town had been founded by immigrants from one area in Italy and, even years later, researchers saw a very closely-knit community where people looked after each other. Rosetans visited each other and frequently organised community celebrations. The households consisted of three generations: old people could be certain that, when they grew old, their experience would be valued and they were going to be respected.

Interestingly, their lifestyles were not ideal: the men smoked and drank alcohol and people's diet was high in fat. But the social network they had created protected them from the pressures of the modern world and its lifestyle-related diseases.

However, even in the 1960s, it was clear that younger Rosetans would not keep up this traditional lifestyle. They soon moved into typical American single-family houses on the outskirts of the town, rejecting traditional social bonds. The consequences followed quickly: the first heart attack of a Rosetan under 45 happened in 1971. Today the Rosetans' vulnerability to heart attack is the same as the national average.

Time reference in the past

3 Read the sentences. Match the verb forms (1-5) in bold with the time references (a-c).

a at the same time as when the study was done
b before the study was done
c in the future when the study was done

1 Cholesterol-lowering drugs **were to appear** many years later.
2 The town **had been founded** by immigrants from one area in Italy.
3 They saw a very closely-knit community where people **looked** after each other.
4 Old people could be certain that when they **grew** old, their experience **would be** valued and they **were going to be** respected.
5 It was clear that younger Rosetans **would** not keep up this traditional lifestyle.

4 Read the sentences. Did the things in bold happen:

a later than I knew?
b before I knew?
c at the same time as I knew?

1 I knew my boyfriend **would be late** for the party.
2 I knew he **was waiting** for a taxi.
3 I knew he **had missed** his bus.
4 I knew he **was going to bring** a surprise present.
5 I knew he **liked** parties.

LANGUAGE CHOICE 32: PAGE 16

5 Complete the sentences with the correct form of the verbs in brackets.

1 Rosetans liked the fact that they ________ (live) in large families.
2 Children were aware that they ________ (have to) take care of their parents one day.
3 Life was predictable, people knew what they ________ (do) when they ________ (get) old.
4 Everyone knew what ________ (happen) in the community the day before.

6 Complete the text with the correct form of the verbs in brackets.

My grandfather was born in a small village in Poland. His family [1]________ (live) there for generations. My granddad always knew that he [2]________ (inherit) his parents' farm one day. However, in 1938 his parents [3]________ (decide) that his sister, who [4]________ (marry) a local boy the year before, [5]________ (stay) on the farm and my grandfather [6]________ (go) to university. When he [7]________ (leave) home in 1939, he [8]________ (not realise) that he [9]________ (never / see) his parents again.

Writing Workshop 5

1 **Look at the photos and read the opinion essay. Is the writer in favour of or against alternative medicine? What arguments does he/she list?**

1 *People are increasingly turning to alternative medicine, such as homeopathy, acupuncture and herbal medicine. In my opinion, alternative medicine is useful as it can help millions of people with illnesses which conventional medicine cannot cure.*

2 *First of all, alternative medicine is 'holistic' since it deals with the whole person, whereas conventional medicine just focuses on the illness. While many conventional doctors rely on quickly prescribing drugs for most problems, alternative therapists tend to have more time to treat their patients. Secondly, treatments like acupuncture have proved successful for problems like back pain, chronic fatigue and asthma when conventional treatment does not work.*

3 *Critics say that there is no scientific proof that alternative therapies actually work; some opponents even claim that they are dangerous due to their side effects and because patients delay proper treatment for serious conditions. Nevertheless, there are many people whose illnesses have been successfully cured by treatments like homeopathy. In addition, alternative medicine actually has fewer side effects than most conventional treatments. Finally, alternative practitioners work with conventional doctors and not against them when dealing with serious illnesses like heart disease and cancer.*

4 *To sum up, although it is not the solution to all health problems, alternative medicine is useful and can help a lot of people. Because of that, I think it should be provided free to patients in this country.*

2 **Which of the arguments that you listed in Exercise 1 do you agree with?**

Text Builder

3 **Match the paragraphs (1-4) in the essay with the functions (a-d).**

a lists reasons to support the writer's opinion
b mentions arguments against and says why the writer does not agree with them
c introduces the topic and states the writer's opinion
d sums up the writer's point of view

4 **Which of the linkers in red in the essay do these things?**

a contrast two pieces of information
b give reasons for something
c list arguments

5 **Use the cues and the words in brackets to write sentences.**

1 treatment is expensive / has nasty side effects / it cures heart disease (nevertheless)

That treatment is expensive and has nasty side effects. Nevertheless it cures heart disease.

2 homeopath talks to me a lot / doctor never listens to me (whereas)
3 homeopathic pills / not expensive / no proof that they work (while)
4 I stopped using those pills / side effects (due to)

6 **Write an opinion essay about a health topic.**

➔ SKILLS BUILDER 26

1 **Write about one of these statements.**

- Health education should be a part of the school curriculum.
- Cigarettes should be made illegal.
- An hour of PE a day should be compulsory in schools.

2 **Write notes for four or five paragraphs:**

- introduction/your opinion
- reasons for your opinion
- arguments against/why you disagree
- conclusion

3 **Use your notes to write your essay.**

7 **Work in groups. Read your partners' essays and have a discussion about the topics.**

Language Review Module 5

1 Talking about health Complete the sentences with the correct form of the verbs below.

break cut do feel tear

1 I was making a sandwich when I ________ myself with the bread knife.
2 Last week my friend ________ his ankle while he was playing football.
3 It's important to ________ regular exercise.
4 Elaine ________ depressed and it's difficult to cheer her up.
5 Terry ________ a ligament in his knee and was in real pain until they took him to hospital. /5

2 Compounds Complete the sentences with one word in each gap.

6 Sports stars who use performance-e________ drugs should be banned for life.
7 The doctor listened to my heart r________ and said it was a little too fast.
8 The speed l________ here is 30 kph.
9 My dad thought he was having a heart a________ but, fortunately, it was something less serious.
10 The problem with doing anything unhealthy is that you don't know what the long-t________ effects will be.
11 Anna's ambition is to break the world r________ for the 5000 metres. /6

3 Comparatives Use the cues to write sentences.

12 exercise / you do, / healthy / you will become
13 hard / you work, / good / you will do in your exams
14 long / you chat, / expensive / your phone bill is
15 late / we are, / angry / Mark will be
16 cheap / clothes are, / bad / quality they are
17 warm / it is, / happy / I feel /6

4 Future Complete the sentences with *will* + infinitive, *will have* + third form or *will be* + *-ing* form.

18 By the end of this film, we ________ (see) about thirty minutes of adverts.
19 This time next week, the operation will be over and you ________ (lie) in a nice comfortable hospital bed.
20 Don't eat so quickly. By the time the film starts, you ________ (finish) all your popcorn.
21 Don't buy anything here. You ________ (find) something better in a different shop.
22 At ten o'clock tonight, we ________ (talk) to our cousins in Australia on the internet. /5

5 Time clauses Use the cues to write sentences. Use the Present Perfect and *will* + infinitive.

23 When / I finish / this homework, / I watch a film
24 You not get paid / until / you be here for one month
25 After / you take these tablets, / you feel better
26 We go for a pizza / after / I try this dress on
27 I meet you / as soon as / I have my dinner /5

6 Justifying opinions Complete the text with one word in each gap.

The National Health Service is great. The [28]r________ for that is that it is free. However, it costs a lot of money and [29]b________ of that, it needs changing. The [30]f________ is that even tourists can get free treatment. That's [31]w________ I feel we should have a health card. Every British person would get one free. [32]T________ no one could complain that it was unfair. Tourists could buy one. It wouldn't be expensive, [33]s________ they wouldn't mind paying for one. /6

7 Time reference in the past Choose the correct words to complete the sentences.

34 I knew what you *were going to/are going to/will* say before you said it.
35 We knew we *would/will/are going to* have to stay at work until late at night.
36 I knew before kick-off that they *won't/wouldn't/aren't going to* win.
37 At the time, sports stars drank, ate unhealthy food and smoked. Changes to their diets *are to/will/were to* appear many years later.
38 It was clear that there *will/is to/would* be trouble later in the day.
39 I *am going to/was going to/would* take my tablet later but I forgot.
40 I thought you *were to/will/were going to* tidy up after the party. /7

Self Assessment

3.16 **Listen and check your answers. Write down the scores. Use the table to find practice exercises.**

Exercise	If you need practice, go to
1	Language Choice 27
2	Language Choice 28
3	Language Choice 29
4	Language Choice 30
5	Language Choice 31
6	Students' Book p.51 ex.11
7	Language Choice 32

LEARNING LINKS: 1 Check Your Progress 5 → MyLab / Workbook page 55. Complete the Module Diary.
2 Sound Choice 3 → MyLab / Workbook page 56. Choose three pronunciation activities to do.

MODULE

6 GENIUS

Objectives: **Read, listen** and **talk about** exceptional people; **read** a story extract; **interview** someone; **write** a description of a person; **learn more about** reference words and modality.

a Stephen Hawking

b Grigori Perelman

c Jane Goodall

TOPIC TALK

1 **Look at the network. What personality adjectives can describe geniuses? Add other adjectives.**

ambitious, ... hard-working, ...

2 3.17 3.18 **Listen to information about the exceptional people in the photos (a-c). What personality adjectives are used to describe them?**

Jane Goodall: dreamy, driven

3 3.19 3.20 **Listen to a description of a person. Complete the information in the network.**

4 3.21 Pronunciation **Listen to the adjectives and underline the schwa /ə/ sounds at the end of the words if you hear them. Then listen and repeat the words.**

1 ambitious	5 eccentric	9 relaxed
2 analytical	6 fearless	10 self-confident
3 clever	7 idealistic	
4 driven	8 meticulous	

LANGUAGE CHOICE 36: PAGE 20

5 **Work in groups. Use the network to describe a person *you* know well.**

Describing people

At first, he/she seems rather [1]_________ but when you get to know him/her you realise he/she's really quite [2]_________.
Sometimes, he/she tends to be slightly [3]_________ but usually he/she is pretty [4]_________.
He/She is fairly [5]_________.
For example, he/she sometimes [6]_________ when talking to people.
He/She is very good at [7]_________ and [8]_________.

Personality
absent-minded, ambitious, analytical, arrogant, articulate, balanced, bright, clever, competitive, creative, dedicated, determined, dreamy, driven, eccentric, energetic, enthusiastic, fearless, idealistic, logical, meticulous, modest, obsessive, reclusive, relaxed, reserved, self-confident, sensible, sensitive, serious, shy, single-minded, thoughtful, witty

Quirks
bites his/her lip, bites his/her nails, blinks, checks his/her mobile, fidgets, frowns, giggles, grins, shrugs his/her shoulders, taps his/her feet, touches his/her hair/nose/ear

Abilities
analysing and solving problems, debating issues, doing puzzles, drawing and painting, getting on with people, making speeches, playing musical instruments, playing sport, singing, telling jokes, working with other people

LESSON 21 DARWIN

Voyage of *The Beagle* 1831-6

Warm Up

1 Look at the map and the pictures. What do you know about Charles Darwin? Which of these things did he do?

1 studied theology
2 travelled to distant places
3 explored the Galápagos Islands
4 worked as a doctor
5 announced a theory of evolution with another scientist

2 Read the article. Check your guesses from Exercise 1. Why is Darwin considered a genius?

3 What other scientists could be called geniuses? Why?

I think Maria Skłodowska-Curie was a genius. She changed scientists' view of physics and chemistry and, being a woman, had to overcome a lot of barriers.

Reference

4 Look at the nouns in bold in the sentences (1-4). Match them with the uses of articles (a-d).

1 He witnessed **an operation** performed on a child. *d*
2 One of the key arguments for natural selection came from **the birds** that Darwin collected from the Galápagos Islands.
3 Darwin's theory of evolution transformed the way we understand **the world**.
4 If **the changes** are great enough, they can produce a new species.

a something unique
b something specific that is described in the same sentence, e.g. with a relative clause
c it is clear from the wider context which thing we refer to, e.g. it has been mentioned before
d one of many things and it doesn't matter exactly which one

3.22

Charles Darwin (1809–1882) developed a revolutionary theory of evolution that transformed the way we understand the world and we see ourselves. In *On the Origin of Species*, published in 1859, Darwin described the process of natural selection. The 'fittest' animals or plants – those with the characteristics best suited to their environment – are more likely to survive and reproduce. They pass on these desirable characteristics to their offspring. Gradually those features become more common, causing the species to change over time. If the changes are great enough, they can produce an entirely new species. *The Descent of Man*, published in 1871, suggested that humans descended from apes.

DID YOU KNOW?

- When Darwin studied medicine, he witnessed an operation performed on a child without anaesthetic. [1]That made him give up medical studies. He then studied theology but, instead of becoming a priest, in 1831 he set off on a five-year scientific expedition around the world. [2]There he collected evidence for his future theory.
- One of the key arguments for natural selection came from the birds that Darwin collected from the Galápagos Islands. The birds were clearly the same species but [3]some had large strong beaks for eating nuts while [4]others had long thin beaks for finding worms in the ground. Darwin realised that [5]all came from a single ancestor but, as they dispersed to different islands, they had adapted to eat the various foods available.
- Darwin developed the theory of evolution in the 1830s but he didn't announce it [6]then. He knew his ideas were radical so he delayed publishing the theory for about twenty years while he assembled more evidence.
- The theory of evolution was actually published a year before *On the Origin of Species*. While Darwin was working on his own theory, another scientist, Alfred Wallace, had independently developed a similar [7]one. [8]Both announced their ideas in two joint articles in 1858: one was an extract from Darwin's future book and the other article was Wallace's paper 'On the Tendency of Species to form Varieties'. Interestingly, after 1858 Wallace never wrote about evolution. The other texts he wrote concerned mainly his explorations in Indonesia and Malaysia.

Galápagos finches

5 **Look at the words (1-8) in red in the text. Find the phrases in the text that they refer to.**

1 *That - witnessing an operation performed on a child without anaesthetic*

6 **Read the sentences 1-4 below. Which of the phrases in bold talk about:**

a one from a pair?
b the remaining ones?
c one of many/one more?
d not the ones already mentioned but different ones?

1 **Another scientist**, Alfred Wallace, had independently developed a similar theory.
2 One was an extract from Darwin's future book and **the other article** was Wallace's paper.
3 **The other** texts he wrote concerned mainly his explorations in Indonesia and Malaysia.
4 His ideas were unfamiliar to **other scientists**.

Practice

7 **Choose the correct words to complete the sentences.**

1 Darwin had ten children but *some/another* died when they were very young.
2 Scientific discoveries are often hard to understand and *all/other* require years of research.
3 Darwin was *a/the* theologian. *There/This* didn't help him in his studies on evolution.
4 My grandfathers are scientists - *another/one* is a physicist and *other/the other* is a chemist.
5 I have to do *another/the other* experiment to complete my research.
6 *The/All* dog breeds come from wolves.

LANGUAGE CHOICE 28: PAGE 18

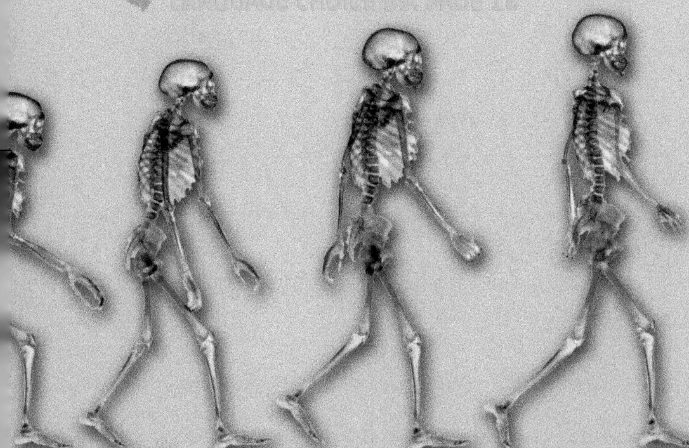

8 **Complete the text with the words below.**

an (x 2) the (x 2) there this
another the other other both

Alfred Wallace was [1] ___*an*___ explorer. He travelled to South America. [2] ________ he studied and catalogued plants and animals and developed his ideas about evolution. On the way back to England, his ship sank, together with his notes and collections. [3] ________forced Wallace to take [4] ________ trip, this time to Indonesia, to collect more data. In 1858, Wallace sent [5] ________ article outlining his theory to Darwin and it was published alongside Darwin's own theory. Even though [6] ________ developed the theory of natural selection at the same time, only one of them, Darwin, is famous to this day while [7] ________ is seldom remembered. However, Alfred Wallace was happy with [8] ________ recognition he received in the scientific community. He made [9] ________ contributions to the development of evolutionary theory, such as [10] ________ concept of how animals adapt to using bright colours to warn off predators.

Grammar Alive

Talking about more than one person

9 3.23 **Listen to the interview. Match the scientists (1-4) with the facts (a-d).**

1 Wallace 2 Lamarck 3 Mendel 4 Watson and Crick

a described DNA
b came to the same conclusions as Darwin
c came up with a theory of evolution earlier than Darwin
d developed the concept of genes

10 **Use the cues to make dialogues.**

1
- Copernicus and Galileo / work in the same period?
- die 1543 / born 1564
- important scientist in Galileo's times?
- Johannes Kepler, a German astronomer and mathematician

A: *Did Copernicus and Galileo work in the same period?*
B: *No, one died in 1543 and the other was born in 1564.*
A: *Were there other important scientists in Galileo's times?*
B: *Yes, a German astronomer and mathematician, Johannes Kepler.*

2
- Michelangelo and Leonardo da Vinci / interested in science?
- mainly a painter and sculptor / an artist and scientist
- great artist in their times?
- lots / e.g. Hieronymus Bosch (the Netherlands), Hans Holbein (Germany)

3
- Louis Pasteur and Robert Koch / French?
- French / German
- important microbiologist in 19th century?
- Ferdinand Cohn, German scientist, classified bacteria

LESSON 22

SKILLS

GOOD AND EVIL

3.24

I had not seen Holmes for some time when he strode calmly into my consulting room on the night of April 24th. I observed him and he looked even more pallid and thinner than usual.
'Can I close the shutters?' My rather eccentric friend tiptoed round the wall and closed them.
'You are afraid of something!' I exclaimed.
'No, I am not a nervous man but one must recognise danger when it is near. I must apologise for calling so late,' he said quietly, 'and I must beg you to allow me to leave your house by climbing over your back garden wall.'
'But what does it all mean?' I asked. I saw that his hands were bruised and bleeding.
'You have never heard of Professor Moriarty?' said he.
'Never.'
'He is the Napoleon of crime. Nobody knows the criminal world like I do but I have found out that Moriarty is the organiser of half of the crime in London. He is the first enemy I have met who is my intellectual equal. He is a brilliant mathematician and an ex-university professor. He is a genius, a philosopher. He does little himself, he only plans and organises. Sometimes his agents are caught but he always escapes. I have been working for months to try to capture Moriarty and I am close. In three days' time, the professor and his gang will be in the hands of the police. But this morning Professor Moriarty came to see me. His appearance was familiar to me. He is extremely tall and thin, has a high forehead and sunken eyes. He looks like a harmless professor but his face moves from side to side like a reptile in a sinister way. He stared at me with great curiosity.
"Please take a chair," I said.
"You must give up your persecution of me, Mr Holmes," he whispered.
"After Monday," I replied.
"Tut, tut! Now I have only one alternative and that is to kill you."
"I am afraid," I said, "I have things to do."
"You will never beat me. And if you destroy me, I will do the same to you," he snarled viciously and went out of the room.

Holmes

Warm Up

1 **Work in pairs. Look at the stills of Holmes, Watson and Moriarty from *Sherlock Holmes: A Game of Shadows*. Make guesses about the personalities of the three film characters.**

I think Holmes looks outgoing and self-confident. He doesn't look like a genius.

2 **Read the descriptions of the film characters on page 105. Check your guesses from Exercise 1.**

Reading

3 **Read the extract from *The Final Problem* by Arthur Conan Doyle. Use the strategies to match the adjectives below with the characters, Holmes, Watson and Moriarty.**

brave brilliant calm dangerous eccentric evil helpful kind likeable loyal sinister threatening

Holmes: brave,

4 **Read the extract again. Choose the best answers to these questions.**

1 Why did Holmes close the shutters?
a he was frightened
b someone might try to kill him
c Moriarty was outside
d it was dark outside

2 What was Holmes' attitude towards Moriarty?
a he liked him
b he was afraid of him
c he admired his behaviour
d he wanted to catch him

3 What is Moriarty's occupation?
a a gang leader
b a murderer
c a professor
d a philosopher

4 Why did Moriarty visit Holmes?
a to get to know him
b to get him to stop investigating
c to threaten to kill him
d to kill him

5 What did Moriarty probably not do after leaving Holmes?
a try to kill him himself
b plan Holmes' death
c organise 'accidents'
d have him followed

6 Which of these things can you not find out about Watson from the text?
a he is married
b he is a good friend of Holmes
c he is good with guns
d he is a doctor

I knew then that I was in terrible danger. At midday, I was in Oxford Street when I was nearly run down by a carriage. Then, as I strolled down Vere Street, a brick came down from a roof and shattered at my feet. Now, on my way here, I was attacked by a thug with a stick. I knocked him down and the police have arrested him.'
'You will spend the night here?' I inquired.
'No, my kind friend, you might find me a dangerous guest. I would like you to come with me to the Continent.'
'I have not got many patients and my wife is away,' I said. 'So I should be glad to come and help.'
'And to start tomorrow morning?'
'If necessary.'
'Oh, yes, it is most necessary.'
Holmes gave me instructions for meeting him and then left over the garden wall.

5 Vocabulary **Look at the Word Builder. Match the words in red in the text with the meanings (a-j).**

a walk quickly with long steps *stride*
b ask someone for information
c watch someone carefully
d walk slowly for pleasure
e walk on your toes
f ask for something in a way that shows you need it badly
g look at something for a long time without moving your eyes
h say something loudly when you are surprised
i say something very quietly
j say something aggressively (like an animal when it is angry)

Word Builder Word families

1 Say/speak: *exclaim, snarl, whisper*
2 Ask: *beg, inquire*
3 Look at: *observe, stare at*
4 Walk: *stride, stroll, tiptoe*

LANGUAGE CHOICE 37: PAGE 20

6 **Use words from the Word Builder to rewrite the dialogue below in a more interesting way. Replace the expressions in italics.**

When Williams *walked quickly* into my office, I *carefully watched* him - he seemed very angry and nervous.
'I've got a terrible problem, Smith. Can I speak to you?' he *asked desperately*. 'We've got a spy and I know who it is!' he *said very quietly*.
'A spy!' I *said loudly* and *looked at* him *for a long time*.
'Don't speak so loudly!' he *said very aggressively*.
'Can I possibly *ask* who it is?' I said.
'It's the boss!' Williams replied.

7 **Look at the expressions (1-2) in bold in the Sentence Builder. Which of them express:**

a the reason for doing something?
b how something is done?

Sentence Builder *by/for + -ing*

1 Please let me leave your house **by climbing** over your back garden wall.
2 Holmes gave me instructions **for meeting** him.

LANGUAGE CHOICE 36: PAGE 20

8 **Match the sentence beginnings (1-5) with the endings (a-e).**

1 Holmes avoided being killed in Watson's house by
2 When he arrived, Holmes made preparations for
3 Moriarty always escapes arrest by
4 After leaving, Moriarty made plans for
5 Moriarty's men tried to kill Holmes by

a killing Holmes.
b leaving through the garden.
c closing the shutters.
d getting others to commit crimes.
e running him over with a carriage.

Your Choice

9 **Work in pairs. Choose a brilliant hero or villain from a film, comic or book. Write notes about:**

- his/her personality
- his/her abilities
- what he/she did

10 **Work in groups. Tell your partners about your character.**

No Comment

'The world is full of obvious things which nobody ever observes.'

LESSON 23

GREAT MUSICIANS

a Benjamin Grosvenor

b Evgeny Kissin

c Maria João Pires

Warm Up

1 Your Culture **Work in pairs. Look at the photos (a-c) and discuss these questions.**

1 Who do you think are the greatest musicians ever from your country?
2 Why were/are they great?

Listening

2 3.25 **Listen to seven answers (1-7) from an interview about the lives of concert pianists. Match them with the questions (a-h). There is one extra question.**

a What sort of workloads do they have?
b What does it take to be successful?
c What sort of pay and conditions do they have?
d What's the best age for starting?
e Do concert pianists get nervous before concerts?
f How many of them actually become successful?
g What's it like preparing to perform a new piece?
h What are the lives of young pianists like?

3 3.26 3.27 **Listen to the full interview. Use the strategies to make notes about three of the topics mentioned in Exercise 2.**

best age for starting: 6-8 – why? to develop physical capacity

4 **Work in pairs. Take turns to use your notes to tell your partner about concert pianists.**

The best age for starting to play the piano is very young – between the ages of six and eight.

5 **Look at the Sentence Builder. Look at the auxiliaries in bold. Which sentence expresses surprise?**

Sentence Builder Emphasis (3)

1 Most people recommend starting between six and eight but some pianists **do** begin a lot earlier.
2 He loves playing in public but he **does** find it exhausting.
3 Wow, he **did** start young!

6 **Work in pairs. Use the cues to talk about your musical interests. Use the auxiliaries *do, does* and *did* for emphasis.**

1 I / not very keen on (type of music) / like (a group)
*I'm not very keen on rap but I **do** like Snoop Dogg.*
2 (name of singer) not my favourite singer / have some good songs
3 last year / not go to any (type of concert) / go to (a type of concert)
4 I usually dislike listening to that (group/singer) / like their/his/her latest record/album
5 our school / not got (big orchestra/jazz group) / have (choir/rock group)

Speaking Workshop

7 3.28 DVD 6 **Listen to or watch the interview with a rock musician. Complete the sentences.**

1 This is the first time Suzy has worked *as a music journalist*.
2 Billy Ray used to be the _________ of a rock group.
3 The group chose their name after their _________ during a storm.
4 The group had _________ in the USA.
5 They gave up the group because they were tired of _________.
6 Suzy thinks that the group should start _________.

8 Look at the Talk Builder. Match the expressions (1-4) with their uses (a-d).

a explaining or commenting on something you have already mentioned
b checking information
c asking the other person to clarify
d checking the other person has understood

Talk Builder Clarifying

1 Is that right? / So that means ... , right? / So, just to recap, you ... , right?
2 What do you mean by that exactly? / I don't quite get that. Could you explain what you mean exactly?
3 Do you see what I mean? / Do you follow me?
4 To put it another way, we ... / In other words, ... / As I said before, there ... / What I mean to say is ...

SKILLS BUILDER 41

9 3.29 Pronunciation **Listen and repeat the expressions.**

10 Complete the dialogue with expressions from the Talk Builder.

A: I am a semi-professional musician. In [1]_________, I have a day job, too.
B: So that [2]_________ you work evenings and weekends?
A: Yes, that's right. [3]_________ said before, we play every Saturday night in a club. We play 'dance punk'.
B: I don't quite [4]_________. Could you [5]_________ you mean exactly?
A: Well, it's a mixture of dance music and punk. To put it [6]_________, we play electronic disco music but with a punk element in it. It's great for dancing. Do you [7]_________?
B: I think so. So, just to [8]_________, you're in a five-piece dance punk band, [9]_________? And you're a local band, too.
A: Yes, and we've just made our first album. Some of the music critics like it but most people haven't heard of it. [10]_________ I mean to say is that it hasn't got onto the radio or anything like that.

11 Work in pairs. Interview a famous musician.

1 **Both choose a real or an imaginary musician (e.g. a composer, singer or guitarist). Find out or make up information about these things:**
- his/her important albums/songs
- how he/she started off
- how he/she became successful
- what he/she enjoys most
- how often he/she plays live
- plans for the future

2 SKILLS BUILDER 42 **Use the strategies in the Skills Builder to write down five of your most common mistakes when speaking.**

3 **Take turns to interview your partner using expressions from the Talk Builder.**

12 Tell the class two or three interesting things about your partner's musician.

She's a folk singer from Scotland who started off playing in clubs in London.

LESSON **24** GRAMMAR

SUCCESS

Steve Jobs

Warm Up

1 What do you know about the person in the photo? In what way was he successful?

2 Read the book synopsis. What are the necessary ingredients for success? Which, in your opinion, is the most important?

3.30

MALCOLM GLADWELL
OUTLIERS
THE STORY OF SUCCESS
'REVELATORY'
THE No. 1 INTERNATIONAL BESTSELLER

We tend to assume that people like Shakespeare or Darwin owe their success to their genius. In his new book, *Outliers*, Malcolm Gladwell suggests that the truth may be more complex. Of course, all successful people are bound to have some natural gifts. But the true ingredients of success are most probably hard work, opportunity, and the environment you grow up in.

First, you need about 10,000 hours of practice before you get really good at something. Mozart's early work was certainly not great or original. He composed his first true masterpieces when he was 21. By that time, he must have spent about ten years composing concertos.

But hard work is not enough, you have to get your chance. Most Silicon Valley tycoons, like Bill Gates or Steve Jobs, were born around 1955. When the personal computer revolution came twenty years later, they were at a perfect age to lead it. Besides, in their teens they enjoyed unlimited access to computer terminals, unlike their less fortunate peers. So by 1975, they had definitely done their necessary 10,000 hours of programming.

Finally, success seems to be easier if you come from a culture that promotes hard work, diligence and industriousness. It can't be a coincidence that Asian children are better at maths than anyone else and Japanese cars are supposed to be the best in the world. Did you know that Japanese kids go to school over 240 days a year whereas the American school year is only 180 days long?

Uncertainty

3 **Look at the sentences (1-4) and compare them to the factual statements in brackets. Do the words in bold make the statements sound:**

a stronger? b less certain?

1 We **tend to** assume that people owe their success to their genius.
(We assume that people owe their success to their genius.)
2 Japanese cars **are supposed to** be the best in the world.
(Japanese cars are the best in the world.)
3 Success **seems** to be easier if you come from a culture that promotes hard work.
(Success is easier if you come from a culture that promotes hard work.)
4 All successful people **are bound to** have some natural gifts.
(All successful people have some natural gifts.)

4 **Look at the sentences with modals (1-3). Which sentence refers to the past? Write the corresponding statements of fact.**

1 The truth may be more complex.
The truth is more complex.
2 He must have spent ten years composing concertos.
3 It can't be a coincidence.

LANGUAGE CHOICE 35: PAGE 18

5 **Rewrite the sentences using the words in brackets.**

1 Perhaps he's got a musical talent. (may)
2 I don't believe they failed the exam. (can't)
3 He is most probably working now. (bound)
4 I think they enjoy studying. (seem)
5 Everybody says that he is the best student at his college. (supposed)
6 Asian kids study more than European schoolchildren. (tend)
7 I'm certain he received a lot of support from his family. (must)
8 Successful people are confident. (seem)
9 Children spend a lot of time doing things they love. (tend)
10 Good students study hard. (bound)

Writing Workshop 6

1 **Look at the picture and read the description. Find three differences.**

1 The first thing you notice about Tom is his height. He is 1.90 m but looks even taller because he is pretty solid. The next thing that strikes you about him is his long, dark hair, which is thick and shiny, and his dark, expressive eyes.

2 When you first meet Tom, he seems shy and serious but you soon realise that he has got a great, dry sense of humour. He has that witty ability to say the right thing at the right time which makes everyone fall about laughing.

3 Of course, Tom has his faults. He tends to be bad-tempered early in the morning and he also fidgets and taps his feet a lot, which can be irritating. However, Tom always has time for other people; he is especially good with young children and works as a monitor in a summer camp. He is brilliant at telling stories and jokes and kids love that.

4 Tom hates dressing up and shopping for clothes and he usually wears black jeans, a heavy metal T-shirt and a denim jacket. He does not feel the cold as most people do so you hardly ever see him wearing a scarf or coat, even in the middle of winter.

5 To sum up, Tom is one of those people who do not seem to care much about what people think of him but who is actually very thoughtful and kind to others. For me, he is someone special because he makes me feel happy and relaxed when I am with him.

2 **Read the description again. What are Tom's talents, quirks and good qualities?**

Text Builder

3 **Match the topics (a-e) with the paragraphs (1-5) in the description.**

a opinion about the person
b habits/behaviour
c personality
d appearance
e clothes

4 **Find words or expressions in the description which mean:**

a to see something (paragraph 1)
b to appear (paragraph 1)
c to make a clear impact on you (paragraph 1)
d to appear (paragraph 2)
e to understand something that you had not noticed before (paragraph 2)
f is often (paragraph 3)
g to put on special clothes (paragraph 4)

5 **Complete the sentences with words from Exercise 4.**

1 One thing you immediately ________ about her is her long, dark hair.
2 Another thing that ________ you is her lovely, soft voice.
3 She is about thirty but she ________ much younger.
4 At first, she ________ quite outgoing and sociable but then you ________ that she is quite shy.

6 **Use the cues to write sentences with relative clauses.**

1 long / dark / shiny / thick / **hair**
He has got long, dark hair which is thick and shiny.
2 pale / round / friendly / expressive / **face**
3 large / blue / sinister / cold / **eyes**
4 soft / deep / attractive / relaxing / **voice**
5 strong / muscular / tattooed / sun-tanned / **arms**

7 **Write a description of someone special that you know.**

SKILLS BUILDER 27

1 **Choose a person and write notes about his/her:**
- appearance
- personality
- habits/behaviour/talents
- clothes

2 **Use your notes to write the description.**

3 **Check your descriptions for mistakes of spelling and grammar.**

8 **Work in pairs. Read your partner's description. Give it a mark from 1 to 5 for:**

- interest
- organisation
- language

Language Review Module 6

1 Describing people **Complete the description with one word in each gap.**

At first my friend Roman [1]s______ quite insecure and shy, but when you get to know him, you [2]r______ that he's really quite outgoing. Sometimes he [3]t______ to be a bit absent-minded. He is [4]f______ modest but he knows that he is very [5]g______ at most school subjects. /5

2 Describing people **Match the beginnings (6-10) with the endings (a-g).**

6 Elaine always bites her
7 Tom often shrugs his
8 My dad hates making
9 I'm very good at solving
10 My mum often tells

a problems.
b jokes.
c speeches.
d shoulders.
e nails.

/5

3 Reference **Complete the sentences with the words below. There are two extra words.**

a all another both other the the other

11 If you don't like this idea, I've got ________ one that you might think is better.
12 There were two people at the meeting. One was very enthusiastic but ________ one wasn't.
13 We interviewed two people. They were ________ excellent.
14 I'm in ________ maths competition at school.
15 ________ final is next week. /5

4 Reference **Complete the text with one word in each gap.**

We're doing [16]________ project at school on geniuses. [17]________ genius I'm writing about is Judit Polgar. She's from Hungary and she became [18]________ chess grandmaster at the age of just fourteen. She's got two sisters and [19]________ of them are great chess players, too. [20]________ three of them can also speak several languages and have got great educational qualifications. /5

5 Word families **Choose the correct words to complete the sentences.**

21 'Thank goodness!' she *begged/exclaimed.*
22 'Please help me,' she *inquired/begged.*
23 Darren *tiptoed/snarled* quietly out of the room.
24 'Do you know who is in charge here?' she *observed/inquired.*
25 I spent ten minutes *staring/observing* at the book but I couldn't concentrate on the words. /5

6 Emphasis (3) **Complete the dialogue with the correct auxiliaries.**

A: Jane is in the final of the piano competition.
B: Well, she [26]________ play really well. You play the piano, don't you?
A: I [27]________ have a few lessons but I gave up.
B: You [28]________ give up a lot of things! What do your parents say?
A: My mum [29]________ get upset sometimes but I [30]________ do judo for for a whole year before I gave that up! /5

7 Clarifying **Complete the dialogue with one word in each gap.**

A: There should be a special school for people like me.
B: What do you [31]m______ by 'people like you' exactly?
A: Well, to [32]p______ it another way, people of above average intelligence.
B: I don't quite [33]g______ that.
A: Well, as I've said [34]b______, geniuses can get bored at normal schools. Do you [35]f______ me?
B: I understand that, but you came nineteenth in the class in our last exams! /5

8 Uncertainty **Choose the correct words to complete the sentences.**

36 Which exercise *are we supposed/are we bound/do we seem* to be doing now?
37 I don't know Carole very well but she *seems/tends/is bound* to be nice.
38 The maths test next week *may/is bound to/must* be difficult. They always are.
39 Ask Paul about your mobile. He *tends to/can't/may* have seen it when he was tidying up.
40 I *can't/must/seem to* have made so many mistakes. Could you check again, please? /5

Self Assessment

3.31 **Listen and check your answers. Write down the scores. Use the table to find practice exercises.**

Exercise	If you need practice, go to
1	Language Choice 36
2	Language Choice 36
3	Language Choice 33 and 34
4	Language Choice 33 and 34
5	Language Choice 37
6	Language Choice 39
7	Students' Book p.61 ex.10
8	Language Choice 35

LEARNING LINKS: 1 Read and listen to a scene from *Hamlet* in Culture Choice 3 on page 110. Then do a project about a famous play or film from your country.
2 Check Your Progress 6 → MyLab / Workbook page 65.
3 Exam Choice 3 → MyLab / Workbook pages 66-68. Complete the Module Diary.

MODULE

7 COMMUNITIES

Objectives: **Read**, **listen** and **talk about** different kinds of communities; **make suggestions** and **evaluate plans**; **write** a story about a personal experience; **learn more about** conditional sentences and the use of *it* and *there*.

TOPIC TALK

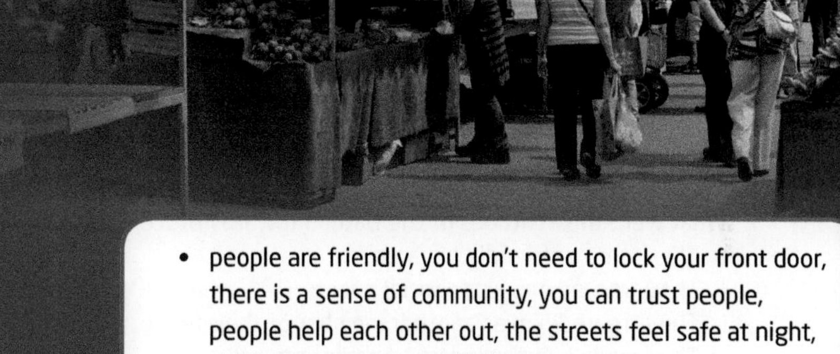

1 Look at the photo. What sort of place do you think it is?

2 4.1 4.2 Listen to three people describing their communities. Which place would you like to live in?

3 4.3 4.4 Listen again to the first person. Complete the information in the network.

4 4.5 Pronunciation Listen and write down the pairs of words. Mark the word stress.

1 *photo; photography*

LANGUAGE CHOICE 40: PAGE 21

5 Work in groups. Use the network to describe *your* local community.

My community

I've lived here for a couple of years and I know [1]*a lot of/quite a few/a few* people. The best thing about living here is that [2]_______ and [3]_______. Another positive thing is that [4]_______.
The worst thing about my area is that [5]_______ and [6]_______.
My area would be better for young people if there were [7]_______. It would also be good if we could [8]_______.

- people are friendly, you don't need to lock your front door, there is a sense of community, you can trust people, people help each other out, the streets feel safe at night, children can go out on their own
- **there are good/lots of** hospitals, libraries, local clubs, local events, parks, playgrounds, schools, shops, sports facilities, volunteer groups
- **there is** a lot of cultural diversity, good public transport, very little crime

- the people are nosy/unfriendly/rude, nobody knows their neighbours, people keep to themselves, there is no privacy
- **there is a lot of** begging, crime, drug abuse, graffiti, heavy traffic, homelessness, litter, pollution, poor housing, poverty, public drinking, unemployment, vandalism
- **there are a lot of** abandoned cars, boarded-up shops, burglaries, burnt-out buildings, muggings, murders, riots, street gangs, traffic accidents
- **there aren't any** good shops, green spaces
- **there is a lack of** clean drinking water, decent sanitation

- more free activities for teens, places for teens to hang out in, better sports facilities (e.g. skate parks), nightclubs for teens
- take part in making decisions about local issues, have a say in the local council, vote in local elections

LESSON 25 SKILLS

NOMADS

Warm Up

1 **Look at the photos and read the first paragraph. Would you like to spend time with an indigenous people? Why/ Why not? Tell the class.**

I would like to live with the Bedouins in the Arabian desert because ...

Reading

2 SKILLS BUILDER 18 **Read the travel book extract and use the strategies to answer the questions.**

1 What is the situation in the extract - the place, the people involved, what they do?
2 What do you think will happen next to the people?
3 What are the relationships between the people?
4 How do they react to events and to each other?
5 What can you guess about their attitudes to life?

3 **Read the extract again. Choose the best answers to the questions.**

1 What was Bruce Parry's situation in Batbayer and Puruhan's family in the Darhad community?
a He visited them every day.
b He lived exactly as they did.
c He worked for them.
d He observed and filmed them.

2 What were the attitudes of the Darhad towards Bruce?
a They were unfriendly towards him.
b They treated him as a special guest.
c They treated him as another member of their team.
d They made him the centre of attention.

3 What did he notice about the Darhad?
a They were very efficient at moving.
b They gave a lot of importance to ceremonies.
c They were not very hard-working.
d They had a modern system of communication.

4 Why were the Darhad moving somewhere else?
a Because they liked moving.
b Because they didn't have enough food.
c Because they needed to be near a lake.
d Because their animals needed grass.

5 What did Bruce think of the Darhad people?
a They were romantic and sentimental.
b They were better than the people in the West.
c They had an easy lifestyle.
d They had a great sense of community.

6 Which of these adjectives does not describe Bruce's habits and lifestyle at home when compared to that of the Darhad?
a busy b generous c selfish d stressful

4.6

In his fascinating book, *Tribe*, the journalist Bruce Parry describes his experiences with indigenous people in Amazonia, Africa and Asia. In Mongolia, Bruce stayed in a ger with Batbayer and Puruhan and their family and saw them make the autumn migration.

I joined in with the daily routine, waking at five in the morning for a breakfast of milky tea, bread and very hard cheese. Then it would be out to help where I could. It was an interesting contrast to my earlier trips, where I'd always been the centre of attention with people watching and hanging around wherever I went. Here, they didn't give a damn; I was there to help so they showed me what to do and I got on with it.

Even as the regular daily work went on, preparations were being made for the big move. Finally, the day came when we were ready to leave. The mysterious system of communication in the steppes was at work again as we were joined at dawn by numerous helpers from other gers. Very quickly the tents came down and were stacked away. At last, totally without ceremony, we were off, a huge herd of mixed animals heading in a straight line along the edge of the mountains.

During the first few days, Bruce watched the animals swimming across a dangerous river and every day observed the mountains getting whiter. Batbayer was worried about snow during the crossing but they were lucky.

The track along the top of the pass was the most treacherous part. Now we horsemen were working hard, cantering off to the sides to bring in stray cattle, helping others who had got stuck in the mud. We were in the saddle for much longer that day, but finally we came to the end of the pass and saw down to the other side. There were the snow-free brown grasslands of the winter pastures. We rode down the gentle slope and into the valley and made camp at the base of the mountains for the last time.
Sadly, in the morning we were going our separate ways; Batbayer, Puruhan and the others heading on down to set up their gers by the lake; the crew and I going back over the pass, then driving back to Ulaanbaatar, before flying home.

Batbayer had said that I looked sad as I rode, and it would be a lie to say I didn't feel more than a few pangs of melancholy leaving my wonderful hosts in that beautiful place. I won't get sentimental and say I don't enjoy my hectic existence at home, but there is a deeply enviable serenity about their lives. I tried desperately not to over-romanticise, but I couldn't help but think that some aspects of their community and its wonderfully generous habits, their hospitality and way of sharing, put my cynical materialistic lifestyle to shame.

'What makes you happy?' I asked Batbayer, in our final chat on camera before we headed back.
He smiled. 'It's very simple: there's the work I have to do, and the peace in my mind.'
'Stress-free living?' I suggested, then listened to the interpreter struggling to translate 'stress'. But he couldn't. It seemed he didn't know if the word even existed in Mongolian.

4 Vocabulary **Look at the Word Builder. Match the words in bold with the meanings (a–i).**

a just continued doing (an activity)
b wait with no particular purpose
c be unable to move
d was not finished
e were taken down
f move towards
g were leaving
h put in a pile
i put up

Word Builder Multi-part verbs (3)

1 There were people **hanging around** and looking at me.
2 I **got on with** the work.
3 The tents **came down** and were **stacked away**.
4 At last, we **were off**.
5 The journey **was not over** yet.
6 They had **got stuck** in the mud.
7 The others were **heading on to** the lake.
8 They **set up** their gers.

LANGUAGE CHOICE 41: PAGE 21

5 **Look at the Sentence Builder. Which of the sentences (1–2) describes observing a <u>completed</u> action?**

Sentence Builder: Verbs of perception + infinitive or *-ing* form

1 Bruce **saw** them **make** the annual migration.
2 Bruce **observed** the mountains **getting** whiter.

LANGUAGE CHOICE 42: PAGE 21

6 **Choose the correct verbs to complete the sentences.**

1 I watched Mary *play/playing* tennis this morning – she won in the end.
2 I noticed Fred *arrive/arriving* at school yesterday because he was wearing a weird new T-shirt.
3 When I get back home, I can often smell my dad *cook/cooking* in the kitchen.
4 I often hear my neighbours *talk/talking* when I am studying.

Your Choice

7 Your Culture **Work in pairs. Choose an annual event in your local community. Write notes to describe it.**

8 **Work in groups. Tell your partners about your event.**

In May, there is always a rock 'n' roll marathon in our town.

No Comment

'One's destination is never a place but a new way of seeing things.' Henry Miller

LESSON **26** GRAMMAR

MATRIARCHY

Warm Up

1 **Look at the photos (a-c). Which activities are typical of men and which of women?**

2 **Read the text. Why does the author think the world would be better if women ran it?**

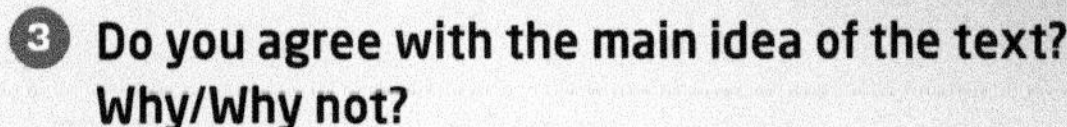
a

3 **Do you agree with the main idea of the text? Why/Why not?**

Viewpoint 4.7

History would have been better if ...

In my opinion, history would have been better if women had been the dominant sex.

History is men getting into trouble. History, as recorded by men, has traditionally been a chronology of wars. But would events have taken the same turn if history had been made and recorded by women? Most certainly not. If we now had a matriarchal society, conflicts between nations would look entirely different. Instead of going to war and killing your enemies, you would hurt their feelings – perhaps you would make remarks about the children in the other country: 'Your children are ugly and have bad table manners.' If you said something like that, both of you would feel so terrible that you'd talk about it. There'd be a lot of communication. Naturally, if women were in charge, the telephone would have been invented very, very early – right after the wheel.

I am not saying a matriarchal society would be perfect. I am saying it would be much more peaceful. No society run by women would send its sons and daughters to be slaughtered by the sons and daughters of another society run by women.

In fact, if roles had been established differently, armed aggression would simply not occur, partly because no one would want anyone else's land. After all, why would you want someone else's land? You can visit. If you own more land, you have to look after it.

Women historians would certainly not define crucial moments in history by events on the battlefield. If they had their way, instead of 'Our glorious victory over XYZ', Chapter 12 of your history book might be 'When We Learned That If You Wash Your Hands You Get Sick Less.' That would start an era.

So when the next election comes, remember: if women run the world, it will be better and a lot less expensive. If I were a man, I would vote for a woman, too – it's time they got their chance.

Conditionals

4 **Match the conditional sentences (1-5) with their meanings (a-e).**

1 If we now had a matriarchal society, conflicts between nations would look entirely different. *a*
2 If women run the world, it will be better and a lot less expensive.
3 If you said something like that, both of you would feel terrible.
4 History would have been better if women had been the dominant sex.
5 If you own more land, you have to look after it.

a unreal present situation
b imaginary past situation
c hypothetical future situation
d possible situation in the future
e a rule describing a permanent reality

5 **Read the conditional sentence from the text. What verb form (*was, am* or *had been*) could be used instead of *were* to mean the same but sound less formal?**

*If I **were** a man, I would vote for a woman, too.*

6 **Read the 'mixed' conditional sentences (1-2). Which of them talks about:**

a an imaginary **past** event or situation and its hypothetical **present** consequences?
b an imaginary **present** situation and its hypothetical consequences in the **past**?

1 If roles **had been formed** differently, armed aggression **would not occur**.
2 If women **were** in charge, the telephone **would have been invented** right after the wheel.

7 **Look at the sentences in Exercise 6. Complete the table with the correct verb forms for 'mixed' conditionals.**

	imaginary condition	**hypothetical consequence**
in the past	Past Perfect	*would* +
in the present		

Practice

8 Write unreal and past conditional sentences about imaginary situations based on these facts.

1 Women are different from men so the world is an interesting place.

If women were similar to men, the world wouldn't be so interesting.

2 Men run the world and there are a lot of international conflicts.
3 The world isn't perfect so not everyone is happy.
4 There have been a lot of wars in the world and a lot of people died in them.
5 A woman is not the president of the USA so I don't believe there are equal opportunities for men and women.
6 Napoleon wasn't a woman so he started a lot of wars.

LANGUAGE CHOICE 43: PAGE 22

9 Use mixed conditionals to answer the questions.

1 What would be the situation now:
   a if your parents hadn't met?

   If my parents hadn't met, I wouldn't be here.

   b if mobile phones hadn't been invented?
   c if the continents hadn't separated?
2 What would have happened in the past:
   a if people were less aggressive?
   b if all people spoke one language?
   c if the Earth was closer to the Sun?

10 Choose the feature from each sentence that describes you. Write three conditional sentences about how these features influenced your past life.

1 I am a boy/a girl.

If I were/was a boy, I would've played more with cars.

2 I am assertive/shy.
3 I like/don't like new experiences.

LANGUAGE CHOICE 44: PAGE 22

Grammar Alive Hypothesising

11 4.8 Listen to a dialogue. Why does Annie think she didn't get the job?

12 Work in pairs. Use the cues to make dialogues.

A: *Are you rich?*
B: *No, I'm not. If I was rich, I would've gone to study abroad.*

A starts	B answers
1 you / rich	1 go to study abroad
2 your girl/boyfriend / assertive	2 get the job at restaurant
3 you / good at languages	3 fail my English exam

B starts	A answers
4 your football team / good	4 lose the last game
5 you / interested in politics	5 take part in yesterday's demonstration
6 you / feminist	6 join a feminist organisation

13 4.9 Listen to another dialogue. Answer the questions.

1 What would make Annie happy?
2 Why does Jim have to work so hard?

14 Work in pairs. Use the cues to make dialogues.

A: *Did you find a job?*
B: *No, I didn't. If I had found a job, I would have some money.*

A starts	B answers
1 you / find a job	1 have some money
2 your parents / strict	2 be a more organised person
3 your dance lessons / good	3 can dance to this rock 'n' roll

B starts	A answers
4 you / pass your driving test	4 can give you a lift
5 you / learn English in primary school	5 speak perfect English
6 you / have a lot of friends as a child	6 be more sociable

LESSON 27 SKILLS

BIKERS

Warm Up

1 Your Culture **Work in pairs. Look at the photos. Answer the questions.**

1 How popular are motorbikes in your country? What races and biker events are there?
2 Is there a 'biker community'? Do bikers have a special style of clothes/tattoos, etc.?
3 Would you like to have a motorbike? Would your parents like you to have one?

Listening

2 4.10 4.11 **Listen and match the people (1-5) with the statements (a-f). There is one extra statement.**

a Non-bikers will never understand us.
b I have two completely separate identities.
c I just love riding really fast.
d There is a sense of community amongst bikers.
e I spend all my social life with other bikers.
f Being on my bike makes me feel that I'm really living.

3 4.10 4.11 → SKILLS BUILDER 6 **Look at the informal expressions in the Skills Builder. Then listen again and list which of them you hear.**

Biker 1: Sure; Go ahead; ...

DVD Choice

4 DVD 7 **Watch the documentary about the woman in the photo and answer the questions.**

1 How is Sasha different from the typical biker?
2 How does she make a living?
3 How does she get away from her small flat?
4 Why has she called her bike 'Tiger Lily'?
5 How do people react when they find out she is a biker?
6 What problems does she have out on the street?

5 DVD 7 **Watch again. Work out the meaning of these statements.**

1 A whole world rolls on two wheels.
2 Let's go and get a big bite out of the Big Apple!
3 An afternoon at the office with Sasha isn't quite what you'd expect.
4 You have to have eyes at the back of your head.
5 Liberty is what it's like to be on the open road.

6 **Would you like to ride a motorbike in New York? Why/ Why not?**

Speaking Workshop

7 4.12 4.13 **Listen to the dialogue. Complete Lucy's diary.**

Saturday 11 April
Go to Mortimer Forest with [1]________.
Leave at [2]________ *and go there in* [3]________.
Tom's dad to pick us up at [4]________.
Have a picnic at [5]________ *place.*
Invite: [6]________, [7]________, [8]________ *and* [9]________.
Go on the ride to the [10]________.

8 Look at the Talk Builder. Which of the reactions (a-h) disagree with the suggestions 1-8?

Talk Builder Making arrangements

Suggestions	Reactions
1 I thought maybe we could ...	a That's a good idea but it means we'd have to ...
2 I think we'd better ...	b Why not?
3 So what about the idea of ... ?	c That'd be great but I'm not so sure about ...
4 What if we asked ... ?	d Cool! That way we ...
5 ... we could maybe ...	e That's fine by me but I'd rather you ...
6 Why don't we invite ... ?	f Okay, I'll see if he wants to come.
7 I suggest we do ...	g That would be nice but ...
8 I'd rather we did something a bit ...	h Okay, let's do that.

SKILLS BUILDER 43

9 4.14 Pronunciation **Listen and repeat the expressions from the Talk Builder.**

10 Complete the dialogue with words from the Talk Builder.

A: I'm organising something for next Sunday. I [1] *thought* maybe we could go to a concert and have lunch somewhere.
B: That's a good [2]________ but it sounds expensive. I think we'd [3]________ go to the rock marathon. It's free.
A: Okay. So what about [4]________ lunch in a café?
B: [5]________ 'd be great but I'm not so sure about going to a café. What [6]________ we took a picnic?
A: Cool! That [7]________ it wouldn't cost very much.
B: And [8]________ don't we invite Judy?
A: Okay. I [9]________ we meet at my place at eleven o'clock. What do you think?
A: I'd [10]________ we met in the centre.
B: Okay, let's do that.

11 Work in pairs. Act out a similar dialogue. Change the times, places and activities.

12 Work in groups. Make arrangements for a group outing.

1 **Choose an activity to do with a group of friends. Write notes like those in Exercise 7 about your plan.**

2 SKILLS BUILDER 44 **Use the strategies to evaluate your plan and think of alternatives.**

3 **Act out the role-play and agree on a plan.**

13 Tell the class what you finally agreed on and why you discounted other alternatives.

We decided to go on a day trip to the coast to go swimming and ... . We decided not to go by train because it's so expensive.

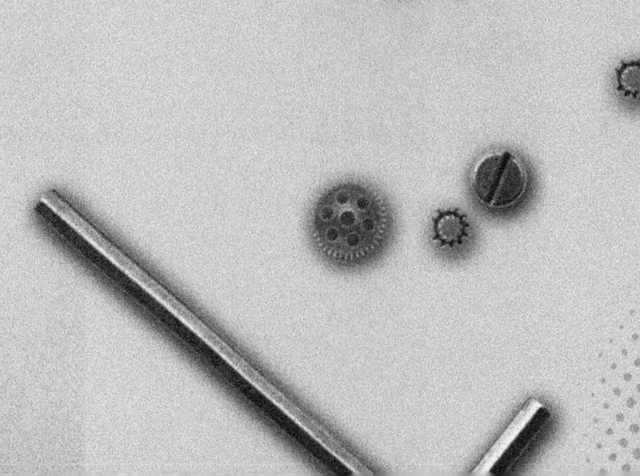

GRAMMAR

EMPATHY

Warm Up

1 **Look at the chimpanzees in the photo. In what ways are they similar to people?**

2 **Read the article. What examples of empathy among animals does the author give?**

(4.15)

We tend to assume that it is natural for people to be selfish and violent. It is often said that altruism is self-interest in disguise. But there is evidence from research on social animals like elephants, dolphins and chimpanzees that there are many species that survive thanks to empathy and cooperation.

Humans are social animals. There is no doubt that since the appearance of *Homo sapiens*, empathy and solidarity have held human groups together. It is true that in both animals and humans empathy is biased: it is always stronger for one's own group than for strangers. However, it can't be denied that compassion is as natural for us as aggression. Simple empathy begins with our bodies: a chimpanzee yawns when it sees another chimpanzee yawning. It is easy to notice similar behaviour in people: when we see pictures of angry faces, we frown; when we see happy faces, we smile.

The highest level of empathy is the ability to think like someone who needs help and offer the kind of help that's required. Humans do this all the time but there are also a lot of examples of such behaviour in animals. An elephant can accompany a dying friend for days, even if it is tempted to leave by the chance of getting food. If a chimpanzee has lost her child, other chimpanzees spend a lot of time looking after the mother.

So maybe it's time to build our society on cooperation and kindness instead of competition. Let's hope it's not too late.

3 **Do you believe that most people are generally:**

a violent and competitive?
b kind and sympathetic?

it and *there*

4 **Read the sentences. Find the word or phrase that *it* refers to. Is it possible in each case? Then choose the correct words to complete the rule.**

1 A chimpanzee yawns when **it** sees another chimpanzee yawning.
2 **It** is true that in both animals and humans empathy is biased.
3 Empathy is biased: **it** is always stronger for one's own group than for strangers.
4 **It**'s time to build our society on cooperation

In English, every sentence *must/needn't* have a subject. In *all/some* sentences the subject has no meaning.

5 **Read the sentences below. Which of them states that something exists?**

1 **There** are a lot of examples of such behaviour in animals.
2 **It**'s not too late.

6 **Translate the sentences in Exercise 5 into your language. How do you translate *it* and *there*? Are these words necessary in your language?**

7 **Complete the sentences with *it* or *there*.**

1 ________ is clear that some animals feel empathy.
2 ________ is a species of monkey that doesn't care about its children.
3 ________ is a social hierarchy among chimpanzees.
4 ________ has been observed that chimpanzees adopt orphaned chimpanzees.
5 ________ are apes that form matriarchal communities.
6 ________ is interesting that chimpanzees and humans differ by only one percent of their DNA.

LANGUAGE CHOICE 45: PAGE 22

8 **Use the cues to write sentences beginning with *It* ... or *There* ... .**

1 possible / observe various forms of communication among animals
It is possible to observe various forms of communication among animals.
2 chimpanzees / in most zoos in the world
3 common / for animals to help one another
4 always an alpha male / in a chimpanzee community
5 true / people's behaviour is quite similar to chimpanzees'
6 little violence / among bonobos

Writing Workshop 7

1 **Look at the picture and read the story. Find three differences between them.**

1 *While walking down the long corridor I could see inside the classrooms and people were turning their heads to see who the head teacher was with. I felt as if I was going to my execution, not starting my first class at the Instituto Antonio Machado.*
2 *As I was opening the door, the students looked up and stared at me. The class teacher, a kindly-looking elderly man with a moustache like a Mexican bandit's, stood up smiling. 'Ah, Chris! Welcome!' He then spoke to the class but I only understood the words 'English' and 'new student' and I felt like a zoo animal standing there in front of everyone. Mr Salazar pointed to a desk and I went to sit down but unfortunately my bag caught on a chair and everything in it fell out onto the floor. I went as red as a beetroot while various students helped me pick up my things, including photos of my girlfriend, my parents and my pet rat, Clarence.*
3 *The rest of the lesson lasted hours but my partner Jorge, a small, pale boy with glasses, explained things to me. During the class, a group of older boys kept pointing at me and laughing, especially a boy in a Real Madrid T-shirt. Afterwards we were outside when Jorge suddenly shouted 'Watch out!' A football was coming fast towards my head. I am not a great footballer but that day I was lucky. Having headed the ball to the ground, I immediately kicked it hard towards the goal. Luckily, the ball went straight through the Real Madrid boy's feet into the goal. Everyone laughed.*
4 *'Now everything's going to be fine,' Jorge said to me and smiled. And everything was after that. It was the start of one of the best years of my life.*

2 **Work in pairs. Answer the questions about the story.**

1 How did the boy feel before going into class? Why?
2 What was embarrassing for him about his first lesson?
3 Who was nice to him on his first day?
4 Which people were not friendly towards him?
5 What made him feel better?

Text Builder

3 **Write the topics for the paragraphs (1-4).**

1 *setting the scene: the situation*

4 **Look at the Sentence Builder. Do the sentences mean the same thing or something different?**

Sentence Builder Sequence linking

1 **Having headed** the ball to the ground, I kicked it towards the goal.
2 **After heading** the ball to the ground, I kicked it towards the goal.
3 **After I (had) headed** the ball to the ground, I kicked it towards the goal.

5 **Rewrite the sentences using the three forms in the Sentence Builder.**

1 I went into the classroom and then spoke to the class teacher.
2 They sat down and then they started doing their projects.
3 He got home and then he turned on the TV.
4 We left the classroom and then went to the playground.

6 **Write a story beginning with the words: *One of the most embarrassing experiences for me was when I ...***

➔ SKILLS BUILDER 28

1 **Write notes about:**
- the situation - where were you, what was happening, your feelings
- what happened and how you felt
- how people reacted and how you felt
- how you feel about it all now

2 **Use your notes to write the story.**
3 **Check your story.**

7 **Work in groups. Read out your stories. Decide which stories are:**

- the funniest
- the most embarrassing
- the best written
- true
- not true

Language Review Module 7

1 Talking about communities **Complete the description with one word in each gap.**

In the countryside you can trust people and you don't need to [1]l______ your front door. Everybody knows each other and people help each [2]o______ out when they have problems. For families with young children, it's great that the streets feel [3]s______ at night and the children can go out on their [4]o______ to play during the day, but when those children are older, it's better for them to have somewhere more interesting to [5]h______ out. /5

2 Multi-part verbs (3) **Rewrite the sentences replacing the underlined words with the correct form of the verbs below. There are two extra verbs.**

be off be over get on with get stuck hang around head on to set up

6 People were standing there, doing nothing.
7 We need someone who will do their work even when nobody is there to tell them what to do.
8 We stopped for a drink but the others continued to the beach.
9 We were late because we couldn't move in the heavy traffic.
10 We didn't realise at the time that our troubles hadn't finished. /5

3 Verbs of perception + infinitive or *-ing* form **Use the cues to write sentences.**

11 I saw / Tom / drive / his dad's car yesterday.
12 Yesterday we listened to / our teacher / talk / about his ideas for a class project.
13 While he was playing a computer game, Paul heard / his parents / discuss / his school report.
14 Have you seen / Brian / draw / people's portraits? He's brilliant.
15 We watched / some people / swim / while we were eating our sandwiches on the beach. /5

4 Unreal and past conditionals **Complete the sentences with the correct form of the verbs in brackets.**

16 This town would be more interesting if there ______ (be) more things for teenagers to do.
17 If you ______ (lock) your front door last night, the burglars wouldn't have stolen your laptop.
18 If more people had gone to the local club, it ______ (not close) last month.
19 If we ______ (not help) our neighbours when they were in trouble, they might not have helped us with our problems.
20 If there was better public transport, the traffic ______ (not be) so heavy. /5

5 Mixed conditionals **Complete the conditional sentence from the notes.**

21 people don't believe government now – lied last year
If the government ______
22 council always listen us – voted for them again
If the council ______
23 safe town – we decided to move here
If this town ______
24 late for work last week – unemployed now
If I ______
25 mum not like motorbikes – dad sold his
If my mum ______ /5

6 Making arrangements **Complete the dialogue with the phrases below. There are two extra phrases.**

but it means I'd rather we I suggest we maybe we could what if I why don't we let's do that

A: I thought [26]______ go to the new shopping centre.
B: That's a good idea [27]______ we'd have to get the bus.
A: [28]______ asked my dad to take us?
B: Cool. [29]______ invite Sam and Kevin, too?
A: Okay, [30]______ /5

7 *it* and *there* **Complete the sentences with *It* or *There*.**

31 ______ is true that bulls are colour-blind.
32 ______ are many animals that can't be tamed.
33 ______ is amazing that red ants and large blue butterflies work together.
34 ______ have been many attempts to reintroduce wild animals, like the wolf, to the UK.
35 ______ has been proved that cows 'moo' in a different accent in different parts of the world. /5

8 Sequence linking **Rewrite the sentences starting with the words in brackets.**

36 After I had read the book, I saw the film. (Having)
37 After resting, we set off for the camp. (After we)
38 After talking to my friend, I felt better. (After I)
39 After waiting for an hour, I went home. (Having)
40 After going to the zoo, I felt sad. (After I) /5

Self Assessment

4.16 **Listen and check your answers. Write down the scores. Use the table to find practice exercises.**

Exercise	If you need practice, go to
1	Language Choice 40
2	Language Choice 41
3	Language Choice 42
4	Language Choice 43
5	Language Choice 44
6	Students' Book p.71 ex. 10
7	Language Choice 45
8	Students' Book p.73 ex. 5

LEARNING LINKS: 1 Check Your Progress 7 → MyLab / Workbook page 77. Complete the Module Diary.
2 Sound Choice 4 → MyLab / Workbook page 78. Choose three pronunciation activities to do.

MODULE 8 LANDMARKS

Objectives: **Read** and **listen about** places and natural and man-made landmarks; **learn more about** making suggestions and discussing arrangements; **write** a description of a place; **learn more about** relative clauses.

TOPIC TALK

a The Jurassic Coast

b Stonehenge

c The Gherkin

1 **Which of the places in the photos (a-c) would you like to visit?**

2 4.17 4.18 **Listen to the description. Where are the places (a-c), how old are they and why are they important?**

3 4.17 4.18 **Listen again. Complete the information in the network.**

Landscape

In my country, there are mainly [1]_______ and [2]_______ in the [3]*south/north/east/west/centre*, although there are [4]_______ in the [5]*south/north/east/west/centre*.
Where I live there [6]*is/are* also [7]_______ .
The area I like most is the Jurassic Coast because it has got beautiful [8]_______ and [9]_______ .
My favourite natural landmark there is Durdle Door which is a [10]*rock arch/mountain peak*.
One of my favourite man-made landmarks is Stonehenge, a [11]_______ .
I also like the Gherkin, a [12]_______ made of [13]_______ and [14]_______ with 5500 [15]_______ .

Types of landscape
deserts, farmland, forest (coniferous/deciduous), grassland (prairie/savanna/steppes/pampas), moorlands, mountains, plains, rainforests, river valleys, tundra

Landscape features
bays, beaches (sandy/shingle), caves, cliffs, estuaries, fjords, glaciers, gorges, hills, lagoons, lakes, marshes, mountains, ponds, rivers, springs, streams, volcanoes, waterfalls

Man-made landmarks
aqueduct, bridge, castle, cathedral, church, lighthouse, palace, skyscraper, stone circle

Materials
brick, concrete, glass, metal, marble, stone, wood

Architectural features
arches, columns, domes, glass panels, stained glass windows, statues, towers

4 4.19 **Pronunciation Listen to the sentences (1-3) twice. Underline the stressed words each time. Match the stressed words with the meanings (a-b).**

1 I think the design's really cool.
 a it's the design I like b that's my personal opinion
2 One of my favourite man-made landmarks is Stonehenge.
 a not natural landmarks b I like lots of them
3 One day, I'd like to visit the restaurant at the top.
 a not the one at the bottom b in the future

LANGUAGE CHOICE 49: PAGE 26

5 **Work in groups. Use the network to talk about landscapes and landmarks in *your* country.**

LESSON 29 VOLCANOES

Volcanoes are dangerous and unpredictable, which makes them terrifying and fascinating at the same time. Here are some famous volcano sites to visit!

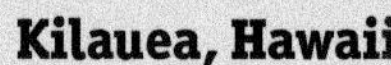
4.20

Mount Vesuvius, Italy

Mount Vesuvius, **whose** last eruption occurred in 1944, is located just east of Naples. The most tragic was its eruption in AD 79, **during which** volcanic ash buried 3360 Romans in the nearby town of Pompeii. The ash helped to preserve everything **that** it fell on, including people and animals. The archaeological site **that** was opened in Pompeii gives an insight into the daily life of the people **whose** lives were ended by the eruption.

Kilauea, Hawaii

Kilauea, **which** is one of the largest volcanoes in the world in width, has been actively erupting since the early 1980s and is an excellent destination for visitors **who** want to see hot lava pouring from a volcano. Although it seems scary, it is one of the safest active volcanoes you can visit. From there, you can go to Mauna Loa, **which** is the world's largest volcano in terms of volume and area covered.

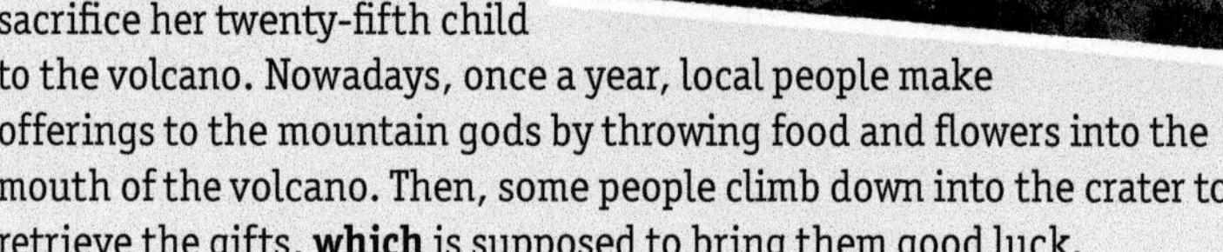

Mount Bromo, Indonesia

Mount Bromo, located in East Java, is an active volcano **that** last erupted in 2000. An old legend says that Princess Roro Anteng, **who** was blessed by the gods with twenty-four children, was required to sacrifice her twenty-fifth child to the volcano. Nowadays, once a year, local people make offerings to the mountain gods by throwing food and flowers into the mouth of the volcano. Then, some people climb down into the crater to retrieve the gifts, **which** is supposed to bring them good luck.

Warm Up

1 What volcanoes have you heard about? What are they known for?

Mount Fuji is the highest mountain in Japan. It's an active volcano.

2 Read the text. Which of the volcano sites:

a has a tradition associated with it?
b has recently influenced people in Europe and North America?
c has caused death and destruction?
d looks dangerous but isn't?

3 Which of the volcano sites would you like to visit? Why?

Relative clauses

4 Read the sentences (1-2). Underline the words to which the clauses in bold refer. Which clause in bold, 1 or 2, gives:

a information that we need to identify the people or things that we are talking about (defining relative clause)?
b extra information about the people or things that we have already identified (non-defining relative clause)?

1 Kilauea is an excellent destination for visitors **who want to see hot lava pouring from a volcano**.
2 Princess Roro Anteng, **who was blessed by the gods with twenty-four children**, was required to sacrifice her twenty-fifth child to the volcano.

5 Look at the sentences (1-3). Which underlined relative clauses are defining (D) and which are non-defining (ND)? Find more examples of both types of clauses in red in the text. Which clauses:

a use commas?
b don't use *that* as a relative pronoun?
c can take no relative pronoun?

1 Kilauea, which is one of the largest volcanoes in the world in width, has been actively erupting since the early 1980s.
2 Mount Bromo is an active volcano which/that last erupted in 2000.
3 It is one of the safest active volcanoes you can visit.

6 Look at the sentences (1-2) below. Which type of clause, defining (D) or non-defining (ND), can have a preposition at the end of the clause?

1 The most tragic was its eruption in AD79, during which volcanic ash buried 3360 Romans.
2 The ash helped to preserve everything it fell on. = The ash helped to preserve everything on which it fell.

Iceland

Iceland, **where** there are about thirty active volcanoes, is a volcanologist's paradise. In 1783, the eruption of Laki created dust clouds and obscured the sun over most of Europe and North America for months, **which** destroyed the crops and caused widespread famine. In the spring of 2010, **when** Eyjafjallajökull erupted, air travel in the northern hemisphere was disrupted for weeks because the volcanic ash could damage plane engines.

Practice

7 Join the sentences using relative pronouns where necessary. Which clauses are defining (D) and which are non-defining (ND)? Use commas where necessary.

1 Visiting Pompeii is an experience. You will never forget it.
Visiting Pompeii is an experience you will never forget. D
2 Popocatepetl has erupted more than twenty times since 1519. It is Mexico's second highest peak.
3 Johannes Kepler thought volcanoes were 'ducts for the Earth's tears'. His main interest was astronomy.
4 Mount Fuji is currently considered a dormant volcano. It last erupted in 1708.
5 There are a lot of travel agencies in Iceland. You can buy trips to Iceland's volcanoes there.
6 1902 saw the worst eruption of Mount Pelée. Over 36,000 people were killed in it.

8 Use the cues to write sentences with non-defining relative clauses.

1 Mount Fuji - the highest mountain in Japan / 60 miles from Tokyo
Mount Fuji, which is the highest mountain in Japan, is 60 miles from Tokyo.
2 Amsterdam - there is the famous Van Gogh museum there / my favourite city in Europe
3 Stonehenge - built 4500 years ago / probably used as a burial site
4 Mount Everest - Tibetan name is Chomolungma / has claimed the lives of over 200 people
5 Istanbul - 13 million inhabitants / the only big city situated on two continents

9 Look at the Sentence Builder. Which relative pronoun is used? What do the underlined clauses do?

a add more information about or comment on the fact/event mentioned in the first part of the sentence
b help identify a person or thing

Sentence Builder Sentential relatives

Volcanoes are dangerous and unpredictable, **which** makes them terrifying and fascinating at the same time.
In 1783, the eruption of Laki created dust clouds and obscured the sun for months, **which** destroyed the crops and caused widespread famine.

LANGUAGE CHOICE 47: PAGE 24

10 Add comments or extra information about these facts.

1 Volcanic eruptions disturb air travel, which ...
2 Popular landmarks are visited by tourists, which ...
3 More people travel to distant locations, which ...

Grammar Alive Adding comments

11 4.21 Listen to the dialogue. How does the woman feel about:

a her holiday plans this year?
b her holiday two years ago?
c the archaeological site in Pompeii?
d not being able to walk down Vesuvius's crater?

12 Work in pairs. Use the cues to make dialogues.

A: *Where did you go last year?*
B: *I visited Pompeii. I went there with my Italian friends, which was fantastic.*

A starts	B answers
Where did you go last year?	1 Pompeii / go there with my Italian friends / be fantastic 2 Iguazu Falls / produce incredible noise / make it impossible to talk there 3 Kilimanjaro / climb to the very top / make some people sick
B starts	**A answers**
Where did you go last year?	4 Egypt / the pyramids be 4500 years old / be hard to believe 5 China / stay with a Chinese family / help me learn a lot about the culture 6 Paris / we not go up the Eiffel Tower / disappointed my sister

LESSON 30 WITHOUT US

a

Warm Up

1 Describe the situation in the drawings (a-b) of New York. What do you think might have happened?

Reading

2 Read the chapter summary. Match the sentences (a-h) with the gaps in the text (1-7). There is one extra sentence.

a With no firefighters either, fires will spread throughout the city and damage even big skyscrapers.
b The building will quickly start to fall down in the next two or three years.
c However, the city's cat population, having gone wild, will survive a lot longer.
d That might be the safest place though, as after about 15,000 years the advance of a glacier will probably have crushed everything underneath it.
e New York's principal weakness is underground. *1*
f The car bridges will only last two centuries but, because of their strength, railway bridges will resist a lot longer.
g However, the paintings in museums like the Metropolitan will have been destroyed by fungi and beetles.
h After a few more decades, even the highest skyscrapers will start to fall as their foundations are weakened by the underground rivers.

3 Read the article again. Are the sentences true (T) or false (F) or is no information given (NI)?

1 New York City would disappear more quickly than we think.
2 Plants would take a long time to start growing in the streets.
3 Fire as well as water would help to destroy buildings.
4 New York's railway bridges would last for five hundred years.
5 Cats will go wild and develop into a new species.
6 The city would probably be completely destroyed by the ice age.

NEW YORK WITHOUT PEOPLE

4.22

What would happen to our planet if humans were to suddenly disappear? This is the basic hypothesis behind Alan Weisman's book *The World Without Us*. Weisman examines how long it would take for humankind's mark on Earth to disappear. In one chapter, there is an analysis of how New York would survive if there were no humans to take care of it.

The size and solidity of New York is such that the very idea that nature could just swallow it up seems absurd. However, New York's vulnerability is greater than it appears and it would take less time for nature to get rid of humanity's terrible impact on the planet than we think. [1]_________ Before the arrival of people there were marshes, lakes, streams and springs and they are still there under the streets. According to New York City engineers, without power to run the pumps the city's subway system will flood within 36 to 48 hours and small ponds and streams will appear on the surface.

Within a few years of the disappearance of people, craters will appear and streets like Lexington Avenue will become rivers again. Plant growth will start immediately and, after five years, trees will have started their colonisation of the streets. After five years with no maintenance, the deterioration of buildings will have begun. [2]_________

After several decades, creepers will have climbed up the sides of the decaying buildings. [3]_________ New York's bridges will also start to suffer with nobody to look after them. First, exposure to hot summers and cold winters will crack concrete and damage the metal structures, which will also be attacked by rust. [4]_________

After 500 years, most of the city will be a forest and coyotes, wolves and foxes will have killed off the last of the city's pet dogs which survived the first few days. [5]_________ Some of the last human structures will be the underground vaults of Manhattan's banks because of the thickness of their walls; the money inside them will be safe but totally worthless. [6]_________ Only the ceramics and the bronze statues will be preserved – that is one of the reasons that we know about the Bronze Age.

New York's great symbol, the Statue of Liberty, is made of bronze and its survival is guaranteed, although it will probably have dropped to the bottom of the harbour. [7]_________
After the departure of the ice, there will be a reddish layer of minerals made up of the metals from the city. The next toolmaker to arrive on the planet might discover and use it but, by then, there would be nothing to indicate who put it there.

4 SKILLS BUILDER 19 **Work in pairs. Use the strategies to write notes about what might happen to *your* town or city without people. Tell the class your predictions.**

If humans disappeared from our town, we think that the first thing to happen would be the flooding of the area near the river.

5 Vocabulary **Look at the Word Builder. Complete it with words in blue from the article and the sentences in Exercise 2.**

Word Builder Noun endings

sis: hypothesis, ________
ity: solidity, ________ , ________
al: arrival, ________ , ________
ance: disappearance, ________ , ________
th: growth, ________
ation: colonisation, ________ , ________ , ________
ure: exposure, ________
ness: thickness, ________

LANGUAGE CHOICE 50: PAGE 26

6 **Rewrite the sentences making the verbs and adjectives in bold into nouns.**

1 That building might not **survive** because there are problems with the roof.

*The **survival** of that building is not very certain because there are problems with the roof.*

2 The **weak** part of that skyscraper is its foundations.
3 Because the bridge is so **solid**, it will last for hundreds of years.
4 After humans have **disappeared**, the planet will go back to its original state.
5 Manhattan has changed a lot since humans **arrived**.

7 **Look at the questions in the Sentence Builder. Which of them emphasise the unlikely nature of a future situation?**

Sentence Builder Conditionals

1 What would happen to the planet if humans **were to disappear** suddenly?
2 What would happen to the planet if humans **disappeared** suddenly?
3 What would happen if our planet **were to become** uninhabitable?
4 What would happen if our planet **became** uninhabitable?

LANGUAGE CHOICE 51: PAGE 26

8 **Work in pairs. Discuss what would happen in these unlikely situations.**

1 aliens arrive on the planet

A: *What would happen if aliens were to arrive on the planet?*
B: *I think they would probably be friendly and ...*

2 a large-scale nuclear war breaks out
3 time travel becomes possible
4 we discover a source of cheap energy
5 humans stop having wars
6 everybody on the planet has enough to eat

Your Choice

9 **Choose two of the 'wonders of the world' on page 130 and read about them. Write notes about them.**

Khufu Pyramid – Great Pyramid of Giza – built in 2560 BC as a tomb for the Pharaoh Khufu

10 **Work in pairs. Ask and answer questions about the places.**

1 When was it built?
2 Who built it?
3 Why was it built?
4 What is it made of?
5 How long would it last without human maintenance?
6 Why would it (not) last a long time?

No Comment

'Nature is indifferent to the survival of the human species, including Americans.'

Adlai E. Stevenson

LESSON 31 SKILLS

BRIDGES

Warm Up

1 What do you know about the bridges in the picture and the photos? Check your guesses on page 130.

Listening

2 4.23 4.24 Listen to a tour guide showing people around Tower Bridge. Match the explanations (1-6) with the places on the diagram (a-g). There is one extra place.

3 4.23 4.24 Listen again. Are the sentences true (T) or false (F) or is no information given (NI)?

1 The towers are built around a wooden structure.
2 The two walkways were used by foot passengers for seventy years.
3 From the western walkway you have good views of the London Eye.
4 The central parts of the bridge are lifted less often than in the past.
5 The steam engines pressurised water for the hydraulic system.
6 The diesel and electric engines are a lot more powerful than the old engines.

4 Look at the Sentence Builder. Which of the expressions in bold:

a recommend doing something?
b discourage someone from doing something?

Sentence Builder Expressions + infinitive or *-ing* form

1 **There's no point in** carrying them around the exhibition.
2 **It's worth** spending some time here and enjoying the views.
3 **It's a good idea to** use the panels to identify the buildings.
4 **It's important to** look right when crossing the road.

LANGUAGE CHOICE 52: PAGE 26

5 Your Culture **Work in pairs. Use the structures in the Sentence Builder to make recommendations about a place in your country.**

It's worth going to the castle.
It's a good idea to wear good walking shoes.

Speaking Workshop

6 4.25 DVD 8 **Listen to or watch a dialogue with a tourist information officer near Tower Bridge. Match the places (1-5) with the descriptions (a-f). There is one extra description.**

1 the Monument
2 the Tower of London
3 HMS Belfast
4 All Hallows Church
5 St Katharine's Docks

a a good place for lunch
b you can buy jewellery there
c good views but you need to be fit
d quick to visit but quite expensive
e a fantastic visit but takes a lot of time
f nearby and free to visit

7 4.25 DVD 8 SKILLS BUILDER 7 **Look at the strategies for listening actively. Listen or watch again. Which of them can you hear or see in the dialogue?**

8 Look at the Talk Builder. Which structures are new for you? How do you say them in your language?

Talk Builder Tourist advice

1 **Can you recommend places to visit near here, please?**
2 **Could you suggest something else to do, please?**
3 **What else would you advise us to do?**
4 **Is there anything else you would suggest doing?**
5 **Is there anywhere that you'd recommend for** lunch?

a **I'd advise you to** go to ... **but it's important to** ...
b **I don't think you should** ...
c **If I were you, I'd go to** ...
d **It's really worth visiting** ...
e **And you mustn't miss** ...
f **There's no point in** ...
g **It's a good idea to visit** ...
h **I think you'd better go to** ...
i **I suggest you** go to ...
j **I'd recommend going to** ...

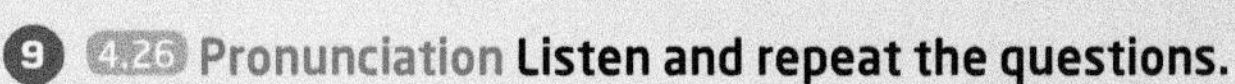

9 4.26 Pronunciation **Listen and repeat the questions.**

10 Use the words in brackets to rewrite the sentences.

1 What else would you advise us to do? (suggest)
What else would you suggest we do?
2 I'd advise you to go to the Design Museum. (recommend)
3 I wouldn't advise you to go to the HMS Belfast. (think / should)
4 If you haven't got much time, I recommend going to the London Eye. (think / 'd better)
5 I suggest you visit the Tate Modern. (if / were)
6 I'd recommend visiting the Tower of London. (good idea)

11 Work in pairs. Act out role-plays asking for and giving tourist advice.

1 **Choose five places for visitors in your town. Write notes with reasons for going there and possible problems.**
the old market: free, lots of interesting stalls – very crowded at this time of year
2 **Use the strategies for active listening from Skills Builder 7 to practise the gestures, sounds and phrases in the dialogue.**
3 **Take turns to ask for and give advice about places to visit in your town.**

12 What are the best places for a tourist to visit in your town? Have a class vote.

We think that the best places to visit are the castle and the old bridge.

LESSON 32

GRAMMAR

THE PANTHEON

Warm Up

1. **Look at the photo below. When do you think this building was built? What is unusual about it?**

2. **Read about the Pantheon. Why is it an interesting building? How does the author feel about it?**

3. **What is your favourite building?**

My favourite building

4.27

In Rome, I saw lots of fantastic squares, fountains, buildings and shops in which you can buy whatever you want. But what I'm going to remember best is the Pantheon.
The Pantheon was built two thousand years ago and has survived intact to this day. Unlike most ancient buildings, it's not rectangular but round. It is not that striking from the outside but what makes an unforgettable impression is the interior.

Its dome is the largest unsupported concrete dome in the world – over 43 metres in diameter. To make the structure lighter, it is partly made of pumice and the stones get thinner closer to the top. What strikes you most is the oculus, a round open hole in the middle of the dome. It is about 9 metres in diameter and the main source of light. The sunlight coming in through the oculus is projected onto the walls and works as a sundial. When it rains, raindrops fall right on the floor and the water is taken away by an ancient Roman drainage system. I can imagine that, on a clear night, you can see all kinds of stars through it.
The immense structure with a round window high above your head makes you feel small and insignificant. I think it reminds us of what we should always be aware of – that we are just a tiny part of the universe. I think the atmosphere here is absolutely magical. Do what you want in Rome but you must not miss the Pantheon!

Emphasis: nominal relatives

4. **Read the examples. Is *what* used to:**

   a mean 'the thing that'?
   b signal a question?

   *It reminds us of **what** we should always be aware of.*
   *Do **what** you want!*

5. **Read the sentences (1-2). Which sentence has an unusual word order and is emphatic? Find two similar examples in the text.**

   1 What strikes you most is the oculus.
   2 The oculus strikes you most.

6. **Read the sentences (1-2) below. Which phrase in bold is more emphatic and can be paraphrased as *everything/anything you want*? Translate the sentences into your language.**

   1 You can buy **whatever you want**.
   2 You can buy **what you want**.

7. **Rewrite the sentences replacing the words in *italics* with *what* or *whatever* and making any other necessary changes.**

   1 I'm going to get you *the things* you need.
   2 You can say *anything that* comes to your mind.
   3 You have to buy *things that* suit you.
   4 You are healthy, you can eat *anything that* you want.
   5 Choose *the thing that* looks best.
   6 I don't read *everything* you advise me to.
   7 I'm not interested in *the things* you do.
   8 You can't buy *everything* you like.

8. **Rewrite the sentences to emphasise the <u>underlined</u> words. Start with *What*.**

   1 <u>The oculus</u> makes the greatest impression.
   What makes the greatest impression is the oculus.
   2 People don't know that <u>the Pantheon dome is thinner at the top</u>.
   3 Tourists don't realise that <u>there is no glass in the oculus</u>.
   4 You need <u>a good guide</u>.
   5 I don't remember <u>the weather on that day</u>.
   6 I really want <u>to have a good time</u>.
   7 You must see <u>the Forum Romanum</u>.
   8 I don't like <u>sightseeing in the rain</u>.

→ LANGUAGE CHOICE [illegible]

Writing Workshop 8

1 Look at the photo and read the description. List three of the main reasons why the writer likes the city so much.

1 Playing football on the beach, samba dancing at night, relaxing with a delicious ice-cold fruit juice in an outdoor café, meeting sociable, hospitable people: this is what I think of when I remember the beautiful city of Rio de Janeiro.

2 Rio is called 'The Marvellous City' for a good reason. It is in an extraordinary location in Guanabara Bay, surrounded by spectacular mountains and by impressive sandy beaches facing south onto the Atlantic. The views from virtually anywhere in the city are breathtaking.

3 There is something to do in Rio 24/7. In the morning, you can visit the centre with its museums and picturesque, historic churches or go up Mount Corcovado to see the eye-catching statue of Christ with its stunning views. In the afternoon, you can relax on the beach and watch the world go by or join in a football game with the welcoming, good-natured locals. Or you can go to the striking Maracanã stadium to watch the professionals play. At night, there is music and dancing everywhere. Even if you are not a brilliant samba dancer, you will have an amazing time.

4 Of course, Rio does have problems. There are enormous areas of depressing slums (favelas) on the hills around the city and violent crime can be a problem, though the situation has improved recently. However, for me Rio is one of the most fascinating places in the world and the Cariocas the warmest people, so I cannot wait to go back!

2 Would you like to go to Rio? Why/Why not?

Text Builder

3 **Match the paragraphs (1-4) with the topics (a-d).**

a the city's landscape
b opinion of the city
c memories of Rio
d what to do in Rio

4 **Match the adjectives in blue in the text with the meanings (a-c). Which of the adjectives do we use to describe people and which to describe food?**

a very attractive to look at
b fantastic or very good
c friendly and pleasant

5 **Replace the adjective *nice* with the adjectives below. There is no one correct answer.**

picturesque amazing beautiful breathtaking delicious fascinating stunning spectacular warm welcoming

One of my favourite cities is Verona in northern Italy. It is a [1]*very nice* city and is in a [2]*really nice* location with [3]*nice* views of mountains in the distance. The [4]*nice* old part of the city is full of [5]*nice* buildings, like palaces and churches. The people are [6]*very nice* and friendly and are always [7]*nice* when you talk to them. Of course, the food is [8]*very nice* too! To sum up, Verona is a [9]*very nice* place with a [10]*very nice* atmosphere.

6 **Write a description of one of *your* favourite places.**

SKILLS BUILDER 29

1 **Choose one of your favourite places. Make a list of things that you want to describe.**
- a city or town
- a famous landmark
- a place in the country

2 **Write notes for four paragraphs.**
- introduction
- physical description of the place
- what to do there
- conclusion

3 **Use your notes to write your description.**

7 **Work in groups. Read each other's descriptions. Which place would you most like to visit?**

Language Review Module 8

1 Talking about landscapes **Complete the description with one word in each gap.**

My town is in a river [1]v_______ . The most famous [2]n_______ landmark is a cliff which is very popular with climbers. There are a few ancient stone [3]c_______ but they aren't as big or famous as Stonehenge. The most famous man-made landmark is the local cathedral which has beautiful [4]s_______ glass windows. There are also some old stone [5]b_______ which cross the rivers. /5

2 Relative clauses **Complete the sentences with a relative pronoun. Add a comma where necessary.**

6 The walks here _______ are short and quite easy, are excellent for inexperienced walkers.
7 The king _______ lived in this castle was very unpopular.
8 Oceanus _______ statue can be seen at the Trevi Fountain in Rome, was a Roman god.
9 There is a small gift shop at the top of Mount Vesuvius _______ you can buy postcards.
10 In 122 BC _______ Mount Etna erupted, many roofs in Catania were destroyed.
11 Mount Etna, under _______ Zeus trapped the monster Typhon, is in the north-east of Sicily. /6

3 Sentential relatives **Rewrite the sentences as one sentence using a sentential relative clause.**

12 4500 years ago, the Santorini volcano erupted. It destroyed the Minoan civilisation.
13 Scientists believe that a part of the Canary Islands may fall into the sea. This could cause a giant tsunami.
14 A large asteroid hit the Earth 65 million years ago. It might have killed the dinosaurs.
15 In 2005, the USA was hit by Hurricane Katrina. It caused 81 billion dollars of damage.
16 In 2010, about 15 centimetres of snow fell on London. It caused Heathrow Airport to close.
17 In January 1963, England had a very cold winter. It caused the River Thames to freeze. /6

4 Noun endings **Complete the sentences with the correct form of the words in brackets.**

18 What is the _______ (populate) of your town?
19 The _______ (arrive) of the French students was an exciting event in our town.
20 The _______ (survive) of our planet depends on all of us.
21 The most amazing thing about this old castle is the _______ (thick) of its walls.
22 How will the _______ (disappear) of the rain forest affect our lives?
23 We're hoping for a _______ (grow) in the sales of electric cars. /6

5 Expressions + infinitive or *-ing* form **Use the cues to write sentences.**

24 worth / read / this guidebook before you go. You don't want to miss anything important.
25 good idea / get / some fresh air and see somewhere different.
26 point / wait / any longer. They aren't going to come now.
27 important / take / the right equipment when walking in the mountains.
28 point / worry / about your exams now. Wait until we get our results.
29 worth / visit / the amusement park. It's great.
/6

6 Tourist advice **Complete the tourist advice with the correct form of the verbs in brackets.**

I've got three days in London but I'm not sure what I should and shouldn't do. Any help appreciated.

30 I'd advise you _______ (go) on the London Eye.
31 It's important _______ (not try) to do too much in one day.
32 It's worth _______ (see) Greenwich.
33 There's no point in _______ (stand) in a queue at Madame Tussauds.
34 You'd better _______ (take) a lot of money – it's an expensive city.
35 I'd recommend _______ (buy) a ticket on one of the tour buses. /6

7 Emphasis: nominal relatives **Rewrite the sentences to emphasise the underlined words. Start with *What*.**

36 You must get <u>a good map</u>.
37 I always worry about <u>missing my plane</u>.
38 People don't understand <u>how the stones got here</u>.
39 I don't like <u>long guided tours</u>.
40 The first thing you notice is <u>the amazing artwork</u>.
/5

Self Assessment

4.28 **Listen and check your answers. Write down the scores. Use the table to find practice exercises.**

Exercise	If you need practice, go to
1	Language Choice 49
2	Language Choice 46
3	Language Choice 47
4	Language Choice 50
5	Language Choice 52
6	Students' Book p.81 ex.10
7	Language Choice 48

LEARNING LINKS: 1 Read and listen to two poems about nature in Culture Choice 4 on page 112. Then do a project about a region from your country.
2 Check Your Progress 8 → MyLab / Workbook page 87.
2 Exam Choice 4 → MyLab / Workbook pages 88-90. Complete the Module Diary.

MODULE

9 BUSINESS

Objectives: **Read, listen** and **talk about** business and work; **watch** an extract from a reality TV programme; **persuade** someone to buy something; **write** a report; **learn more about** reported speech and infinitives.

TOPIC TALK

1. Your Culture **What are the most important companies in your country?**

2. 5.1 5.2 **Listen to a local radio business report. Complete the notes.**

1 Big UK company profits _up_ by about ________ %
2 Local youth unemployment: ________ to ________ %
3 UK video game sales: ________ by ________ %
4 Blue Rock profits: ________ by ________ %

3. 5.3 5.4 **Listen and complete the information in the network below.**

4. 5.5 Pronunciation **Listen to the words below in sentences. Underline the stress. Where does the stress fall for verbs and nouns: the beginning or the end of the word?**

1 update 3 present 5 decrease 7 export
2 update 4 present 6 decrease 8 export

LANGUAGE CHOICE 53: PAGE 27

5. **Work in pairs. Tell your partner your opinions about companies *you* like and dislike, *your* work experience and *your* ambitions.**

Business and work

I think most [1]_______ give good value for money but a lot of [2]_______ offer poor [3]*services/products.*
My favourite company is Funk because its [4]*products/services* are [5]_______ and [6]_______ .
I dislike Alpha Telecom because its [7]*products/services* are [8]_______ and [9]_______ .
There are [10]*a lot of/few/hardly any* job opportunities for young people now.
I [11]*have done/would like to do* [12]_______ .
My ambition is to [13]_______ .

banks, bus/train companies, cafés, cinemas, clubs, clothes/computer/computer game/phone manufacturers, internet/mobile phone network providers, publishers, shops (chain stores/corner shops/department stores/discount stores/hypermarkets)

Products: (un)attractive, (in)efficient, hi-tech, good value for money/overpriced, good/poor quality, (un)reliable, (un)safe, well-made
Services: (in)efficient, (in)expensive, good value for money/overpriced, (un)punctual, (un)reliable, (un)safe

part-time work as a shop assistant, waiter/waitress
summer/holiday work as a life guard, monitor
voluntary work: abroad, community service, environmental
work experience in a company as a programmer, secretary

be a civil servant, be self-employed, set up my own business/company, work for a family business/multinational company/small company, work for an NGO (non-governmental organisation)

SKILLS

LESSON 33 ENTREPRENEURS

a Mark Zuckerberg

b Stella McCartney

c Bill Gates

Warm Up

1 Look at the photos of famous entrepreneurs and try to answer the questions. Check your guesses on page 130.

1 What kind of business did he/she start?
2 When did he/she start his/her business?
3 Why was it successful?

Reading

2 SKILLS BUILDER 20 **Use the strategies to think of five questions to ask about the magazine profiles. Then read the profiles and try to answer them.**

3 Work in pairs. Ask and answer your questions from Exercise 2 about the people.

4 Read the text again. Choose the best answers to the questions.

1 What new thing did Vanessa think she could offer parents?
  a More advice about teens.
  b Useful advice from teens.
  c Online advice from parents.
  d A blog with her own advice.
2 Why has she been successful?
  a She has built a well-known brand.
  b She knows her customers personally.
  c She employs a lot of people full-time.
  d Parents like her website's advice.
3 What new thing did Jamal offer music lovers?
  a Videos of rappers singing and dancing.
  b Professionally produced videos and interviews.
  c Videos and interviews of a new style of music.
  d Live concerts broadcast online.
4 Why has Jamal been successful?
  a He produces exciting material.
  b He has only filmed famous singers.
  c He has gone into record production.
  d He has become a media mogul.

YOUNG ENTREPRENEURS

5.6

Growing up in Los Angeles, ***Vanessa Van Petten*** *got into trouble so often that her mother and father began buying parenting advice books. During one of her frequent groundings, Van Petten glanced through several of the books and spotted what she considered two major problems. First, the books provided useless advice. More importantly, they were written by adults with no input from teenagers.*

That's when Van Petten decided to take matters into her own hands. At the age of sixteen, she wrote a book for parents from the teenage perspective: *You're Grounded: How to Stop Fighting and Make the Teenage Years Easier*. By the age of twenty-one, she had created RadicalParenting.com, an online community for parents and teens. That's where, with two full-time employees, Van Petten's 120 bloggers aged twelve to twenty answer questions from parents. The site generates revenue through advertising and sponsored links to other websites.

Vanessa's advice:

Get advice and help: 'Everyone said I was too young to start a company but I used online resources, read books, attended conferences and got advice from people I know. That's how I learnt about the business so quickly.'

Reach new audiences: 'Social media is a great way to get in touch with new users – that's why we went on sites for mums and personally emailed videos to big users in each community.'

Do something that works: 'Most importantly, we offered advice that actually works. Parents increasingly began spreading our quirky and sometimes controversial articles by word of mouth. We want to build a brand that is not only interesting but also life-changing.'

5 Vocabulary **Look at the Word Builder. Match the expressions (1-8) with the meanings (a-h).**

a reach a particular number
b has a good result
c by someone telling you
d do something yourself
e can't go out
f later in the future
g there were good opportunities
h stop you seeing clearly

Word Builder Idiomatic language (2)

1 You're **grounded**.
2 She decided to **take matters into her own hands**.
3 They spread it **by word of mouth**.
4 The **door was wide open**.
5 His attitude is **paying off**.
6 The channel has **clocked up** 50,000 subscribers.
7 It will **cloud your vision**.
8 It is bad for you **in the long run**.

LANGUAGE CHOICE 54: PAGE 27

*After **Jamal Edwards** got a video camera for Christmas, he filmed foxes in his west London garden, uploaded the film and got 1000 views. That's what got him started as a film-maker and, at the age of sixteen, Jamal began SBTV, an online broadcaster of music promos, video interviews and live performances from the UK rap scene.*

At the time, grime music, a hybrid of hip hop and UK garage, was just starting. You wouldn't find grime on mainstream TV channels, so artists put videos of their work on YouTube. The door was wide open for an online channel dedicated to grime music.

Edwards started filming London rappers freestyling (improvising) on the street, backstage at gigs or in the back seats of cars. The performances, delivered straight to camera and posted online within days, are raw and thrilling. But Edwards didn't want to restrict himself to local unsigned talent or the grime scene so he has filmed other singers. Recently, he and his eight-strong team have been filming the likes of Ellie Goulding, Nicki Minaj, Bruno Mars and even Justin Bieber. Jamal's attitude appears to be paying off for the channel. Jamal says that SBTV has clocked up 50,000 subscribers and a total of 39 million video views. Last month, he signed a deal with Sony RCA to create his own imprint within the label. Suddenly, the bio on Edwards's Twitter account – 'media mogul' – doesn't seem like an exaggeration.

Jamal's advice:

Don't copy the competition: 'Chase your dream not the competition, because looking at the competition will cloud your vision and be bad for you in the long run.'

6 **Look at the Sentence Builder. Find the expressions in red in the text. What situations do they refer to?**

1 *when she realised that parental advice books were no good*

Sentence Builder Reference

1 **That's when** Van Petten decided to take matters into her own hands.
2 **That's where** the bloggers answer questions from parents.
3 **That's how** I learnt about the business so quickly.
4 **That's why** we went on sites for mums.
5 **That's what** got him started.

LANGUAGE CHOICE 55: PAGE 27

7 **What experiences have influenced you? Write five sentences about them and their effects. Tell the class.**

Once I was ill after eating seafood. That's why I hate it!

Your Choice

8 Your Culture **Work in pairs. Choose two of the questions to discuss.**

1 What famous entrepreneurs are there from your country? What business did they start?
2 What personal qualities do you think entrepreneurs in your country need to have?
3 Do you think you would be a good entrepreneur? Why/Why not?
4 What would be a good sort of business to start in your town or city? Why?

9 **What did you agree about? Tell the class.**

We agreed that you need to be hard-working and have initiative to start your own business.

No Comment

'I work for myself, which is fun. Except when I call in sick, I know I'm lying.'

Rita Rudner

LESSON 34 GRAMMAR WORK EXPERIENCE

5.7

Youth unemployment is on the rise. The number of 16 to 25-year-olds without a job is reported to have reached 1 million last week. It is believed that the situation is not going to improve soon.
The government is trying to ease the problem by creating training programmes. Unpaid apprenticeship and work experience schemes are expected to help young people gain necessary professional experience. However, some employers are sceptical: 'Young people today are known to have very high expectations. It's often said that they want to work less and earn more,' says Mark Harmon, chairman of West London Shopkeepers' Union.

Warm Up

1 Look at the photos (a-b). Which job would you like to do?

2 Read the short article. Answer the questions.

1 What problem does it describe?
2 What solutions are offered?
3 What is the employers' opinion?

3 Read the comments about the article. Whose experience is positive and whose is negative?

Reporting

4 Complete the table with the original sentences.

Reported sentence	Original sentence
1 They said they didn't need any new staff.	
2 They warned me that they wouldn't pay me.	
3 They said they had been looking for a job for weeks.	

5 Read the sentences. Why has the tense in the underlined part not been changed to the past tense? Match the sentences (1-3) with the explanations (a-c).

1 My grandfather always **said** that <u>any job is better than no job</u>.
2 They **think** <u>I'm unsuitable</u>.
3 They **said** <u>they usually hire people with some experience</u>.

a the reporting verb is in the present tense
b we report a general truth
c we report a statement that is still true at the moment of reporting

Comments

5.8

I want to become a hairdresser. My teachers advised me to look for an unpaid apprenticeship and I found a job in a hair salon, though they said they usually hire people with some experience. They warned me that they wouldn't pay me but at least I'm learning some practical skills.
Ian Dawson, 18, London

I did some work experience in a restaurant. When I inquired when they were going to pay me, they threatened to fire me. A lot of my friends admit they can't afford to work for free so they can't get any work experience.
Tom McLane, 20, Norwich

The media accuses young people of being lazy but that's not true. I recently employed three young men on unpaid work experience. They said they had been looking for a job for weeks. They work so hard that I've offered to pay them.
Alex Harrison, 52, Liverpool

I went to an interview once but when I said I don't have any GCSEs they said they didn't actually need any new staff. People think I'm unsuitable just because I don't have English and maths GCSEs!
Lizzie Moore, 19, York

I graduated in Public Relations. At first, I applied for the jobs I really wanted but my grandfather always said that any job is better than no job so I looked for other jobs. Yesterday, there were 60 applicants for one job behind a bar and the manager jokingly suggested that anyone less attractive than Brad Pitt should give up.
Mike Mitchell, 24, Newcastle

6 **Match the statements (1-8) with the reporting verbs in red in the text.**

1 You should look for an unpaid apprenticeship.
2 If you don't look like Brad Pitt, give up.
3 I'll pay you.
4 Young people are lazy.
5 We can't pay you.
6 When are you going to pay me?
7 Be careful, we can fire you.
8 To be honest, I can't afford to work for free.

LANGUAGE CHOICE 56: PAGE 28

7 **Look at the sentences below. Do they report:**

a a general/impersonal opinion/statement?
b the words/opinion of a particular person?

1 **It is believed** that the situation is not going to improve.
2 **It's often said** that they want to work less and earn more.
3 Work experience schemes **are expected** to help young people.
4 Young people today **are known** to have very high expectations.
5 The number of 16 to 25-year-olds without a job **is reported** to have reached 1 million.

8 **Look at sentences 3-5 from Exercise 7. Answer the questions.**

a Are the verbs in **bold** passive or active?
b Do they describe an opinion held in the present or the past?
c What verb form in red are they followed by: a tense, an infinitive or an *-ing* form?
d Which verb form in red refers to an opinion about the past and which about the present or the future?

Practice

9 **A businessperson lost all his money yesterday. Report what he said last week. Where do you not need to change the tense?**

1 'My name is Michael Wallenberg.'
He said his name is Michael Wallenberg.
2 'I'm rich.'
3 'Money doesn't bring happiness.'
4 'I'm going to give £5 million to charity.'
5 'I have three children.'
6 'My business is in perfect shape.'

10 **Use the beginnings to rewrite each sentence in two ways.**

1 Everyone supposes that banks will give fewer loans.
Banks are supposed to be giving fewer loans.
It is supposed that banks will give fewer loans.
2 Experts expect that unemployment is going to rise.
Unemployment ______________________
It is ______________________
3 Everyone knows that economic problems started a long time ago.
Economic problems ______________________
It is ______________________
4 People believe that good education gives better job opportunities.
Good education ______________________
It is ______________________
5 People say that colleges have stopped teaching practical skills.
Colleges ______________________
It is ______________________

LANGUAGE CHOICE 57: PAGE 28

Grammar Alive Impersonal reporting

11 5.9 **Listen to the news item. Complete the sentences with things reported in the programme.**

1 A hundred new businesses are reported *to be registered every week*.
2 It is reported that young businesspeople are ________ .
3 It is believed that the most successful businesses ________ .
4 It is supposed that the new trend ________ .
5 The IT business is expected to ________ .

12 **Use the cues to write short news items.**

1 Inflation / report / reached 5% last month - expect / will go up to 8% next year
Inflation is reported to have reached 5% last month.
It is expected that it will go up to 8% next year.
2 Steve Jobs / believe / was the biggest visionary in business - say / his company is not going to be so creative without him
3 know / employers look for experienced workers - work experience programmes / expect / help young people find jobs - hope / a lot of teenagers will benefit from them
4 Bill Gates / know / started his business as a teenager - his company / believe / earned billions of dollars throughout the years - Gates / know / given a lot of money to charity

LESSON 35 SKILLS

BUSINESS IDEAS

Warm Up

1 Work in pairs. Look at the network. Which of the stages do you think is the most difficult? Which activities would you find most interesting?

Business

1 Product design
- brainstorm ideas
- find a gap in the market
- identify potential customers/users
- identify customer needs
- produce a prototype

2 Marketing
- do market research
- study the competition
- list unique selling points
- produce a poster/video
- write a sales talk

3 Selling
- sell the product to retailers
- get orders/make sales
- increase sales
- make a profit/a loss

Listening

2 5.10 5.11 Listen to a phone-in programme about starting up a business. Order Sir George's underlined advice in Exercise 1.

1 *list unique selling points*

3 5.10 5.11 Listen to the programme again. Complete the sentences.

1 Sir George Pitcher appears on TV and is a *businessman* from East London.
2 You need to think about how your product is different ________ .
3 A sales talk should explain how your product is useful for your ________ .
4 You should prepare your presentation well, ________ and be enthusiastic.
5 A prototype is a ________ of your product that you can test out and improve.
6 You can either make a prototype yourself or pay for the ________ .
7 To find a possible area for a new business, identify situations where ________ don't work very well.
8 When doing market research, it's important to ________ the competition.

4 What part of Sir George's advice do you think is the most useful? Tell the class.

I think his most useful advice is to decide how your product is different from the rest.

DVD Choice

5 DVD 9 Watch the documentary without sound. Are the sentences true (T) or false (F)? Watch the documentary again with sound and check your guesses.

1 *Junior Apprentice* is a reality show about a business competition.
2 The participants' task is to design and sell a product for university students.
3 Hannah and the boys develop a trolley and sled for music festivals.
4 Adam and the girls design a plastic storage unit with games.
5 Adam's team get slightly fewer sales than Hannah's team.

6 DVD 9 Watch again and answer the questions.

1 What sort of person is Lord Sugar looking for as the winner?
2 What kind of person is Lord Sugar?
3 Which of the two teams works better? Why?
4 What are the unique selling points of the two products?
5 What reason is given by the final shop for not making an order?

7 Would you buy either of the products? Why/Why not?

Speaking Workshop

8 5.12 5.13 **Listen to a dialogue about the product in the photo above. What are its main advantages? Would you buy one? Why/Why not?**

9 5.12 5.13 SKILLS BUILDER 8 **Listen to the dialogue again. Use the strategies to decide whether the statements about the situation are true (T) or false (F).**

1 Danny and Mrs Atkinson don't know each other very well.
2 The dialogue takes place in the school hall.
3 Danny is selling things to get money for himself.
4 Danny is outgoing and likes selling things.
5 Mrs Atkinson is convinced by the T-shirts from the start.
6 Mrs Atkinson's children are called Angela and Tommy.
7 She is in a hurry to go somewhere else.

10 Look at the Talk Builder. Do the structures in bold make the sentences more or less emphatic?

Talk Builder Convincing someone

1 **That's what** makes them so special.
2 And **even better is** the guitar T-shirt.
3 **What's brilliant about them is** that you can ...
4 They're great ... because **all you need is** ...
5 **Another thing that's fantastic about them is** that ...
6 **What's also good is** that they're ...
7 But **it's the price that** will just amaze you!
8 They don't ... but they **do have** ...

SKILLS BUILDER 46

11 5.14 Pronunciation **Listen and repeat the sentences.**

12 Complete the description with words from the Talk Builder. Would you like to use the app?

This is a great new mobile phone app to study English with. [1]________ fantastic about it is that it has lots of interactive exercises. [2]________ thing that's great is the recording facility - [3]________ what makes it great for improving your speaking. [4]________ also good is the dictionary with translations in twenty languages. And [5]________ better is the automatic language checker which tells you your mistakes and gives you the correct version. The app can't show films but it [6]________ have lots of things to listen to. But it's the material [7]________ you'll love - it's fun and up-to-date. Now [8]________ you need is your mobile phone and you can study English anywhere!

13 Work in pairs. Act out a role-play to sell something.

1 **Imagine you are selling something to raise money for a good cause (e.g. cancer research). Choose a second-hand or new object to sell. Write notes about:**
   - what it is
   - what it does
   - its advantages
   - its price
   - possible questions about it

2 SKILLS BUILDER 47 **Look at the strategies for playing for time. Which is the most useful in your opinion?**

3 **Act out the role-plays. Take turns to sell your object.**

14 Did your partner convince you? Why/Why not? Tell the class.

Anna really convinced me about her ...

GRAMMAR

DECISIONS

Warm Up

1 Read the article. Which strategy is more effective in decision-making: relying on intuition or analysing a lot of data?

5.15

We believe that in order to take the right decision we need to collect as much information as possible. Imagine you want to buy a computer: you analyse the advantages and disadvantages of tens of models and finally buy one. You may have chosen thoughtfully but, surprisingly, you could have made an even better decision without so much thinking.
George Soros, a famous businessman, is known to have been helped by intuition in many of his successful investments. Similarly, experienced stockbrokers often 'know' what is the right thing to do even before they see the available data. How is that possible?
We don't need loads of information to make the right decision – but we need the right kind of information. When we have to go through a lot of data, we waste time. Instead, the key information can be selected intuitively from our experience and can help us make an absolutely correct choice. When decisions have to be made fast, our first impressions can give us very effective guidelines, especially if we have had a lot of experience in this field. The more experience we have had, the more correct our intuitive judgment is. Experiments suggest that conscious analysis of all the pros and cons makes sense when our decision is relatively straightforward, such as choosing between two T-shirts in a shop. But when the choice is complex, like whether to marry someone or not, snap decisions can be more effective. So when your intuition seems to be telling you to do something, it may be a good idea to take it seriously.

2 How do you make choices? Are you a quick or a slow decision-maker?

Infinitives

3 Look at the infinitives in red in the sentences (1-5). Are they simple (S), passive (PS), continuous (C) or perfect (PR)? Look at other infinitives in red in the text and describe them in a similar way.

1 They know what is the right thing to do.
2 You may have chosen thoughtfully.
3 George Soros is known to have been helped by intuition in many investments.
4 Decisions have to be made fast.
5 Your intuition seems to be telling you to do something.

4 Look at sentences 2 and 5 in Exercise 3. Which infinitive talks about something that:

a happened earlier, before other events?
b is/was going on at the time of other events?

5 Read the sentences (1-5) and match them with the situations (a-e).

1 They seem to employ students here.
2 They seem to be employing some students here.
3 They seem to be employed here.
4 They seem to have employed some students here.
5 They seem to have been employed here before.

a They probably employed students in the past.
b They are probably employing students.
c They are probably employed here.
d They were probably employed here.
e They probably employ students.

➜ LANGUAGE CHOICE 58: PAGE 28

6 Use the beginnings provided and the correct infinitives to rewrite the sentences.

1 It seems that we took a very good decision.
We seem to ______________________.
2 It's possible that his fortune was acquired illegally.
His fortune may ______________________.
3 I don't like it when people question my decisions.
I don't like my decisions ______________________.
4 I think they are thinking about a new strategy.
They could ______________________.
5 I'm happy that I'm working here.
It's good to ______________________.

7 Complete the text with the correct infinitive form of the verbs in brackets.

The world seems [1]_______ (dominate) by famous labels. Every teenager wants [2]_______ (have) designer shoes and jeans. But it's good [3]_______ (know) how these products are made. You may [4]_______ (dream) about the expensive computer on your desk for years but remember that it could [5]_______ (produce) by Chinese or Indonesian teenagers. They may [6]_______ (work) all day in horrible conditions. They may [7]_______ (pay) so little that they can hardly survive. And they may never [8]_______ (use) a computer in their life.

Writing Workshop 9

1 Which of the following paid jobs do you think young people (aged 18-25) can get abroad?

- work on nature conservation projects
- cleaner in a hotel
- language teacher
- work in a hospital
- grape picker
- group leader or monitor of children
- bar or restaurant worker
- sports instructor
- work with disabled children
- life guard

2 Read the report and check your answers from Exercise 1.

Summer Jobs Abroad

The objective of this report is to list summer jobs abroad for young people from 18 to 25 in full-time education. To produce the report, research was carried out on the Net and ten people with experience of working abroad were interviewed.

Resort jobs

The most common jobs are in holiday resorts, hotels and campsites in European countries, especially France and Spain. Bar, restaurant and hotel jobs can be found for applicants with a reasonable level of the local language. Another alternative is being a monitor organising free-time activities but it is vital to have qualifications for working with children.

Summer camp

Group leaders, monitors and life guards are wanted for summer camps, particularly in the USA. Moreover, there is work for qualified instructors in outdoor pursuits like climbing and horse-riding. First-aid qualifications are essential.

Other jobs

Grape picking in France is a popular job although it is hard work and does not pay well. Teaching English on summer courses is another option providing you have done a basic one-month course.

Volunteering

Provided that you do not need the money and can pay for your trip, you can do 'voluntourism': travel and work on community projects, help disabled children, work with endangered animals or help out in hospitals.

Useful tips

- For European jobs, only your passport is needed. However, you have to get a working holiday visa as well for jobs in the USA and Australia.
- It is important to get a job before you go abroad. The best places to find jobs are websites, like www.seasonworkers.com.
- Never lie in your application and do not apply unless you have the right qualifications.

Text Builder

3 Find this information in the report.

a the methods used to get the information *lines 3-4*
b the purpose of the report
c advice about getting jobs
d the list of possible jobs
e holidays with voluntary work

4 Find expressions in blue in the text meaning:

a the purpose of
b necessary (x 3)
c a different choice (x 2)

5 Find linking words in red in the text that have the same meaning as:

a if (x 2)
b but (x 2)
c in addition to that
d in particular (x 2)

6 Write a report about jobs or courses.

SKILLS BUILDER 30

1 **Choose one of the topics below. Make a list of information you want to find out.**

- part-time and summer jobs for young people in your area
- courses for learning English abroad
- courses in your area (fitness, outdoor pursuits, arts and crafts)

Jobs for young people: what kind? pay? hours and conditions?

2 **Use your questions from Stage 1 to look for information on the Net and interview people. Write more notes.**

3 **Use your notes to write a report. Use headings and organise it in this way:**

- introduction: objective/methods used to collect data
- list options and alternatives
- useful advice/tips

4 **Check your report for spelling, vocabulary and grammar.**

7 Work in groups. Read each other's reports. Tell the class the most interesting information you have learnt.

Language Review Module 9

1 Talking about business and work **Complete the description with the words below.**

experience opportunities part
punctual value voluntary

When I left school, there weren't many job [1]________ for people like me without many qualifications. I did some [2]________ work in a local hospital and I got a [3]________ -time job in a restaurant but I really wanted to work in fashion. At school, we had done some work [4]________ in a department store and I really enjoyed it. In the end, I set up my own internet clothes shop. I offer good [5]________ for money and the shop is doing well. My cousin works for me. She is full of ideas and always [6]________ for work and for meetings. /6

2 Idiomatic language (2) **Replace the underlined part of the sentences with an idiomatic expression including the correct form of the word in brackets.**

7 News of our website has spread by people talking about it to each other. (mouth)
8 I was very pleased when my blog was visited by its 1000th visitor. (clock)
9 Eventually this job will lead to great opportunities. (run)
10 Her positive attitude to work is leading to good things for her. (pay)
11 Don't rely on other people. You should do things for yourself. (matters)
12 Inventors shouldn't worry about anything which will make things less clear for them. (vision) /6

3 Reference **Complete the sentences with *That's* + *when, why, where, what* or *how*.**

13 I worked as a shop assistant last summer. ________ I didn't go on holiday.
14 There's a new clothes shop in the town centre. ________ I bought this dress.
15 My friend had a great idea for an internet business. ________ he made his fortune.
16 My friend worked on a farm in Italy last year. ________ I'd like to do next year.
17 Last week I helped my aunt in her shop. ________ I realised that I didn't want to be a shop assistant. /5

4 Reporting verbs **Report the sentences using the verbs in brackets.**

18 'You are late,' said Mr Davies to Mark. (accuse)
19 'I overslept,' said Mark. (admit)
20 'I'll get someone else,' said Mr Davies. (threaten)
21 'You should get more sleep,' said Mr Davies. (advise)
22 'I'll be watching you,' said Mr Davies. (warn)
23 'I can work late,' said Mark. (offer) /6

5 Reporting **Complete the sentences with the correct form of the words in brackets.**

24 (It / known) ______that success is difficult.
25 (It / believe) ______ that young people are lazy.
26 Unemployment (expect / become) ______ worse.
27 (It / say) ______ that shops will disappear.
28 Prices (report / rise) ______ by six percent this year.

/5

6 Convincing someone **Complete the text with the words below. There is one extra word.**

also another better it's need
that's what's

[29]________ great about these shoes is that they are totally practical. [30]________ thing [31]________ brilliant is that they actually help your feet to breathe and they [32]________ have a five-year guarantee. You'll love them but [33]________ the price which will astound you. They are a complete bargain at only £20. Even [34]________, if you buy one pair, you can get a second pair half price.

/6

7 Infinitives **Rewrite the sentences using the words in brackets and an infinitive.**

35 I work during the holidays so that I can save money. (I / in order)
36 My ambition is to become very rich. (I / want)
37 I enjoy working for myself. (It / good)
38 It's possible that Mark lost his job last week. (Mark / may)
39 It appears that we were employed to do the boss's shopping. (We / seem)
40 We know this money was stolen. (This / known)

/6

Self Assessment

5.16 **Listen and check your answers. Write down the scores. Use the table to find practice exercises.**

Exercise	If you need practice, go to
1	Language Choice 53
2	Language Choice 54
3	Language Choice 55
4	Language Choice 56
5	Language Choice 57
6	Students' Book p.91 ex.12
7	Language Choice 58

LEARNING LINKS: 1 Check Your Progress 9 → MyLab / Workbook page 99. Complete the Module Diary.
2 Sound Choice 5 → MyLab / Workbook page 100. Choose three pronunciation activities to do.

MODULE 10 DESIGN

Objectives: **Read, listen** and **talk about** design, fashion and technical problems; **discuss** problems and solutions to them; **write** a formal letter of inquiry; **learn about** expressing regrets and **learn more about** modality.

TOPIC TALK

a Coffee pot for masochists

b Flat chair

c 'Le Million' mobile phone

d Gold Collection dress

1 **Work in pairs. Look at the photos (a-d) and the network. Describe the objects and say what you think about them.**

I think the coffee pot is impractical because ...

2 5.17 5.18 **Listen to the dialogue. Write down five opinions that you agree with.**

1 *Things should be good quality.*

3 5.17 5.18 **Listen again. Complete the information in the network for Brian.**

Style

I think things should [1]________ and [2]________.
My favourite object is my [3]*iPhone/bracelet/watch* because it [4]________ and [5]________.
What I don't like is stuff that [6]________ and [7]________.
I [8]*am/am not* very style-conscious [9]*and/but* I like clothes that are [10]________.
The clothes that suit me best are [11]________, [12]________ [13]*trousers/jackets/shirts/dresses/tops/jerseys.*

Good features

look(s) appealing, classy, elegant, original, simple, sleek, sophisticated, striking, stylish, trendy, up-to-date

be (is) durable, environmentally friendly, functional, good quality, innovative, long-lasting, practical, useful, user-friendly, valuable

Bad features

look(s) bizarre, cheap, dated, dull, old-fashioned, ordinary, ostentatious, tacky, tasteless, unoriginal, weird

breaks easily, costs a fortune, doesn't last, doesn't work properly, is impractical, is poor quality, is useless

Clothes adjectives

casual, colourful, cute, different, elegant, feminine/masculine, outrageous, rebellious, smart, stylish

checked, flowery, plain, striped

beige, burgundy, chocolate, cream, crimson, dark blue/green, etc., gold, light blue/green, etc., purple, scarlet, silver, turquoise

baggy, close-fitting, loose, tight

long/short-sleeved, round-necked, V-necked

corduroy, cotton, denim, leather, linen, silk, velvet, wool

4 5.19 Pronunciation **Listen to how these words are pronounced in the sentences. Listen again and repeat the sentences.**

1 by a
2 be odd
3 there are
4 not into
5 you know
6 don't you
7 suit you
8 blue and
9 aren't you
10 do you

LANGUAGE CHOICE 62: PAGE 32

5 **Work in groups. Use the network to talk about *your* style.**

LESSON **37** GRAMMAR

DESIGN ICONS

a Jonathan Ive - classic iPod

b Philippe Starck - citrus fruit juicer

Warm Up

1 **Look at the objects on this page. Which one do you like most? Why?**

2 **Read the blog. What does the author like about each of the objects?**

3 **Think of the objects you use every day. Choose one that you really like and one you don't like and explain why.**

Regrets

4 **Read the sentences (1-4) and match them to the meanings (a-b). Translate the sentences into your language.**

1 I **could have bought** it at a good price (but I didn't).
2 I **could have asked** her to save it for me (but I didn't)!
3 He **should have got** a Nobel Prize.
4 I really **should have got interested** in design earlier.

a we are talking about a missed opportunity in the past
b we are talking about a mistake made in the past

5 **Read the sentences below and answer the questions. Then complete the table.**

1 I **wish** my school canteen **had** these chairs.
  a Does my school canteen have Arne Jacobsen chairs?
  b Am I happy about it?
2 I **wish** he **had designed** all my other gadgets.
  a Did Jonathan Ive design my other gadgets?
  b Am I happy about it?

Time	Tense
regret about the present	*wish* + _______
regret about the past	*wish* + _______

HOME DIRECTORY ABOUT AWARDS LINKS

(5.20)

Everyday objects shape our tastes and habits. Well-designed and functional things fill us with positive emotions and make everyday activities easier. Yet we often don't know the people behind the beautiful and practical things around us. I wish the designers' names were put on everything we buy. Today, I pay tribute to some of them.

1 I'm sure you recognise this classic chair. The Danish architect Arne Jacobsen, who designed it in 1955, should have got a Nobel Prize for it. It's light, comfortable and has universal appeal. I wish my school canteen had these chairs instead of the white plastic monsters.

2 The man who designed the iPod, Jonathan Ive, is a genius. I wish he had designed all my other gadgets. The iPod is easy to navigate and the size is perfect, it fits your hand like nothing else. And it's beautiful.

3 This desk lamp, created by Michele De Lucchi and Giancarlo Fassina in 1986, is an icon of modern Italian design, a favourite with designers and architects. It's simple and elegant. It makes you want to sit down and start working. I wish I had had one on my desk when I was studying for my exams.

4 It's hard to believe Philippe Starck's futuristic-looking elegant tripod is a fruit juicer. No surprise it's a cult object among design freaks. I could have bought it at a good price when I was in Italy but I didn't realise then that it was so famous. I really should have got interested in design earlier. The only problem with Starck's designs is the price – they are usually quite expensive.

5 Le Corbusier, the famous French architect, designed a few chairs, too. This comfortable armchair was created in 1929 but the design still looks very fresh and has been repeatedly copied. My grandmother used to have one of his armchairs but she gave it away when she sold her house. I could have asked her to save it for me!

e Arne Jacobsen - chair 3107

c
Le Corbusier - LC2 armchair

d
Michele De Lucchi and Giancarlo Fassina - Artemide Tolomeo desk lamp

Practice

6 Choose the correct paraphrase.

1 I regret I am not an industrial designer.
  a I wish I had been an industrial designer.
  b I wish I wasn't an industrial designer.
  c I wish I was an industrial designer.
2 I regret I didn't buy that armchair.
  a I shouldn't have bought that armchair.
  b I wish I hadn't bought that armchair.
  c I could've bought that armchair.

7 Use the words in brackets to rewrite the thoughts of a famous designer.

1 I didn't become an architect. (could)
2 I didn't get my children interested in design. (should)
3 I haven't designed any toys. (could)
4 I have always worked too much. (should)
5 I've never worked with other designers. (should)
6 I didn't create my own school of design. (could)

LANGUAGE CHOICE 59: PAGE 90

8 Use *I wish* and the correct tense to rewrite the sentences.

1 I regret I don't have any designer objects in my room.
  I wish ...
2 I regret I spent so much money on this carpet.
3 I hate my school building! It's so ugly.
4 I regret I didn't visit the Museum of Modern Art when I was in New York.
5 It's a pity there aren't many interesting designers in my country.
6 What a pity that we haven't been taught art and design at school.

LANGUAGE CHOICE 60: PAGE 90

9 Use *I wish* to write sentences about three objects you don't like in your town, school or home.

I wish the lampposts in my town weren't made of concrete. I wish they had been designed by someone creative.

Grammar Alive Expressing regrets

10 5.21 Listen to two dialogues. Complete the table with Donna's and Louise's regrets about the past and the present.

	present	past
Louise regrets that she	doesn't have a bike like Donna's	
Donna regrets that she		

11 Work in pairs. Use the cues to make dialogues.

A: *I love your bag.*
B: *I bought it in Milan.*
A: *I wish I had gone to Italy with you last year.*

A starts	B answers
1 • bag • I / go to Italy with you last year	1 bought it in Milan
2 • headphones • my headphones / better	2 comfortable
3 • notebook • I / go shopping with you	3 bought it yesterday
B starts	**A answers**
4 • mobile • I / not lose my old mobile	4 old
5 • umbrella • my umbrella / bigger	5 very big
6 • pen drive • I / get some nice presents at Christmas	6 a Christmas present

12 Use *wish* to write about three things you regret about the present and three things you regret about your past.

I wish I didn't have to share a room with my brother. I would have more room for my gadgets.
I wish I hadn't bought that ugly lamp. It was really expensive and I don't like the colour anymore.

LESSON **38** # SMART VEHICLES

Warm Up

1 **Work in pairs. Look at the photos (a-c) and the words below. Describe the vehicles and make guesses about them. Then check your guesses on page 130.**

- city car, racing car, sports car
- motorbike, skateboard
- diesel/electric/hydrogen/petrol engine

It looks like a racing car with a ...

Reading

2 SKILLS BUILDER 21 **Read the review of the EN-V. Use the strategies to match the paragraphs (a-g) on page 99 with the gaps (1-6). There is one extra paragraph.**

3 **Read the article again. Answer the questions about Mike Rutherford's attitudes and opinions.**

1 Did he enjoy testing the EN-V? Why/Why not?
2 What does he think of electric cars?
3 What are his conclusions about the EN-V?
4 Do you think he is interested in new technology? Why/Why not?
5 What sort of car do you think he probably drives?

4 **Work in pairs. Would *you* like to own or drive an EN-V? Why/Why not?**

I'd love to have one and come to school in it.

5 Vocabulary **Look at the Word Builder. Find more examples of words in blue with these prefixes in the article and the paragraphs (a-g) on page 99. Then match the prefixes (1-8) with the meanings below.**

- not enough *8*
- not (x 2)
- again
- too
- before
- very
- on its own

Word Builder Prefixes

1 **auto**pilot, ________, ________
2 **in**secure, ________
3 **over**ambitious, ________, ________
4 **pre**-charged, ________
5 **re**invent, ________
6 **ultra**-modern, ________
7 **un**sure, ________
8 **under**used, ________

LANGUAGE CHOICE 63: PAGE 32

a EN-V

5.22

GM's clever EN-V concept is a two-wheeled, two-seater solution to urban transport. *Telegraph Motoring's* Mike Rutherford has a preview and takes it for a spin.

1 ________

That's because of the nature of the EN-V. Last week, I drove one of these, though it was more like flying a small plane than driving. In terms of wackiness, originality, smiles per mile and fun at the controls (I can't say behind the wheel because I didn't find one, or any pedals come to that) it gets 11 out of 10 from this sceptical fan of electric vehicles.

2 ________

Sure, it's an effective mobility machine for one or two people travelling around cities. But it's far less like a car than the Renault Twizy which has four wheels and needs a fully-qualified car driver.

3 ________

When I asked the company last week, GM said it was unsure what legal category it will be in. I'd call it a 'Personal Urban Mobility Pod'. It's less than 60 inches* in length, as wide as it is long, able to drive itself or be driven, has a 25 mph top speed, a range of 25 miles, and is supposed to be uncrashable thanks to its sensors.

4 ________

While they are doing homework en route, an insecure parent can watch thanks to the on-board CCTV facilities. Then, after delivering its human cargo, driving itself back home and parking itself neatly, it would be time for one or more of the parents to climb in for the morning commute to the office. After that, the EN-V can recharge its battery, a process that takes only two to six hours.

5 ________

GM insists that today's typical car, with its five seats and internal combustion engine, is 'inefficient' and 'over-engineered' for city driving, even if it is very green. A conventional car capable of doing 100 mph plus is underused and expensive for customers, millions of whom live in overcrowded cities with average speeds of 8–12 mph.

6 ________

*1 inch = 2.5 cm

b DTV Shredder

a So, what's the problem with the ultra-modern EN-V? Why does it fail in its mission to reinvent the automobile? That's because, er, it's not a car.

b How much cheaper? GM says the price for EN-V cars will 'only be about £10,000'. Personally, I enjoyed driving the EN-V and would like to own one. Even so, I would not buy an EN-V for that price.

c Alternatively, EN-Vs could be described as ultra-efficient butlers. A typical day for a family of EN-V owners in the future might start like this: at 7.45 a.m. a parent might put their kids inside and put the pre-charged vehicle into autopilot mode before sending them to school.

d General Motors claims that it is completely reinventing the automobile. However, it has failed to achieve this overambitious goal with its new product, the EN-V (Electric Networked Vehicle).

e Having said that, the EN-V is not a motorbike with a roof either. A motorcycle tends to have one wheel in front of another, rather than side by side, EN-V-style.

f GM thinks we underestimate how much future city vehicles will change and that they will be a lot smaller, lighter and less expensive. 'EN-Vs will be much less costly than conventional cars.'

g With all this in mind, when the owner is at work they could allow the EN-V to earn money by hiring it out as a sort of automated taxi. EN-Vs will be better value for money because of low running costs, lower parking fees and cheaper insurance due to their low maximum speeds and collision avoidance systems.

c Electric Super Car

6 **Look at the linkers in the Sentence Builder. Which of them can be used instead of *although* and *nevertheless*?**

Sentence Builder *even*

1 The traditional car is inefficient, **even if** it is very green.
2 EN-Vs will be less expensive, **even though** it's not clear how much cheaper.
3 Personally, I enjoyed driving the EN-V and would like to own one. **Even so**, I would not buy an EN-V for that price.

7 **Work in pairs. Complete the sentences about the advantages and disadvantages of the vehicles. Think about these things:**

- expensive/cheap to buy/to run
- fast/slow
- (un)safe
- quick/slow to recharge
- (un)comfortable
- (in)efficient
- clean/polluting

1 Hydrogen cars *have very efficient engines and are very clean*. Even so I wouldn't buy one because they are *expensive and difficult to recharge*.
2 Sports cars ________ . Even so, I wouldn't drive one because they are ________ .
3 Electric cars ________ even though they ________.
4 Motorbikes ________ even if they ________ .
5 Large utility vehicles, like Range Rovers, ________ even if they ________ .

Your Choice

8 **Work in pairs. Choose a car that you know and write notes about it. Use the Net to help you if necessary.**

Skoda Yeti Greenline
Size: length 4.2 metres, height 1.6 metres
Advantages: efficient engine, good on bad roads, good for a family

9 **Work in groups. Tell your partners about your car.**

We've chosen the Skoda Yeti Greenline. It's a great car because it's ....

No Comment

'Somebody actually complimented me on my driving today. They left a note on the windscreen. It said, "Parking Fine".'

Tommy Cooper

LESSON 39 SKILLS GLITCHES

a Intel Pentium chip, 1993

b Stock Exchange crash, 1987

Warm Up

1 **What technical glitches have you had with the machines you use? Were they caused by design faults or because you used them wrongly? Tell the class.**

I have problems with my bike because of the gears.

Listening

2 5.23 5.24 SKILLS BUILDER 9 **Look at the photos (a-b) and listen to the documentary. Read the Skills Builder. In what ways (1-4) does the speaker organise information? How clear is her explanation?**

1 chronologically (time)
2 by topic or sub-topic
3 by place or people
4 by importance (e.g. less important to more important)

3 5.23 5.24 **Listen to the documentary again. Choose the best answers to the questions.**

1 What causes most technical problems?
 a computer glitches
 b design faults
 c inappropriate use
2 Why does the speaker think there are more glitches now?
 a we have more technology
 b trains use more technology
 c computers always make mistakes
3 What kind of problem did the Pentium chips have?
 a they made mistakes dividing some numbers
 b some of them didn't work at all
 c they couldn't do a lot of mathematical calculations
4 What did not cause Black Monday?
 a automatic selling by computers
 b dealers buying shares
 c computers crashing

4 **Which of the glitches do you think is the most interesting or worrying? Why?**

5 **Look at the Sentence Builder. Match the sentences (1-2) with the situations (a-b).**

a Our appointment is in half an hour. We've got to leave now.
b You haven't been looking well for weeks. You should go to the doctor.

Sentence Builder *It's time ...*

1 **It's time** (that) *you went* to the doctor.
2 **It's time** *to go* to the doctor.

LANGUAGE CHOICE 65: PAGE 32

6 **Use the cues to write sentences.**

1 It's 8.00 a.m. It's time / get up / go to school
 It's time to get up and go to school.
2 It has been really difficult to log on to the internet at school for ages. It's time / improve the wi-fi at school
3 It's been freezing at school for days. It's time / repair the school central heating
4 It's one o'clock. It's time / have lunch
5 You have put on a lot of weight recently. It's time / stop eating so many snacks
6 It's midnight. It's time / go home / go to bed

Speaking Workshop

7 5.25 DVD 10 **Look at the photo. What is the situation? What has just happened? What are they going to do? Listen or watch and check your guesses.**

8 5.25 DVD 10 **Listen or watch again. Match the sentences with the people: Beth (B), Tina (T).**

1 Thinks they will win the competition.
2 Thinks the problem could be the controls.
3 Suggests trying a different battery.
4 Doesn't want to take it to pieces.
5 Suggests building a new motor.
6 Manages to repair the car.

9 **Look at the Talk Builder. Which of the sentences (1-12) talk about the problem and which talk about possible solutions to it?**

Talk Builder Problem-solving

1 So, what do you think the problem is?
2 It might be a problem with the ...
3 Whenever you try to ...
4 That could be the cause of the problem but I doubt it. Another issue is the ...
5 We could try ...
6 That might work but we should ...
7 The problem with doing that is ...
8 One solution would be to ...
9 Another option would be to ...
10 Maybe, but it might take a long time to do that.
11 It would be good to ...
12 What do you think would be the best thing to do?

SKILLS BUILDER 46

10 5.26 Pronunciation **Listen and repeat the sentences.**

11 **Rewrite the sentences using the words in brackets.**

1 What should we do now (best thing)
What do you think is the best thing to do now?
2 A possible problem is the fuel. (might be)
3 It makes a strange noise as you turn it on. (whenever)
4 What about changing the battery? (one solution)
5 We could also try buying new controls. (another option)
6 But that would cost a lot. (the problem with that)

12 **Work in pairs. Act out a problem-solving role-play.**

1 **Imagine you are designing something for a competition and it does not work. Choose the object (e.g. a rocket, plane, robot).**
2 **Write notes about:**
- what the object is
- the problems with it
- the possible solutions
3 **Act out the problem-solving role-play. Agree on the solutions.**

13 **Tell the class about:**

- what you wanted to design
- what problems you had
- what solutions you decided on

Our design was a robot house cleaner. The problem was that it kept falling over. We decided to change the design and use wheels instead of legs.

No Comment

'To make mistakes is human, but to really foul things up you need a computer.'

Paul Erhlich

LESSON 40

GRAMMAR

THE DRESS

Warm Up

1 **Look at the photo. What do you know about Marilyn Monroe?**

2 **Read the article. Are the statements about the dress true (T) or false (F)?**

1 It was specially designed for Marilyn Monroe.
2 It was made to cover the actress's legs.
3 It has never been copied.

5.27

If you've never seen it, you ought to watch this iconic scene: Marilyn Monroe standing over a subway grate in a white dress. The scene comes from the 1955 film *The Seven Year Itch*, directed by Billy Wilder.
The dress, created by William Travilla, has a simple design. The truth is he didn't have to do much – Marilyn looked stunning anyway. So he designed a halter dress with a long pleated skirt below the waistband. The fabric needed to be lightweight so that it could flutter upward in the breeze and reveal Marilyn's legs. She had to hold the dress so as not to show too much. It was white to portray innocence.
The scene was shot in New York City. It was exciting because at that time Hollywood film makers were required to avoid showing too much bare flesh. Fans and the press were allowed to watch the filming. Surprisingly, onlookers were also permitted to take photos. Each time the director tried to shoot the scene, hundreds of camera flashes went off and he had to stop. Apart from that, the onlookers couldn't be forbidden to talk so there was a lot of noise. In the end, they were forced to rebuild the scene on a set of 20th Century Fox.
In the last 50 years, replicas of the 'subway' dress have been worn by many characters, including Fiona in *Shrek 2* and Barbie dolls. It was auctioned in 2011 for more than $5.6 million.

3 **What other famous items of clothing can you think of? Why are they famous?**

Modality

4 **Complete the table with the verbs and expressions in red in the text.**

obligation/necessity	*was obliged*
permission/possibility	
prohibition	*couldn't*
lack of obligation	*didn't need to*
advice	*should*

5 **Use the verbs in brackets and the beginnings to rewrite the sentences.**

1 I have to wear a uniform at school. (require)
2 We can't wear miniskirts. (forbid)
3 I could wear what I wanted. (allow)
4 I had to put on a Harry Potter costume. (oblige)
5 I should read about the history of fashion. (ought)
6 I wasn't required to cut my hair short. (have)

6 **Choose the correct verbs to complete the text. Use the picture to help you.**

In the 1940s and 1950s, Hollywood fashion designers [1]*ought to/had to* create thousands of dresses for their stars. They [2]*were forced/didn't have* to follow Parisian styles so they created their own version of glamour. Their designs were often very simple but they were [3]*allowed/forbidden* to use expensive fabrics, like silk, velvet and fur. As a result, their dresses looked timeless and elegant.

Women were [4]*permitted/obliged* to follow strict fashion rules. They [5]*had to/were forbidden to* wear knee-length dresses or skirts. They were [6]*not allowed/required* to leave their homes without a hat, gloves and a handbag. However, women were [7]*forbidden/allowed* to have permed hair.

LANGUAGE CHOICE 61: PAGE 30

7 **Choose a period in history and write three sentences to describe the style rules at that time. Use the words below.**

allowed required obliged forbidden permitted forced

Before the First World War in Europe, men were required to wear long trousers, long jackets and hats. They were allowed to wear colourful ties but they ...

Writing Workshop 10

LEONARDO DA VINCI
DESIGN SCHOOL

10-DAY SUMMER COURSE IN MILAN WITH WELL-QUALIFIED, ENGLISH-SPEAKING TEACHERS

- Five optional areas: fine art, fashion, interior design, graphic design, product design
- Excursions to cities like Verona and Venice
- Air-conditioned classrooms with the latest digital technology
- Workshops, studios and library with 20 computers and 10,000 books
- Individual accommodation in student residence

For more information: Pia Posio ldvds@gmail.com
Price: from €750

1 Look at the advert. Would you like to go on the course? Why/ Why not? What other summer course would you like to do?

2 Read the letter. Which of these things does Jane want more information about?

a getting around Milan
b food
c the total cost of the course
d the dates of courses in August
e if rooms are individual or shared
f the kind of course to choose
g visits and trips

From: Jane Henderson
To: Pia Posio

Dear Ms Posio,
1 I am writing in order to ask you for more information about your summer course which I saw advertised online.
2 First of all, I would like to know which course you think would suit me. I have just finished my A levels (art, English and maths) and want to study design and technology at university. Therefore, I would like to do an introductory design course so that I can be prepared for next year. Could you tell me which of your courses in August would be best for me?
3 Another query I have is related to accommodation. There are no photos on your website and as a result it is difficult to know what sort of rooms there are. Also, could you tell me if there is a kitchen in the residence so I can cook some of my own meals since I am a vegan?
4 I would also be grateful for more information about the price because your website is not very clear about it. Could you tell me if the price includes food and study materials?
5 My last question is about excursions as I am interested in Italian art. For example, I would like to visit the Uffizi Gallery so I would love to go to Florence. Could you send me a calendar of excursions to look at?
6 I look forward to hearing from you soon.

Yours sincerely,

Jane Henderson

Text Builder

3 Write headings for the paragraphs (1-6) in the letter.

1 *Reason for writing*

4 Look at the linking words in red in the letter. Match the groups of linkers (1-3) with the uses (a-c).

1 to, in order to, so that, so
2 since, as, because
3 therefore, so, as a result

a to express the result of something: *It rained - we stayed inside.*
b to explain the purpose of something: *We stayed inside - to avoid the rain.*
c the reason for something: *We stayed inside - it was raining.*

5 Choose the correct linkers to complete the sentences.

1 I am writing to you *in order to/so that* get information about courses.
2 I want to improve my English *since/so* I am interested in your summer course.
3 My level is not very high *as/therefore* I never studied English at school.
4 I would like to have a single room *therefore/so that* I can study at night.

6 Write a letter asking for information about a course.

SKILLS BUILDER 31

1 **Choose the type of course that you are interested in and look for an advert on the Net.**
2 **Make notes about your queries.**
3 **Use your notes to write a letter of enquiry. Use the paragraph structure in the Skills Builder.**
4 **Check your letter for style.**

7 Work in pairs. Read your partner's letter. Then act out a telephone conversation asking for and giving information.

Language Review Module 10

1 Talking about style **Complete the description with one word in each gap.**

I bought a shirt last week. It's got long [1]s_______ and it cost a [2]f_______ . It [3]s_______ me. I like buying nice clothes which [4]l_______ more than a few weeks. I only stop wearing clothes because they look [5]d_______ and old-fashioned, not because they are falling apart. My brother loves things which are [6]c_______ , so he's always looking for bargains. /6

2 *could/should* **Use the cues to write sentences.**

I bought this dress last Saturday but now I'm not sure it was a good idea.

7 I / should / try / it on in the shop.
8 I / could / buy / two dresses in the market for the same price.
9 I / should / ask / my friends for their opinion.
10 I / should / keep / the receipt so I could change it. /4

3 *wish* **Complete the sentences with the correct form of the verbs in brackets.**

11 I wish I _______ (not buy) this watch.
12 I wish I _______ (check) on the internet.
13 I wish I _______ (not drop) it on the floor.
14 I wish I _______ (discuss) it with my parents.
15 I wish I _______ (not find) that shop.
16 I wish I _______ (not be) in such a hurry. /6

4 Prefixes **Complete the words with the correct prefix.**

17 I prefer clothes designed by _______known designers rather than famous ones.
18 The fashion show doesn't start until tomorrow but we were able to see a short _______view yesterday.
19 Most people _______estimate his abilities but I know he's a genius.
20 The shopping centre gets so _______crowded on Saturdays that it can be difficult to move.
21 These heaters are very _______ efficient. They are expensive and the house is still cold.
22 Don't forget to _______ charge your camera batteries overnight. We'll need them tomorrow. /6

5 *even* **Complete the sentences with *even if, even though* or *even so.***

23 The hotel room cost a lot of money. _______ , it was still good value for money.
24 I wouldn't buy a sports car _______ I was rich.
25 Dad walks to work every day, _______ it's raining.
26 We can't get our invention to work _______ we've had a lot of help. /4

6 *It's time ...* **Choose the best sentence.**

27 The alarm's ringing.
a It's time to get up.
b It's time we got up.
28 They're closing the playground.
a It's time to go home.
b It's time we went home.
29 These jeans are really old.
a It's time I bought some new jeans.
b It's time to buy some new jeans.
30 Your dad is going to fall asleep in a minute.
a It's time to stop and have a rest.
b It's time he stopped and had a rest. /4

7 Problem-solving **Complete the dialogue with the phrases below. There is one extra phrase.**

you could buy   one solution would be
that might work   the cause of the problem
the problem is   the problem with doing that

A: This DVD keeps stopping. What do you think [31]_______ ? Is the DVD player broken?
B: That could be [32]_______ .
A: I could take it back to the shop.
B: Well, [33] _______ is that it would probably cost more to fix than to buy a new one. [34]_______ a new DVD player, but the real problem is that your DVDs are scratched and dirty. [35]_______ to put your DVDs away when you've finished using them. /5

8 Modality **Rewrite the sentences using the words in brackets.**

36 We have to be home by ten o'clock. (required)
37 It wasn't necessary for us to wear coats. (have)
38 We weren't allowed to talk. (forbidden)
39 It was wrong for you to leave early. (shouldn't)
40 My dad had to work all night. (obliged) /5

Self Assessment

5.28 **Listen and check your answers. Write down the scores. Use the table to find practice exercises.**

Exercise	If you need practice, go to
1	Language Choice 62
2	Language Choice 59
3	Language Choice 60
4	Language Choice 63
5	Language Choice 64
6	Language Choice 65
7	Students' Book p.101 ex.11
8	Language Choice 61

LEARNING LINKS: 1 Read and listen to extracts from *The Devil Wears Prada* in Culture Choice 5 on page 114. Then do a survey about clothes and fashion.
2 Sound Choice 6 → MyLab / Workbook page 109. Choose the pronunciation activities to do.
3 Exam Choice 5 → MyLab / Workbook pages 110-112. Complete the Module Diary.
4 Check Your Progress 10 → MyLab / Workbook page 113.

Culture Choice 1

1 Your Culture **Are there any groups of people in your country which are discriminated against now or have suffered from discrimination in the past?**

West Indian immigrants in the UK suffered discrimination in the 60s and still have problems.

2 6.1 6.2 **Listen to a talk and complete the notes.**

Civil Rights Movement in the USA 1945–1970

Early 20th century: 'Jim Crow' laws in the South meant segregation in [1] public transport, public places. Few Afro-Americans able to [2] ________ and had little protection from [3] ________ extremist groups (e.g. Ku Klux Klan).

After World War II: Change of attitude when [4] ________ GIs (soldiers) came home.

1955: Montgomery [5] ________ Boycott led by Martin Luther King. Sit-ins, [6] ________ and 'freedom rides' throughout the South.

[7] ________: March on Washington with [8] ________ people. Luther King's famous 'I have a dream' speech.

[9] ________: Civil Rights Act ended segregation.

[10] ________: Voting Rights Act enabled blacks to vote.

1968: Luther King assassinated + race riots in major US [11] ________. Summer Olympics: athletes made [12] ________ Power salute.

3 6.1 6.2 **Listen again. Answer the questions.**

1 How were Afro-Americans second-class citizens?
2 How did Afro-American soldiers feel after the war?
3 What were the 'freedom rides'?
4 How did Martin Luther King see the USA's future?
5 How did many Afro-Americans feel in 1968?

4 **Read about Langston Hughes on page 107. Which of these things do you think most influenced his work?**

a his family
b his race
c a style of music
d his political views
e his travels

5 6.3 **Read and listen to the poem *Will V-day Be Me-day Too?* Check your guesses from Exercise 4.**

6 **Read the poem again and answer the questions.**

1 Who is the letter written by and who is it addressed to?
2 How have Afro-American soldiers helped the US war effort?
3 Who have they been fighting against?
4 What has the writer promised his dying friend?
5 What is he worried about when he gets home?
6 What is he asking his fellow white soldiers to do?

7 **Work in pairs. Discuss the questions about the language in the poem.**

1 Find words that rhyme in the first five verses.
Verse 1: letter/better; Yank/tank; through/too
2 What do 'V-Day' and 'Me-Day' mean?
3 Who is 'GI Joe'?
4 Who or what is 'Dixie'? What does Dixie do to black people?
5 Find the four references to 'Jim Crow' in the poem. In which of them are these images used?
   a a train for carrying prisoners
   b an authoritarian person
   c a sinister animal
6 Why does the poet use capital letters to say 'WILL V-DAY BE ME-DAY TOO?'

My Culture Project

8 **Work in pairs. Choose a period of your country's history. Use the Net to find information and write notes under headings like these:**

- the situation
- the issues
- the leaders
- the result

9 **Tell the class about the period in history.**

We chose the late 19th century, when women campaigned to get the vote in the UK ...

James Langston Hughes was born in Missouri in 1901. His parents soon divorced and he lived with his grandmother for a few years before going to Illinois to live with his mother and her new husband. He began writing poetry at school and, after leaving, did different jobs and travelled around the world as a seaman. He came back to the USA in 1924 and went to university. Langston Hughes lived in New York most of his life and wrote poems, plays, short stories and novels. He loved jazz and its rhythms can be seen in his poems about the lives of working class blacks. In his writing, he attacked racial stereotypes and fought for Afro-American rights. He died in 1967.

Glossary

antiquated: (adj) old-fashioned
buddy: (n) friend (US English informal)
cattle: (n) cows and bulls
comrade in arms: (n) someone who has fought with you
crow: (n) a black bird
defeat: (n) when you lose a war
Dixie: (n) south-eastern states of USA that belonged to the slave-owning Confederacy and the white people living there
face: (v) deal with something difficult
folks: (n) people (colloquial)
glow: (n) soft, warm light
harm: (n) damage, injury or trouble
herd: (v) to move animals
ill-fated: (adj) unlucky
lap: (n) the upper part of your legs when you are sitting down
lay: (v) to put something somewhere
lynch: (v) to kill someone without trial because you think they have done something wrong
might: (n) power, strength
munitions: (n) military supplies, like bombs
native: (adj) your native town/country, etc. is the place you were born
stevedore: (v) load and unload ships and lorries
tan-skinned: (adj) with dark brown skin
Yank: (n) American (informal)

Will V-Day Be Me-Day Too?

Over There,
World War II.

Dear Fellow Americans,
I write this letter
Hoping times will be better
When this war
Is through.
I'm a Tan-skinned Yank
Driving a tank.
I ask, WILL V-DAY
BE ME-DAY, TOO?

I wear a US uniform.
I've done the enemy much harm,
I've driven back
The Germans and the Japs,
From Burma to the Rhine.
On every battle line,
I've dropped defeat
Into the Fascists' laps.

I am a Negro American
Out to defend my land
Army, Navy, Air Corps –
I am there.
I take munitions through,
I fight – or stevedore, too.
I face death the same as you do
Everywhere.

I've seen my buddy lying
Where he fell.
I've watched him dying
I promised him that I would try
To make our land a land
Where his son could be a man –
And there'd be no Jim Crow birds
Left in our sky.

So this is what I want to know:
When we see Victory's glow,
Will you still let old Jim Crow
Hold me back?
When all those foreign folks who've waited –
Italians, Chinese, Danes – are liberated.
Will I still be ill-fated
Because I'm black?

Here in my own, my native land,
Will the Jim Crow laws still stand?
Will Dixie lynch me still
When I return?
Or will you comrades in arms
From the factories and the farms,
Have learned what this war
Was fought for us to learn?

When I take off my uniform,
Will I be safe from harm –
Or will you do me
As the Germans did the Jews?
When I've helped this world to save,
Shall I still be colour's slave?
Or will Victory change
Your antiquated views?

You can't say I didn't fight
To smash the Fascists' might.
You can't say I wasn't with you
in each battle.
As a soldier, and a friend.
When this war comes to an end,
Will you herd me in a Jim Crow car
Like cattle?

Or will you stand up like a man
At home and take your stand
For Democracy?
That's all I ask of you.
When we lay the guns away
To celebrate
Our Victory Day
WILL V-DAY BE ME-DAY, TOO?
That's what I want to know.

Sincerely, GI Joe.

Culture Choice 2

1 A TALE OF TWO CITIES
by Charles Dickens (1859)
200 million copies

2 THE LORD OF THE RINGS
by J.R.R. Tolkien (1949)
150 million copies

3 AND THEN THERE WERE NONE
by Agatha Christie (1939)
100 million copies

1 Your Culture **Look at the list of best-selling novels above and discuss these questions.**

1 What are the best-selling books in your country at the moment? Which of them do you like?
2 How important are advertising and marketing when creating a best-seller?
3 What are the all-time best-selling books in your language? Which is your favourite?

2 **Which of this advice about producing a best-seller do you think is true?**

1 To start with, write an exciting story with very good characters.
2 It is good to get publicity in the media for your book.
3 Get a book cover that looks like a lot of other books.
4 Include a summary of the story on the back of the book.
5 Get a famous person to say that they like your book.
6 Use tricks to get your book into best-seller lists.
7 Use blogs only to tell people all the good things about your book.
8 Social media is a good tool to sell your book.

3 6.4 6.5 **Listen to an interview with a marketing expert. Check your guesses to Exercise 2.**

4 6.4 6.5 **Listen again. Answer the questions.**

1 How is luck important in making a book into a best-seller?
2 How did Agatha Christie get attention for her books?
3 What things make a reader pick up a book in a bookshop?
4 What are blurbs and what should they do?
5 How have people manipulated best-seller lists?
6 What things should writers do online to help promote their book?

5 **Read about Jane Austen on page 109.**

1 Why did she never become famous in her lifetime?
2 What is 'Austen mania' and when did it start?
3 Why do you think her books and films based on them are so popular?

6 6.6 **Read and listen to an extract from *Pride and Prejudice*. Which of these sentences are true (T), false (F) or is there no information (NI) to decide?**

1 The Bennet girls wanted to marry Mr Bingley because he was rich.
2 Mr Bingley made a good impression on everyone at the dance.
3 People did not like Mr Darcy much because he was not very good-looking.
4 Bingley was an extroverted and outgoing sort of person.
5 Darcy did not want to dance with other people because he was a bad dancer.

7 **Read the extract again. Answer the questions.**

1 Why were people at the dance so interested in Bingley and Darcy?
2 How were the characters of the two men different?
3 Why did Darcy make such a bad impression on Elizabeth?
4 What sort of person was Elizabeth?

My Culture Project

8 **Look at the book blurb for *Pride and Prejudice*. Choose a book and write notes about it (type of book, story and characters). Write a short book blurb about it.**

The best-selling classic novel *Pride and Prejudice* is about five sisters. The eldest, Jane, meets the wealthy Mr Bingley and they soon fall in love, but Bingley's friend Darcy makes a bad impression on Jane's sister, the clever and independent Elizabeth. But what are the two men <u>really</u> like? Will the two girls ever find true love and happiness?

9 **Work in groups. Read each other's blurbs and discuss the books. Which ones would you like to read?**

PRIDE *and* PREJUDICE

(1775-1817) came from a well-off English family and started writing as a teenager. In her short life, Austen wrote six novels about life and romance in polite English society, particularly from a woman's point of view. The books sold well but Austen had to publish them anonymously because writing novels was not considered the occupation of a lady. Since the 1990s, there has been an outbreak of 'Austen mania' and her novels have consistently been in the best-seller lists. As well as sequels and prequels of her books, there have been best-sellers based on Austen's stories like *Bridget Jones's Diary*. The novels have been adapted for television and there have been Hollywood films like *Pride and Prejudice* (2005) starring Keira Knightley and Matthew Macfadyen.

When a wealthy young man, Mr Bingley, comes to live in the area, Mrs Bennet is excited because she thinks that he might fall in love with and marry one of her five daughters. She persuades her husband to visit him and, a few days later, the Bennet family go to a local ball where they see Mr Bingley with a group of people.

Mr Bingley was good-looking, gentlemanlike and friendly. His sisters were fine women and very fashionable. His brother-in-law, Mr Hurst, looked a gentleman; but his friend Mr Darcy soon drew the attention of the room by his fine, tall person and his handsome features. Within five minutes of coming in, rumours spread around that he had ten thousand pounds a year. Darcy was looked at with great admiration until people realised that he was unfriendly and reserved.

Mr Bingley had soon got to know everyone in the room; he was lively and outgoing, danced every dance, was angry that the ball closed so early, and talked of giving one himself at his new house. What a contrast between him and his friend! Mr Darcy danced only once with Mrs Hurst and once with Miss Bingley and didn't want to be introduced to any of the young ladies. Nobody liked him and Mrs Bennet disliked him the most because he was rude to one of her daughters.

Elizabeth Bennet had been obliged, by the lack of gentlemen, to sit down for two dances and she overheard a conversation between Mr Bingley and Mr Darcy.

> 'Come, Darcy, I hate to see you standing about by yourself in this stupid way. You should really dance.'
> 'I certainly shall not. You know how much I detest it, unless I know my partner. Your sisters are engaged, and there is not another woman in the room whom it would not be a punishment to me to dance with.'
> 'Well, I have never met so many pleasant girls in my life as I have this evening; and several of them are really pretty.'
> Mr Darcy looked at the eldest Miss Bennet, Jane.
> 'You are dancing with the only handsome girl in the room,'
> 'Oh yes! Jane is the most beautiful creature I've ever seen! But there is one of her sisters sitting just behind you who is very pretty too. Let me ask Jane to introduce you.'
> 'Which girl do you mean?' Mr Darcy turned round and looked for a moment at Elizabeth, till catching her eye, he withdrew his own. 'She is okay but not handsome enough to tempt me. And I don't feel like dancing now.'

Darcy then walked off rudely. Naturally, after that, Elizabeth did not have very friendly feelings towards the arrogant Mr Darcy but she told the story to her friends and made the whole thing into a joke as she had a good sense of humour.

However, over the next few weeks Darcy and Elizabeth keep meeting at local parties and dances and Darcy begins to find himself attracted to her because of her intelligence and charm. Little did Elizabeth know when she first met this strange, proud man that Darcy was eventually to be the love of her life.

Culture Choice 5

1 **Look at the portrait of Shakespeare below. Do you think the sentences are true (T) or false (F)?**

1 He was about sixty years old when the portrait was painted.
2 He lived in about 1600.
3 He had quite a lot of money.
4 He was conservative and conventional.
5 He was very shy and nervous.

2 6.7 6.8 **Listen to a conversation about Shakespeare. Check your guesses from Exercise 1.**

3 6.7 6.8 **Listen to the conversation again. Complete the notes.**

William Shakespeare

Born in Stratford-upon-Avon in 1 *1564*.
Learned 2______ and 3______ at local grammar school.
In 4______, married Anne Hathaway and had 5______ children.
In the mid or late 6______, went to London to become an 7______ and then a writer.
By the late 8______, was a prosperous 9______.
Died in 10______ and left his 11______ to his wife.
He wrote 12______ plays and 13______ poems. Contributed 14______ new words to English and lots of famous 15______ like 'vanish into thin air' (to disappear completely).

4 Your Culture **Work in pairs. Discuss the questions.**

1 Who was the greatest writer (novelist, poet or playwright) ever from your country?
2 Why were they great?
3 How well-known are they abroad?
4 What influence have they had on your culture?
5 Do you like their work? Why/Why not?

Portrait of William Shakespeare

5 6.9 **Read and listen to the last scene from *Hamlet*. Order the sentences (a–j) to summarise the scene.**

a Claudius then poisons Hamlet's wine to make sure he is killed.
b Gertrude drinks Hamlet's poisoned wine by mistake.
c Hamlet asks Horatio to tell everybody what has happened and then dies.
d Gertrude dies from the poison and Laertes confesses his and Claudius's plan.
e Claudius organises a fencing competition to kill Hamlet. *1*
f Laertes wounds Hamlet with the poisoned sword, then Hamlet does the same to Laertes.
g Laertes poisons his sword before the competition starts.
h Laertes apologises to Hamlet and then dies.
i Hamlet gets the first hit in the competition.
j Hamlet wounds Claudius with his sword and makes him drink the poison.

6 **Read the scene again. Answer the questions.**

1 Why does Laertes want revenge from Hamlet?
2 How does Hamlet explain all the bad things he has done to Laertes's family?
3 Who is the real villain of the play? Why?
4 Why does Hamlet kill Claudius?
5 Why are Hamlet and Laertes not to blame for what they have done?
6 What does Hamlet do before dying?

7 **Work in pairs. Discuss the questions.**

1 Did you enjoy the scene from Hamlet? Why/Why not?
2 What are your favourite/least favourite characters from it?
3 What alternative endings to the play can you think of?

My Culture Project

8 **Work in pairs. Choose a scene from a famous play or film from your country. Write notes about:**

- which play/film it is in
- the characters
- what happens
- famous lines
- why you like it

9 **Work in groups. Tell your group about your scene.**

My favourite scene is from Garcia Lorca's Blood Wedding: when the bridegroom finds the bride and Leonardo together ...

HAMLET'S DEATH

King Claudius, Hamlet's uncle, the killer of Hamlet's father and the new husband of Hamlet's mother Gertrude, organises a fencing match between Hamlet and Laertes. Laertes is the son of Polonius who Hamlet killed by mistake and the brother of Ophelia, Hamlet's ex-girlfriend who has killed herself because Hamlet treated her badly. Laertes wants revenge and Claudius persuades him to poison his sword in order to kill Hamlet. Before the fight, Hamlet talks to his friend Horatio and then Claudius comes in with Gertrude, Laertes and other courtiers.

Claudius: Come and shake hands with Laertes, Hamlet.
Hamlet: *(to Laertes)* I'm sorry. I've done you wrong. Everyone here knows – and I'm sure you've heard – that I'm mad. When I insulted you it was due to insanity.
Laertes: My feelings are satisfied – even though what you have done to my father and sister should make me want revenge. But when it comes to my honour, I cannot forgive you so quickly.
Hamlet: Well, let's play this friendly fencing match.
Claudius: Give them the swords, Osric. Since Laertes is better than Hamlet, he needs three more hits to win the match. *(to Osric)* Put the wine glasses on that table. If Hamlet is winning, I'll drink to his health and poison his wine. Come on, let's start.

Hamlet and Laertes start to fence.

Hamlet: That was a hit.
Osric: One hit to Hamlet.
Claudius: Let's drink to Hamlet. *(He puts poison in the wine.)* Give him this.
Hamlet: No, put it down for a moment. Let's play. Another hit. What do you think?
Laertes: You got me, I admit it.
Claudius: Hamlet is going to win this.
Gertrude: No, he's tired. Hamlet, take my handkerchief and wipe your forehead. The queen drinks to your good luck and happiness, Hamlet.

Gertrude lifts the glass with the poison.

Claudius: Gertrude, don't drink that.
Gertrude: I'll drink it if I want to. *(She drinks.)*
Claudius: *(to himself)* That was the poisoned drink. It's too late now.
Hamlet: Get ready for the third hit, Laertes. You're just playing around.
Laertes: You really think so? Come on.

Laertes wounds Hamlet. Then in a scuffle they end up with each other's swords and Hamlet wounds Laertes. Gertrude then collapses.

Hamlet: What's wrong with the Queen?
Claudius: She fainted at the sight of the blood.
Gertrude: No, it was the drink! Oh, Hamlet! I've been poisoned. *(She dies.)*
Hamlet: Who has done this?
Laertes: It's partly my fault. Hamlet, you're dead. No medicine in the world can cure you. You don't have more than half an hour to live. I poisoned the sword that you've got now. And your mother's been poisoned. But the king's to blame for that.
Hamlet: The sword was poisoned! Then get to work, poison!

Hamlet wounds Claudius with the sword.

Hamlet: Here, you murderer, now drink this. Follow my mother.

Hamlet makes Claudius drink and he dies.

Laertes: He got what he deserved. Please forgive me as I forgive you, Hamlet. You're not to blame for my death and my father's, and I'm not responsible for yours. *(He dies.)*
Hamlet: *(to Horatio)* God will free him from blame. I'll follow him to heaven in a minute. I'm dying. Horatio, tell everyone the truth about what happened here.

They hear the sound of an army approaching.

Osric: Young Fortinbras is returning in triumph from Poland.
Hamlet: I'm dying, Horatio! This poison's killing me. I will not live but I vote for Fortinbras to be the new King of Denmark. Tell him that – the rest is silence.
Horatio: Now a noble heart is breaking. Good night, sweet prince. May the angels sing you to sleep.

Glossary

blame: (n) responsibility for something bad
blame: (v) to say or think that someone is responsible for something bad
courtier: (n) an important person at a royal palace
deserve: (v) to have earned something by doing something good or bad
faint: (v) to suddenly become unconscious
fencing: (n) the sport of fighting with a long, thin sword
forehead: (n) the part of your head above your eyes and below your hair
handkerchief: (n) a piece of cloth that you use for drying your nose or eyes
heaven: (n) the place where good people are believed to go when they die
hit: (n) when a sword hits the other player in fencing
in triumph: (adv) with victory
play around: (v) to not take something seriously
poison: (n) a substance that can kill you or make you very ill if you eat or drink it
revenge: (n) something you do to punish someone who has done something bad to you
scuffle: (n) a short physical fight
sword: (n) a weapon with a long pointed blade and handle
wipe: (v) clean something with a cloth
wound: (v) to cause an injury to someone

Culture Choice 4

1 Your Culture **Which region in your country has:**

1 the most beautiful landscape?
2 the best quality of life?
3 the highest standard of living?

2 6.10 6.11 **Look at the photo and map of New England below. Then listen to a tour guide describing the region. Choose the best answers to the questions.**

1 How big is New England?
  a bigger than Texas
  b as big as the state of Washington
  c a bit bigger than England
2 What is the population of the region?
  a 4.5 million b 14 million c 40 million
3 What type of landscape is most common?
  a prairies and grasslands
  b coniferous forests
  c deciduous forests
4 When is the most popular time to visit?
  a autumn b summer c spring
5 What is special about New England?
  a it has little contact with the rest of the States
  b its food and buildings are distinctive
  c it was the first area settled by the English

3 6.10 6.11 **Work in pairs. Listen again. Write notes on the topics below. Then ask and answer questions about them.**

Student A
- geography (area, population, cities)
- tourism (things to do, see)
- influence on US culture

Student B
- landscape and vegetation
- special identity
- influence on US politics

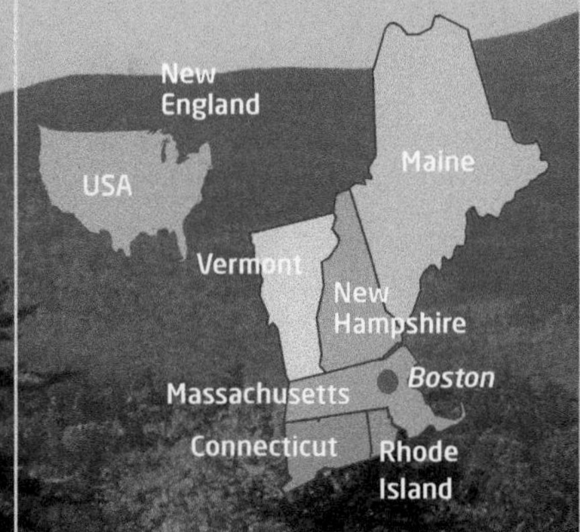

4 **Read about two New England poets on page 113. What similarities and differences are there between their lives?**

5 6.12 **Read and listen to the poems. Match the sentences to the poems: Poem 1 (P1), Poem 2 (P2) or both (B).**

a It is set in winter in the New England countryside. *B*
b It is probably in the middle of the day.
c The poet is alone with his/her horse.
d The poet is galloping on his/her horse.
e The poet has stopped to look at the woods.
f The poet is thinking about the beauty of nature.
g The horse gives the poet strength and energy.
h The poet would like to stay but has things to do.

6 **Read the poems again. Answer the questions.**

1 What words in the first poem rhyme with these words?
  a flight b sun
2 What words in the second poem rhyme with these words?
  a Verse 1: know; here b Verse 2: shake; sweep
3 Find lines in the first poem where the poet says these things:
  a 'I love speed!'
  b 'There are times when you feel you can never die.'
  c 'I feel part of nature.'
4 Match the images (a-c) in the second poem with their possible meanings (i-iii).
  a the woods i death
  b sleep ii obligations in life
  c promises iii beauty and danger

My Culture Project

7 **Choose a region from your country (not your own). Write notes about the things in Exercise 3 (e.g. geography).**

8 **Work in groups. Ask and answer questions about your regions.**

Amy Lowell was born in Massachusetts in 1874. She came from a wealthy family and, after leaving school, she travelled and became a popular socialite. When she was 28, she started writing poems and published her first book of poetry in 1912. She died in 1926.

1

A Winter Ride
by Amy Lowell

Who shall declare the joy of the running!
Who shall tell of the pleasures of flight!
Springing and spurning the tufts of wild heather,
Sweeping, wide-winged, through the blue dome of light.
Everything mortal has moments immortal,
Swift and God-gifted, immeasurably bright.
So with the stretch of the white road before me,
Shining snow crystals rainbowed by the sun,
Fields that are white, stained with long, cool, blue shadows,
Strong with the strength of my horse as we run.
Joy in the touch of the wind and the sunlight!
Joy! With the vigorous earth I am one.

Robert Frost was born in 1874 in California but, after his father's early death, his family had no money and they moved to live with his grandfather in New England. For much of his life, Robert was a farmer in New Hampshire and wrote poems in the early mornings before starting work. He died in 1963.

2

Stopping by Woods on a Snowy Evening
by Robert Frost

Whose woods these are I think I know.
His house is in the village, though;
He will not see me stopping here
To watch his woods fill up with snow.
My little horse must think it queer
To stop without a farmhouse near
Between the woods and frozen lake
The darkest evening of the year.

He gives his harness bells a shake
To ask if there is some mistake.
The only other sound's the sweep
Of easy wind and downy flake.
The woods are lovely, dark and deep,
But I have promises to keep,
And miles to go before I sleep,
And miles to go before I sleep.

Glossary

bright: (adj) with a lot of light
declare: (v) to say something
deep: (adj) going far in from the outside
dome: (n) a round shape
downy: (adj) with fine hairs
flake: (n) a piece of snow (snowflake)
harness: (n) a piece of equipment for controlling a horse
heather: (n) a low plant with purple, pink or white flowers
God-gifted: (adj) given by God
immeasurably: (adv) incredibly
immortal: (adj) living forever
joy: (n) great happiness or pleasure
mortal: (adj) not living forever
queer: (adj) strange
rainbow: (n) large curve of different colours that can appear in the sky when there is both sun and rain
shadow: (n) the dark shape that something makes on the ground when it is between the light and the ground
shining: (adj) full of light
spring: (v) to jump over
spurn: (v) to ignore
stained: (adj) coloured or marked by
stretch: (n) part of a road
sweep: (v) moving fast through
swift: (adj) fast
tuft: (n) a bunch of grass, etc. growing together at the base
vigorous: (adj) strong and energetic
wide-winged: (adj) with wings stretched like a bird flying

Culture Choice 5

1 Your Culture **What well-known fashion brands and designers do you know of from your country?**

Zara and Mango are well-known Spanish brands and Agata Ruiz de Prado is a famous Spanish designer.

2 6.13 6.14 **Listen to a discussion about fashion. Listen again and match the sentences (1-8) with the people: Alex (A), Suzie (S), both of them (B) or neither of them (N).**

1 Buys her clothes from designer clothes shops.
2 Thinks that big clothes companies treat their workers badly.
3 Thinks the fashion industry is good for the economy.
4 Thinks adverts should show normal-sized women.
5 Thinks fashion design involves a lot of creativity.
6 Thinks that the fashion industry is bad for the environment.
7 Likes wearing the same clothes all the time.
8 Likes going clothes shopping.

3 **Work in pairs. What are your opinions about the fashion industry?**

A: *I think it's very creative and is good for our country's economy.*
B: *I disagree. I think that ...*

4 **Read about Lauren Weisberger on page 115. Where did she get material to write her first novel?**

5 6.15 **Read and listen to the extracts from *The Devil Wears Prada*. Are the sentences true (T) or false (F)?**

1 Alex rings with bad news and thinks Andrea should come home immediately.
2 If Andrea doesn't stay on in Paris, she will definitely lose her job.
3 Andrea is only expected to look after Miranda's work affairs.
4 Miranda wants her daughters to fly to Paris just for a party.
5 Miranda imitates Andrea's reply because she thinks it is funny.
6 Andrea tries to think of ways to solve the passport problem.
7 Miranda is furious at Andrea's reaction to her order.
8 Andrea decides to get a flight immediately after the party.

6 **Read the extracts again. Answer the questions.**

1 Why do you think Andrea feels guilty when Alex asks her if she is coming home?
2 What sort of person do you think Miranda is? Give examples.
3 Why do you think Andrea refuses to deal with Miranda's order about the passports?
4 What do you think Miranda is going to say when Andrea interrupts her?
5 How do you think Andrea feels as she leaves the fashion show?
6 What can you guess about Lauren Weisberger's opinions about the fashion industry?

7 **Work in pairs. Discuss the questions.**

1 Have you seen the film *The Devil Wears Prada* or would you like to?
2 How accurate do you think Lauren Weisberger's description of the fashion world is?
3 How do bosses treat their subordinates in your country? How do you think they should behave?

My Culture Project

8 **Work in pairs. Write six questions about one of the topics below.**

- people's tastes in terms of clothes (styles, colours, materials)
- the styles, materials and colours that are 'in' this year for young people
- people's opinions about the fashion industry

1 *What kind of clothes do you like wearing when you go out with your friends at the weekend?*

9 **Work in groups or go around the class. Ask your questions and answer your partners'.**

10 **Write notes with your results. Use your notes to tell your results to the rest of the class.**

Lauren Weisberger was born in 1977 in Pennsylvania and studied English literature at Cornell University. Her first job was working as assistant to Anna Wintour, the editor-in-chief of *Vogue*, the famous fashion magazine. Lauren then began writing for another magazine and wrote a best-selling novel based on her experiences at *Vogue* called *The Devil Wears Prada*. Since then, she has published three more successful novels. She lives with her husband in New York City.

Andrea (Anne Hathaway) with her boss, Miranda Priestly (Meryl Streep)

After university, Andrea becomes personal assistant to Miranda Priestly, British editor of a fashion magazine. Andrea is accompanying Miranda to Paris when she receives a call from her boyfriend in New York: her best friend, Lily, has had a car accident and is in a coma.

'When are you coming home?' asked Alex. When I was silent for a moment, he continued. 'You are coming home, aren't you? You're not seriously considering staying there while your best friend on earth lies in a hospital bed, are you?'
'What are you suggesting, Alex? Are you suggesting it is my fault because I didn't see it coming? That she's lying in a hospital bed because I'm in Paris right now? That if I had known that she was hanging out with Benjamin again none of this would have happened?' …
'No, I didn't say any of that. Why don't you call me when you know what flight you're on?' …
I couldn't point out the obvious to him, namely, that if I left early to come home I'd be fired immediately. …

Andrea stays on and Miranda gives her orders while going to the Dior fashion show.

'Ahn-dre-ah, leave a message at Horace Mann that the girls will be missing school on Monday because they will be in Paris with me, and make sure you get a list of all the homework they'll need to make up. Also, push back my dinner tonight, until eight thirty. If they're not happy about that, then just cancel it. Have you located a copy of that book I asked you for yesterday? I need four copies – two in French, two in English – before I meet them at the restaurant. Oh, and I want a final copy of the menu for tomorrow's party. …

At the show, Andrea is watching when Miranda comes up to her.

'Ahn-dre-ah, we have a very serious problem here. You have a serious problem. It seems that the twins' passports expired last week.'
'Oh really,' was all I could manage but that clearly wasn't the right response. Her hand tightened around her bag and her eyes began to bulge with anger.
'Oh really?' She mimicked. … 'That's all you have to say? … You'll need to figure out how to renew the passports in time for their flight tonight. I will not have my own daughters miss this party tomorrow night, do you understand me?'

There was virtually nothing I couldn't find, fix or arrange, but securing federal documents while in a foreign country in less than three hours was not happening. Period. She had finally made her very first request of me in a full year that I could not accommodate.

I yanked out my cell phone and punched in a number and watched as Miranda became increasingly livid.
'Ahn-dre-ah!' she hissed. … 'What do you think you're doing? I'm telling you that my daughters need passports immediately, and you decide it's a good time to chat on your phone?'
My mother picked up on the third ring but I didn't even say hello.
'Mom, I'm getting on the next flight I can. I'll call you when I get to JFK.' … I clicked the phone shut before she could respond and looked up to see Miranda. …

'Ahn-dre-ah, you realize what you're doing, do you not? You do know that if you simply leave like this I'm going to be forced to …'
'So sorry, Miranda,' I announced, 'but I don't think I'll be able to make it to the party tomorrow. You understand, don't you? I'm sure it will be lovely so do enjoy it. That's all.' And before she could respond … I strutted outside to hail a cab. I couldn't remember feeling better than at that particular moment. I was going home.

Glossary

accommodate: (v) to deal with a request
be fired: (v) to lose your job
bulge: (v) to stick out
cancel: (v) to stop an arrangement
(in a) coma: (n) being unconscious for a long time due to an accident or illness
expire: (v) when an official document can no longer be used
figure something out: (v) to think about a problem until you find a solution to it (US English)
hail a cab: (v) to stop a taxi in the street
hiss: (v) to whisper aggressively (like a snake)
livid: (adj) very angry
make up: (v) to work on something because something has prevented you doing it before
mimic: (v) to imitate somebody's voice
miss: (v) not go somewhere or do something
period: (n) US English for 'full-stop': .
punch in: (v) dial a number
push back: (v) to postpone or put an arrangement later
renew: (v) to arrange for an official document to continue for a further period of time
secure: (v) to obtain or get
strut: (v) to walk proudly
twins: (n) two children born at the same time to the same mother
yank something out: (v) take something out violently

Listening

1 Identifying facts and opinions
Page 20, Exercise 3

- A fact is something that is known to be true or to exist, for example:
  - A figure or statistic: e.g. *3.7 million animal experiments a year*
  - A date: e.g. *Cosmetic testing on animals was banned in 2008.*
  - A statement based on knowledge rather than feeling or opinion: e.g. *She is a researcher at Cambridge University.* not *She's pretty.*

  Be careful of vague language and statements without specific information to back them up: e.g. *There are **a lot of** animal experiments.* (No information on exactly how many)
- An opinion is the belief or judgement of one or more people.
  - Expressions to show opinions: *I don't think that ... , In my opinion, ... , I'm in favour of ... , I'm against ... , We should ... , Activists claim that ...*
  - Opinion adjectives: *It's **cruel**., It's **natural**., It's **depressing**., It's **good**., It's **horrible**.*
  - Other words or expressions with clear connotations: Negative: *cruelty, discrimination, that's silly* Positive: *courage, It helps ... , It's good for ...*
- The first time you listen, write down three facts. Use abbreviations to write notes.
- Listen again and write down three opinions.

2 Working out the meaning of words from context
Page 30, Exercise 3

- Listen the first time to get the general idea. If there is no task, write down important words that you do not understand. (e.g. *spokesperson*)
- Then look at the words and try to guess the meanings of them before you listen again. Answer these questions:
  - What is the context? What do you know about the subject?
  - Are there any words in your language that look similar? Do you think the meaning is similar?
  - What part of speech does the word look like? (e.g. *noun, verb, adverb, adjective*)
- When you listen again, use the context and the part of speech to try to guess the meaning of the words. Use any explanations and definitions given to help you (e.g. *a person who has been chosen to speak officially for a group, organisation or government*).
- After listening, write down a translation of the word with an example sentence.

3 Identifying speakers' intentions
Page 40, Exercise 3

- When you listen the first time, pay attention to the speakers' intonation that shows their mood, e.g. relaxed, irritated, tired, angry, happy.
- Pay attention to functional expressions that do these things:
  - Make requests: *Can you ... ?/Could you ... ?*
  - Make suggestions: *Let's .../Why don't we ... ?*
  - Give advice: *You should .../If I were you...*
  - React: *That's a good idea./I'm sorry but ...*
- Remember that people often don't express directly what they want. Particularly in English, people often say things indirectly (e.g. *It's a bit cold, isn't it?* meaning *Could you close the window?*)

4 Matching (identifying opinions)
Page 51, Exercise 8

- Before you start, read the opinions. Underline key words and think of possible synonyms for them. Example: *we need to/we should*
- Listen the first time to get the general idea. Try to identify the people's general position about the topic.
- Listen out for these things:
  - Expressions that show opinions: *in my opinion*
  - Negative and positive words: *junk food*
  - Facts in favour or against arguments: *40% of cancer is caused by lifestyle.*
- When you listen again, listen out for the given opinions expressed in a different way.
- Pay attention to people agreeing or disagreeing with the other person to identify their opinions.

5 Making notes
Page 60, Exercise 3

- Before you listen, draw an empty network to complete or use topics that are given to draw it.
- When you listen the first time, list topics and complete some information.
- When you listen again, write down important information related to each topic. Do not try to write down everything you hear.
- Leave out unnecessary words (e.g. pronouns) and use abbreviations: *2 yrs 2 mths*
- If you don't catch a particular word or phrase, try to guess the general meaning and write something similar: *to become strong* for *develop physical capacity*
- After listening, add any other information to the network that you remember.

6 Identifying informal style
Page 70, Exercise 3

- Notice informal style when you listen (formal language in brackets):

Greetings *Hi, Hi there, Hello, How's it going?*
Short replies *Yeah (yes), Sure, Okay, No problem, Go ahead, Fire away*
Short forms *Thanks (Thank you), Bye (Goodbye), No probs (No problem)*
Leaving out words *(You) Know what I mean?, (It was) A pleasure, (Of) Course*
Addressing people First names: *Mary*
Abbreviations: *Tom (Thomas), Sue (Susan)*
Familiar forms: *love, darling* (not used between men), *mate* (used between men)
Informal words *cool (lovely, very nice), kid (child), cash (money), wild time (good fun), awesome (very good), laid-back (relaxed)*
Vague language *kind of, sort of, you know, you know what I mean*
Non-standard language *It's great, innit? (Isn't it?)*

7 Listening actively
Page 81, Exercise 7

- When you are listening to someone, use gestures (e.g. nodding) and facial expressions to show you are following.
- Also use sounds to show that you are listening: *mmm, uh-huh, hmm.*
- Use short expressions to show you are listening: *right, yeah, I see, okay, etc.*
- Use expressions to show these things:
  - Interest: *Really?, Interesting, I see.*
  - Surprise: *Wow!, Oh no!, Really?*
- Repeat words and expressions to show interest or surprise: *311 steps*!
- When you are not clear about something you can also repeat words: *The Tower of London?*
- Use questions and exclamations to show interest or surprise: *Is it?, It isn't!*

8 Identifying the context
Page 91, Exercise 9

- First, identify the basic situation. Use any sound effects to help you. Listen for clues: e.g. references to where they are.
- Listen out for information about what has happened beforehand.
- Ask questions about the people:
  - Who are they? (What are their jobs/roles?)
  - What is the relationship between them? How well do they know each other?
  - What do they call each other?
  - What sort of language (formal/informal) do they use when they speak to each other?
  - What is their attitude towards the other person? How polite or friendly are they?
  - What do they want from the conversation?
- Listen closely to the intonation of the speakers to identify feelings.
- Also listen out for hesitation, sighing or yawning, that show their mood.

9 Understanding the organisation of information
Page 100, Exercise 2

- Information can be organised in different ways:
  - Time (from the past to the present, from the present to the past)
  - Topic/sub-topic (e.g. design: interior design, technical design, fashion design, etc.)
  - People/places: what different people do/did, what happens/happened in different places
  - Order of importance: from less to more serious examples or the other way round
- When you are listening, focus on organising expressions:
  - *Today, I'm going to talk about ...*
  - *First of all ... , Then ... , After that ... ,*
  - *One interesting person is ... , Another writer is ...*
  - *Even more serious than that was ... ,*
- After listening, evaluate how clear the speaker was:
  - very clear and well-organised
  - not always clear
  - not very clear at all

Reading

10 Mapping a writer's argument

Page 6, Exercise 4

- Draw a table with headings like these:

MAIN ARGUMENT Communication technology can be bad for us and we need to learn how to use it better.	
Reasons	**Information and examples supporting it**
1 communication technology can be addictive	a woman cannot resist the red light that shows a new message
2 communication technology is bad for relationships between people	
3	
4	

- Read the text and identify the main argument.
- Read it again and list the writer's main reasons.
  Examples: *1 communication technology can be addictive, 2 communication technology is bad for relationships between people*
- After listing the writer's main reasons for his/her opinions, read the text again and list the information (e.g. facts and statistics) or practical examples that the writer mentions to support his/her point of view.
  Example: *a woman cannot resist the red light that shows a new message*
- Use the table to evaluate the writer's argument. Are all the reasons supported by facts or examples?

11 Identifying informal style

Page 13, Exercise 4

- Notes, emails, letters and postcards to friends or family have an informal style. Blogs and chats on the internet are also usually informal.
- Some features of informal style include:
  - Informal ways of starting letters: *Hi, Hi there, Hello, How are things?, How are you?*
  (Formal: *Dear Sir/Madam, Dear Ms Smith*)
  - Informal ways of finishing letters: *Write soon, See you, Take care, All the best, Love, Kisses*
  (Formal: *Yours sincerely, Yours faithfully, With kind regards, With best wishes*)
  - Colloquial words: *cool, mate, okay, anyway*
  - Contractions: *I'm (having a great time), I'll (be back)*
  - Punctuation:
  capital letters: *AMAZING*
  exclamation marks: *Brilliant!!!*
  dashes: *I'm really busy – I've got two exams tomorrow.*
  emoticons: *It's going to be a busy week* ☹.

12 Identifying writers' opinions

Page 18, Exercise 4

- Read the text quickly to get the general idea.
- Read the text again more slowly. Underline words and expressions that clearly show opinions:
  - Adjectives: *popular, courageous, unjust*
  - Adverbs: *brutally*
  - Nouns: *discrimination*
  - Verbs: *had to*
- Underline quotes from people that give an opinion about what happened (e.g. *you feel part of something*).
- Underline examples of positive and negative behaviour that the writer mentions (e.g. *government in Poland sent tanks onto the street* = negative).

13 Identifying facts and opinions

Page 28, Exercise 2

- Look at the information about facts and opinions in Skills Builder 1. Then read this information about written texts.

  Facts
  In reports and articles, the sources of information are often given: e.g. ***According to UNESCO****, there are seven million children without …*
  Hypertext is also used to give more information in online texts: e.g. *Animals are often transported by lorry for long journeys of up to ten hours.*

  Opinions
  When other people's opinions are quoted in written texts, these expressions are often used:
  Supporters *of factory farming* ***claim that*** *it is cheaper and more productive.*
  Critics say *that it is bad for the environment.*

14 Evaluating the reliability of news reports

Page 26, Exercise 4

- Read the text quickly and identify where it is from (e.g. newspaper, blog, social media). Does it come from an established organisation (e.g. the UN, the BBC) with a reputation for objectivity or is it written by an individual or a group who want to influence people's opinions?
- What is the writer trying to do?
  - report what happened
  - give an opinion about what happened
- Underline opinions mentioned in the texts (e.g. *Some local residents thought that* ...). Find other words that clearly show the writer's opinion (e.g. *This came as a surprise to a lot of people but not to me*).
- Does the writer express claims without facts or evidence (e.g. *the criminal lie that is global warming*)?
- What is the writer's tone (emotional, angry, relaxed)? Look out for 'extreme' words (e.g. *criminal, disgraceful, intolerable, a disgrace).*
- Does the report give different points of view or only one side of the argument?
- If you are not sure about the reliability of a report, find two or three other reports about the same event and compare them.

15 Evaluating advertisements

Page 39, Exercise 4

- Good adverts should be honest, give clear and accurate information and should not manipulate people's feelings.
- When you read an advert, ask questions about these things:
  - Is it clear from the format that it is an advert or does it look like something else (e.g. an article)?
  - Does the advert have extra information which is easy to miss (e.g. in small print)?
  - Does the advert show stereotypes of people (e.g. women cleaning, men being in charge)?
  - How does the advert make people feel about themselves? Does it make them feel they need the product to be happier, more confident, etc.?
  - How reliable does the information look? Does it include vague claims with no figures or sources?
- If you are actually thinking of buying something, check out the information in other sources (e.g. online product reviews). Compare the information before you buy the product.

16 Identifying formal style

Page 43, Exercise 4

- In formal, written English we do not use these things:
  - Contractions (e.g. *I'm writing to you*)
  - Colloquial words and expressions (e.g. *it's cool*)
  - Direct requests (e.g. *I want you to send me* ...)
- Instead we use formal expressions like these:
  - Starting formal letters:
    Dear Sir/Madam, Dear Mr/Ms Smith,
  - Reasons for writing:
    I am writing to complain about/ask about/tell you about ...
  - Making requests:
    I would be grateful if you could give me a full refund/give me information about ...
  - Making demands:
    Not only would I like you to repair it but I would like a complete refund, too.
  - Making threats politely:
    Unless I receive a satisfactory reply within the next month, I will have to take further action.
  - Finishing the letter:
    I look forward to hearing from you.
  - Signing off:
    Yours faithfully, Yours sincerely, With best wishes, With kind regards,

17 Analysing characters

Page 58, Exercise 3

- Read the story extract and underline adjectives that describe the person physically (e.g. *more pallid and thinner*) and their personality (e.g. *eccentric*).
- Underline adverbs (e.g. *calmly*) or expressions (e.g. *in a sinister way*) which describe how the characters do things.
- Read the dialogues again and underline the statements or opinions which tell us about the character, e.g. Watson: *So I should be glad to come and help.* (kind).
- List the actions which show us something about the character. In a good novel or story, the author shows the characters' personalities through their actions, e.g. *Holmes defends himself against a man with a stick.* (brave).

18 Understanding the context

Page 66, Exercise 2

- First, read any questions and use the title and any photos to guess answers.
- Read the text quickly. Identify where it takes place and the people involved.
- When reading again, try to picture the situation in your mind. It can help to close your eyes to imagine the characters and the place.
- Look for clues in the text that tell you about what happened before or after (e.g. references to any previous experiences or plans).
- Look for clues that tell you something about the characters' personalities, their relationships with other people and their cultural attitudes:
  - Direct descriptions of people and their attitudes (e.g. *generous*)
  - How they treat other people (e.g. Are they kind/unhelpful/aggressive?)
  - How they behave and how they react to events (e.g. *worried about snow*)
  - What they say (e.g. Batbayer: *the peace in my mind* – answering the question *What makes you happy?*)
- After answering the questions, work with a partner and compare your answers.
- Remember, there is often not just one 'correct' interpretation of the situation.

19 Applying information from a text

Page 79, Exercise 4

- Read the text and write notes about the general conclusions and principles mentioned in it. For example:
  - *cities without humans – first thing to happen: flooding (underground tunnels, etc.)*
  - *growth of plants – pavements*
- Evaluate these conclusions. Do they make sense? If necessary, check information elsewhere (e.g. the durability of bronze objects).
- Apply the principles and conclusions to another situation (e.g. what would happen in my town if people disappeared?). Write notes about it, for example:
  - *first thing: flooding of area near the river in spring*
  - *growth of plants: grass on streets, creepers on walls of buildings*
- Compare your notes and conclusions with another student, pair or group.

20 Asking questions before reading

Page 86, Exercise 2

- Look at any photos or headings to guess what the text is about. If this is not possible, read the first paragraph.
- Decide what you know about the subject, if anything, and write notes. For example:
  young entrepreneurs: more common in the hi-tech sectors
- Then think about what you would like to know about it. Write five questions. For example:
  1 How did he/she start off?
- Read the text to answer your questions. Write notes with the answers. For example:
  1 Vanessa: writing a book for parents
- Sometimes you will not be able to answer your questions.
- Evaluate how useful the information in the text was for you: 5 – very useful, 1 – not very useful.

21 Matching (paragraphs with gaps in a text)

Page 98, Exercise 2

- Read the main text first quickly to get the general idea. What is it about?
- Read the text again and list paragraph topics (e.g. the nature of the EN-V). Do the same with the paragraphs removed from the text. (e.g. the problem of the EN-V).
- Try to match the paragraphs with the gaps. First, think about the topics and the arguments in the text. Decide whether the topic of the paragraph removed from the text fits in between the topics of the paragraphs before and after the gap.
- Look for linking words in the paragraphs (e.g. *even so, alternatively, not, either*) which refer to things mentioned in the previous paragraph.
- Also look for references to previous paragraphs (e.g. *I drove one of* ***these****, having said* ***that****, while* ***they*** *are doing their homework*) to help you.
- Once you have matched all the paragraphs with all the gaps, read the whole text again to check that it sounds logical and coherent.
- When you have finished, check if the extra paragraph still does not match any gap.

Writing

22 An informal email

Page 13, Exercise 7

KEY
linkers
informal style

informal beginning

Hi there Fred!

How are things? I'm sorry for not writing back sooner but I've been really busy – actually I haven't had time for anything.

news, problems and plans

As you know, I'm in the school play and I've got lots of school work too for all my subjects, especially for geography ☹. How are you getting on at school?

I'm also trying to decide what to study at university. My parents want me to do medicine but I'm not keen on it – in fact, I can't STAND the sight of blood!!!! How are you getting on with your plans?

Anyway, I also wanted to tell you about Sue – things aren't great between us and she's always telling me what to do and complaining ☹. To be honest, I'm really fed up. What do you think I should do?

By the way, I met Jennie Smith in the street last week. Do you remember her from Year 6? She was that tall girl with black hair – she's quite good-looking now and she's got a great sense of humour. In fact, I haven't laughed so much for AGES!!! Would you like to meet up with her when you come over in the holidays?

informal ending

I hope all's well with your family and with Kate. Send them my love.

All the best,
Tom

23 A 'for and against' essay

Page 23, Exercise 6

KEY
linkers
expressing opinions

introduction to the topic: defining what it is, basic facts about it

Nuclear power involves the splitting of uranium atoms to produce energy. According to the Worldwatch Institute, there are 439 nuclear plants operating worldwide and in some countries, like France, they produce most of the electricity (68%).

arguments for something

The main argument for nuclear power is that, apart from being cheaper than many other methods of generation, it provides energy without producing large quantities of carbon dioxide emissions (Nuclear Energy Authority 2006). Another argument is that it uses a small amount of fuel so it is easy to store unlike coal, gas or oil. Moreover, it is much more reliable than renewable energies like solar and wind which depend on the weather.

arguments against something

On the other hand, critics of nuclear power say that it is fundamentally unsafe. For instance, there have been major accidents like Three Mile Island in 1979, Chernobyl in 1987 and Fukushima in 2011. Furthermore, nuclear power is not as cheap as its defenders claim as they do not take into consideration the building of the power stations or the treatment of nuclear waste. According to Amory Lowins and Imran Sheik (2012), per kilowatt nuclear energy costs 14 cents and wind energy only 7. Finally, anti-nuclear activists point out the danger of terrorist attacks as well which has grown in the last few years (US State Department).

conclusion (your opinion)

To sum up, despite producing reliable energy and not causing a large amount of carbon dioxide emissions, nuclear energy has a lot of dangers. In my opinion, we should close all nuclear power plants although it means that a bigger investment in renewable energy sources is required.

KEY
linkers
showing result
useful expressions

24 A TV series review

Page 33, Exercise 6

introduction - basic information about the programme

The first series of the spoof documentary *Twenty Twelve* showed on BBC 4 in the first half of 2011. The comedy makes fun of London's preparations for the 2012 Summer Olympics and stars Hugh Bonneville as the boss of the preparation committee, Olivia Colman as his secretary and Jessica Hynes as the public relations chief.

good things about it

The best thing about this spoof is definitely the acting as there are some excellent performances by Bonneville as a self-important but incompetent boss and Hynes as a PR woman who only speaks in jargon. There are some funny jokes and so many good dialogues that the programme is nearly always amusing.

bad things about it

However, the satire is a bit too mild to be really funny and there is so much repetition about traffic that it starts to become dull. There is also such a lot of voiceover in the show that it distracts from the dialogue and tries to explain too much. Finally, the production is just too stylish to be convincing and give it that cheap documentary feel.

conclusion

To sum up, this show has some funny bits but it does not get off the ground because it is just not critical enough and is too mild. In fact, Seb Coe, the real Olympics organiser, appears in one show. If *Twenty Twelve* had been more critical, no politician would have gone near it!

KEY
linkers
emphasis
formal language
useful expressions

25 A letter of complaint

Page 43, Exercise 7

Dear Sir or Madam,

reasons for writing/ product information

I am writing to you about a series of problems that I have had with my new ZTAB2 tablet. I bought the computer from your website for €300 on 10 May (product number ZT87625HT) and it arrived five days later. I enclose copies of the guarantee and receipt.

what went wrong/ false advertising claims

In your advertising, you claim that the ZTAB2 tablet has more power and speed than the original ZTAB. However, I have been using it for three weeks and it seems virtually the same. Not only do apps load quite slowly but the graphics are not very fast either and this affects gaming quality. Finally, I have had connectivity problems and the ZTAB2 is not compatible with my TV and printer.

problems with customer service

When I phoned your customer service department, after waiting for half an hour I was put on to a technician who told me that I was wrong about the ZTAB2 and she hung up as soon as I asked to speak to the manager. Since then I have phoned your office twice and written a letter but nobody has responded to my complaints.

what you want/ further action

Not only would I like you to refund my money but I would like compensation for wasting my time. Unless I receive a satisfactory reply within the next three weeks, I will have to take further action. I have already been in contact with my local consumer protection office and they have recommended that I take legal action if I do not get full satisfaction.

I look forward to hearing from you.
Yours faithfully,

Paul Davies (Mr)

26 An opinion essay

Page 53, Exercise 6

KEY
reason, contrast and addition linkers
other useful linkers and expressions

introduction: definition of the subject and personal opinion

Alternative therapies are treatments, like homeopathy and acupuncture, which are unscientific since they are not based on evidence but on beliefs whereas conventional medicine comes from scientific research. In my opinion, alternative medicine is of very little use in treating illness.

reasons for opinion

First of all, there is no scientific proof that alternative medicine works. Although clinical trials have demonstrated the benefits of acupuncture for back pain, all other alternative medicine is no better than a placebo – something of no medical value but with some psychological effects. Secondly, alternative medicine can actually be dangerous due to its side effects and as patients delay proper treatment. For example, many patients who use homeopathic pills to avoid malaria have actually contracted the disease.

argument against and reasons you disagree

Supporters claim that alternative medicine cures health problems, like back pain or asthma, which conventional medicine cannot deal with. They say that these therapies have fewer side effects and work better. Nevertheless, conventional treatments have higher success rates than alternative therapies in all areas. In addition, even though herbal treatments are called 'natural', they can have very dangerous effects on patients. Finally, alternative practitioners usually refuse to participate in clinical tests because they know what the results will be.

conclusion: personal opinion

In conclusion, most alternative therapy is closer to magic than science. While some treatments can work there is no scientific evidence to justify its use in the public healthcare system and it should be more closely regulated by the government.

27 A description of a person

Page 63, Exercise 7

KEY
useful expressions

appearance

The first thing you notice about Judy is her long, blond hair which always looks clean and shiny. The next thing that strikes you about her is her infectious smile and her large blue eyes which always seem to be laughing and happy.

first impressions/personality

When you first meet Judy, she seems a bit vague and absent-minded but you soon realise that she is very quick and bright and has an amazing ability to understand other people. She has the capacity to always say the right thing when people are upset and need a bit of comfort.

habits/behaviour/talents

Of course, Judy has her faults. She tends to be a bit too laid-back and she always leaves things until the last moment which can be a bit stressful. She also giggles too much which can be irritating. However, Judy is usually great with people. She's also an excellent artist – she is brilliant at drawing and has done some great portraits of her friends.

clothes

Judy loves dressing up and shopping for clothes and she usually wears colourful dresses or matching skirts and tops. You hardly ever see her wearing jeans, jumpers or T-shirts, even at the weekend.

opinion about the person

To sum up, Judy is one of those people who you underestimate when you first meet them. She seems a bit lost and disorganised but she is actually very observant and does not miss anything. For me, she is someone special because she is always a great friend to me.

28 A story

Page 73, Exercise 6

KEY
linkers (time/comment)
sequence linking
useful expressions

setting the scene: the situation

While going to the Christmas party on the bus, we were looked at strangely by the other passengers. My friend Sue and I were both dressed up as aliens with green skin, four arms and two heads. We felt we were going to have a fantastic time at a friend's flat and that we might even win the fancy dress competition.

what happened: the feelings of the people

As the door to the flat opened and we walked in, everybody turned and stared at us. They were all dressed normally and nobody else in the room was wearing fancy dress! I felt a bit angry and immediately went over to speak to Anne, whose party it was. Unfortunately, one of my arms caught on the Christmas tree and it fell over on top of me and the decorations went everywhere. After going as red as a beetroot, I tried to pick everything up.

what happened next: how people reacted

Later we found out that the competition had been cancelled but we had not been told about it. During the meal, people kept making jokes about aliens which was rather irritating. After we had started dancing, everybody looked at us. Suddenly, I saw a very good-looking boy dressed as Mr Spock from *Star Trek* who I had not seen before. He came up and started dancing with me and we had a fantastic time. Luckily, he had a motorbike and took me home with him when the party finished.

what happened in the end

Having arranged to meet, we started going out together. We are madly in love with each other and I am now pleased that I went to the party dressed as an alien!

29 A description of a place

Page 83, Exercise 6

KEY
linkers
descriptive adjectives
useful expressions

memories of the place

Swimming in the sea, playing beach volleyball, eating delicious fresh sardines at a pretty outdoor café, meeting sociable, hospitable people: this is what I think of when I remember the lovely seaside city of San Sebastian in the Basque Country in northern Spain.

the landscape

San Sebastian (Donostia in Basque) is in an extraordinary location on the Bay of Biscay with two impressive bays and the beautiful island of Santa Clara on one side and striking green hills on the other side. The views from virtually anywhere in the city are breathtaking.

what to do there

There are lots of things to do in San Sebastian. In the morning, you can chill out on the spectacular Concha beach and go swimming, surfing or windsurfing. At lunchtime, you can walk around the picturesque old town and eat the best tapas in the world. In the afternoon, you can go walking or mountain biking in the hills or visit the marvellous aquarium and the amazing science museum. There is some great nightlife in San Sebastian with lots of cafés, bars and clubs. Even if you cannot speak Spanish or Basque, you will have an amazing time.

opinion of the place

Of course, San Sebastian has had its problems and it used to have violent political demonstrations. However, everything is much quieter now. For me, San Sebastian is one of the most fascinating places in the world with some of the most welcoming people and I cannot wait to go back!

30 A report

Page 93, Exercise 6

KEY
linkers
useful expressions

introduction

possible jobs

voluntary work

advice

Part-time Jobs in Herefordshire

The objective of this report is to list part-time jobs in Herefordshire for young people in full-time education. To produce the report, research was carried out on the Net and twenty people with experience of working part-time were interviewed.

1 Hospitality

The most common part-time jobs available are in cafés, pubs, restaurants and hotels, particularly in Hereford. Moreover, there is some work for catering staff for special events like the Hay-on-Wye Festival. Previous experience and basic health and safety qualifications are essential.

2 Retail and office work

There are some part-time opportunities in shops, especially supermarkets in Hereford. Weekend jobs can be found as shop assistants and cashiers. Another alternative is working in an office but it is vital to have ICT and accounting skills.

3 Other jobs

Some part-time farm work is available although it does not pay well. Being a sports instructor is another option providing you have the qualifications. Finally, charity fundraising is a possibility although you will need a driving licence.

4 Volunteering

Provided that you do not need the money you can do voluntary work for local NGOs: working at animal centres, doing conservation work and organising events.

Useful tips

- For most part-time jobs you will just need to be over eighteen. However, for some jobs, like administrative work, A levels are needed.
- It is important to put your name on databases. The best places to find jobs are websites like www.part-timework.com.
- Never lie in your application and do not apply unless you are qualified.

31 A letter/email of enquiry

Page 103, Exercise 6

KEY
linkers of result, reason and purpose
formal language
useful expressions

reason for writing

queries: courses, accommodation, price, excursions

signing off formally

From: Tom Barker
To: Maria Suarez

Dear Ms Suarez,

1 I am writing in order to ask you for more information about your Spanish courses in Granada which I saw advertised online.

2 First of all, I would like to know which course you think would suit me best. I did Spanish at university but I have not used it for five years or so. Therefore, I am not sure what my level is now. Can I do an online test so that I can check what my level is?

3 Another query I have is related to accommodation. The information on your website is a bit vague and as a result it is difficult to know if rooms are shared or individual. Also, could you tell me if there are any sports facilities there so I can do regular exercise since I am training for next year's football season?

4 I would also be grateful for more information about prices. Your website is not very clear because it just mentions 'price from €750'. Could you tell me if this includes excursions and lunch?

5 My last question is about excursions as I am interested in visiting Seville and Cordoba. Could you send me a calendar of excursions to look at?

6 I look forward to hearing from you.

Yours sincerely,

Tom Barker

Speaking

KEY
linking expressions to organise presentation
describing statistics and trends
other linking words and expressions

32 Giving presentations

Page 11, Talk Builder

introduce topic

In this talk we're going to look at families and households in the UK and how they have changed in the last few years.

main points

The first interesting trend to point out is that fewer couples are getting married. For example, only fifty-six percent of British families now have married parents. That figure is down from the 1970s when seventy percent of parents were married.

Another area to comment on is the number of stepfamilies. Twelve percent of families are now stepfamilies and the number has gone up by over a third in the last ten years.

However, there are more unmarried couples with stepchildren than ever before. For example, the percentage of unmarried stepparents went up from twenty percent to over forty percent in 2006. The number of lone or single parent families is up too, by about ten percent and now one in four British children live with just one parent, usually their mother.

Another interesting area is the number of single-person households, which has increased to about a third of all households. One of the main reasons for more people living on their own is that people are choosing to live alone. At the same time, the numbers of widows and widowers is up as people live longer than before.

summary/questions

So to summarise, British families are changing and there are fewer traditional families and more new types of families. So that's it. Has anyone got any questions?

33 Preparing presentations (strategies)

Page 11, Exercise 12, Stage 2

- Choose a topic that you think is interesting and that you know something about.
- Write down four or five areas to talk about related to the topic. Example: *changes in marriage*
- Use a search engine, like Google, to find three or four useful websites.
- Write notes with information about the different areas of the topic. Example: *Number of children (per couple): gone down (1990 - 3.2, 2010 - 2.1)*
- Organise your notes using a flow diagram.
- Practise giving your presentation by yourself or with your partner. Go through it again just before you are going to give it.

34 Having discussions

Page 21, Talk Builder

A: **There's no doubt that** all kinds of hunting are cruel.

B: **I'm afraid I don't agree with that at all. Actually**, it is important to control animals like foxes. **In my opinion, we should** hunt species that damage the environment.

A: **That's a valid point** but you don't need hunting for that. **It's clear that** animals suffer so that people can have fun hunting. People pay a lot of money to do it.

B: **Absolutely! I completely agree** with that. **It's definitely true that** hunting provides jobs – and we need them now.

A: **Exactly**, we need jobs **but what about** jobs for people looking after the environment? **Frankly, I think** that hunting should be banned.

B: **I don't think so. In fact**, there are opportunities for more hunting. **Personally, I think** we could increase tourism with hunting trips.

A: **I'm sorry, but that's just not true**. Very few people go on hunting trips. **Surely** environmental tourism would be better?

B: **I'm afraid I'm not convinced. It's obvious that** hunting is something natural. **Don't you think so?**

A: **No, I wouldn't say that.** I think it's cruel.

35 Preparing for a discussion (strategies)

Page 21, Exercise 12, Stage 2

- Read the statement to be discussed. Brainstorm ideas in favour of it and against it. You need to know the arguments that the other person will use so that you can react to them. Example:
  FOR: *Hunting provides jobs in the country.*
  AGAINST: *We could create other jobs to look after the environment.*
- Use a table to organise your argument (see Skills Builder 10 Mapping a writer's argument).
- Work with your partner. Rehearse expressing your opinions.

36 Describing scenes

Page 31, Talk Builder

Well, **the scene starts off with** Ricky lying on the sofa half asleep reading a magazine. **Then** the camera focuses on Suzie coming in. **First of all**, Suzie screams and frightens Ricky so that he jumps. Then Suzie goes into the kitchen. **At first**, you think she is making a drink for herself with lots of ice. But **it's just hilarious because** Suzie pours it onto Ricky's head. Anyway, **eventually**, Ricky gets off the sofa and goes into the kitchen to help with the dinner. **Unfortunately**, there isn't any food in the fridge **so Ricky immediately** phones for a pizza. **It's so funny because**, when he's talking to the pizza place, Suzie is miming to describe the sort of pizza she wants. **The next thing that happens is that** the dog starts jumping up on Ricky. **It's ridiculous because**, **as soon as** the dog does that, Ricky starts shouting down the phone. **Eventually**, the woman puts the phone down and they decide to go out for a hamburger.

In the end, they have a great time. The dog **finally** eats most of Suzie's hamburger so he's happy, too.

37 Describing scenes (strategies)

Page 31, Exercise 12, Stage 3

- To tell jokes or describe scenes, use present tenses: *This guy goes into this shop and ...*
- When you are describing a scene, don't use long sentences. Use short sentences organised with linkers: *She arrived at the check-in desk.* (pause) ***First of all**, she asked a question.* (pause) ***After that**, she dropped her bag.*
- When you don't know a word in English, don't stop speaking. Use vague language or gestures to describe the word or describe it in words: *She passed her one of those sort of passes that you need to get on a plane.*
- Comment on what you think is funny: *It was hilarious because ...*

38 Leaving out words

Page 41, Talk Builder

- Short questions with *any, anybody/anything*:
  A: **Any news** of your brother? (~~Is there~~ any news of your brother?)
- Condensed questions as replies:
  A: We're going to the cinema.
  B: When? (When ~~are you going to the cinema~~?)
- Echo questions (to express interest or surprise):
  A: I'm going to start doing judo.
  B: Are you? (Are you ~~going to start judo~~?)
- Short replies:
  A: Can you help me with this maths problem, please?
  B: Of course, no problem. (Of course, ~~I can help~~. ~~That's~~ no problem ~~for me~~.)
  A: Have you been to Rome?
  B: Yes, I have. (Yes, I have ~~been to Rome~~.)
- Exclamations:
  A: I met Sue yesterday.
  B: You didn't! (You didn't ~~meet Sue~~!)

39 Justifying opinions

Page 51, Talk Builder

- **I think that** we should ban junk food. **I think so because** it causes so many health problems. **Actually**, more people die from a bad diet than from smoking or drinking.
- As far as I'm concerned we should educate people. **The reason for that is that** most people just don't know what food is good for them. **The fact is that** people don't eat enough fruit and vegetables.
- It's difficult to get people to change their habits. **So I think** the government should make supermarkets only sell healthy food.
- People should know what they're eating. **Therefore**, I think we should get the fast food chains to provide information about ingredients.
- The fast food companies put lots of sugar, salt and fat in their food.
- **Because of that**, people get addicted to it. **That's why I think** we should control fast food chains.

40 Discussion strategies

Page 51, Exercise 12, Stage 2

- Before the discussion, think about your ideas and write notes. Think of reasons and find facts to back up your opinions.
- Practise expressing your opinions based on facts: *I think ... because ... , ... therefore I think ...*
- Ask other people about their opinions: *Don't you agree?, Don't you think?*
- If somebody else tries to dominate, use polite expressions to interrupt: *Can I just say something, please?*
- To stop someone interrupting a lot, use polite expressions: *Could you let me finish, please?*
- Use polite expressions to disagree: *That's true but ... , That's an interesting point but ...*

41 Clarifying

Page 61, Talk Builder

A: We're from Australia and we only started the band six months ago. **To put it another way**, we're a pretty new band.
B: **So that means** it's your first time here, **right**?
A: Yes. We've got gigs and some studio time.
B: **What do you mean by that exactly**? Are you making another record?
A: Maybe. We've arranged some sessions. **In other words**, we're going to lay down a few opera tracks.
B: **I don't quite get that. Could you explain what you mean exactly?**
A: **What I mean to say is** that we've got ideas for an Aboriginal rock opera. **Do you follow me**?
B: I think so. So, you're going to record it here?
A: No, **as I said before**, we'd like to record some of the songs for it. **Do you see what I mean**?
B: Yes. **So, just to recap** a couple of things – you're a new Australian rock band, **right?**

42 Correcting yourself (strategies)

Page 61, Exercise 11, Stage 2

- If you know you have made a simple mistake, correct yourself. Use expressions like: *I mean ...* or *Sorry ...*
- If you think you might have made a mistake, ask about it: *Is that correct? Is that right*?
- If you are really not sure, carry on speaking. The most important thing is to communicate.
- If the other person does not understand you, try to say it in a different way: *I mean ... , What I mean is ...*
- Write down a list of your most common mistakes with their corrections.

43 Making arrangements

Page 71, Talk Builder

A: **I thought maybe we could** go up to the mountains on Sunday.
B: **That's a good idea but it means we'd have to** go by bus and there aren't many on Sundays. **I think we'd better** get someone to take us there. **What if we asked** your mum?
A: **Why not? So what about the idea of** skiing?
B: **That'd be great but I'm not so sure about** the snow. How about going for a walk?
A: **Cool! That way we** could go all the way up to the lake. **We could maybe** take a picnic, too.
B: **That's fine by me but I'd rather you** made it.
A: Okay. And **why don't we invite** a couple of friends, like Tom?
B: **Okay, I'll see if he wants to come.**
A: **I suggest we** meet at your place at 10. What do you think?
B: **That would be nice but** it's a bit late. **I'd rather we met up a bit earlier**. Say half past eight.
A: **Okay, let's do that.**

44 Evaluating plans (strategies)

Page 71, Exercise 12, Stage 2

- First, write notes with plans for doing something. Think about what to do and about practical things like food, transport, money, times, etc.
- Read your notes again and think of possible problems with the arrangements:
  – The club might be very crowded.
  – The bus might arrive late as they aren't very reliable.
  – It might rain and spoil the picnic.
- Think of alternative plans of action to deal with the problems and the advantages and disadvantages:
  – We could go to the cinema. (cheaper but less fun)
  – We could go by car. (more convenient but parents might be busy)
  – We could have lunch at a café. (easier but more expensive)

45 Tourist advice

Page 81, Talk Builder

A: **Can you recommend places to visit, please?**
B: **I'd advise you to** go to the Prado. **It's important not to** miss the Velazquez rooms. And I **don't think you should** miss Goya, either.
A: **Could you suggest something else to do, please?**
B: **If I were you, I'd go to** the old part of town. **It's really worth visiting. And you mustn't miss** the Royal Palace, either.
A: What about going to somewhere like Segovia?
B: **There's no point in** leaving the city.
A: **What else would you advise us to do?**
B: **It's a good idea to visit** the Retiro Park.
A: **Is there anything else you would suggest doing?**
B: **I think you'd better go to** the Thyssen museum.
A: **Is there anywhere that you'd recommend for** lunch?
B: **I suggest you** go to the area around the Cava Alta. **I'd recommend going to** Casa Lucio.

46 Convincing someone

Page 91, Talk Builder

A: This is a dog running machine and it's completely automatic. **That's what** makes it so special. It's got a screen with different landscapes. **Even better are** the animals that your dog can chase. **What's brilliant about this is** that your dog has a great time when you're out. **All you need is** a minute to programme the treadmill. **Another thing that's fantastic is** that it gives the dog treats.
B: But what happens if there is a problem?
A: That's a very good question. Just let me check that ... There is a sensor and, if there are problems, it automatically stops. **What's also good is** that the treadmill can talk to the dog. But **it's the price that** will just amaze you! It's a bargain at two hundred pounds.
B: How much does delivery cost? Is that included?
A: Erm, let me think ... No, actually it isn't but you **<u>do</u> get** five kilos of dog treats.
B: Great! I'd like one. My dog, Freya, will love it!

47 Playing for time (strategies)

Page 91, Exercise 13, Stage 2

- When you are speaking in your own language and in another language you often need time to think about what to say.
- One way of gaining time is using sounds of hesitation (*mmm, err*) and expressions (*well, right, you see, you know*).
- Another way is directly asking for more time: *Let me think. Just let me check.*
- You can also use phrases to respond to the other person and give you time to think at the same time:
  - Replying to a question: *That's a good question. That's a very interesting question.*
  - Reacting to a suggestion: *That's a possibility. That's an interesting idea. That's a good suggestion.*

48 Problem-solving

Page 101, Talk Builder

A: Oh no, our robot's stopped working. **So, what do you think the problem is**?
B: **It might be a problem with the** controls. Or it could be the electric motor. **Whenever the robot starts to move, the motor stops**, then starts again.
A: **That could be the cause of the problem but I doubt it. Another issue is the** design of the robot's legs. They don't move very well. Now we've got a real problem.
B: **What do you think would be the best thing to do?**
A: **One solution would be to** change the design and use wheels instead of legs.
B: **The problem with doing that is** the cost. We'd have to buy the wheels. **We could try** taking out the motor and looking at it.
A: **That might work but we should** check out the robot's legs first.
B: **Another option would be to** make the legs shorter. If they were shorter, it might walk better.
A: **Maybe, but it might take a long time to do that.**
B: **We could** ask my dad about what to do. He's good with machines.
A: Great. **It would be good to** get another opinion.

STUDENT A/B ACTIVITIES MODULES 1-6

M1, Lesson 3, Exercise 12

Teenage usage of communication technology in the USA

	December 2000	November 2004	September 2009
Use the internet	73%	87%	93%
Go online every day	42%	51%	63%
Go online weekly	45%	35%	26%
Get news online	68%	76%	62%
Buy things online	31%	43%	48%
Have a cell phone	no data	45%	75%
Have an MP3 player	no data	51%	79%

Teenage socialising and social media use in the USA

	November 2006	September 2009
Spend time with friends socially every day	31%	33%
Talk on the home phone every day	39%	30%
Send text messages every day	27%	54%
Talk on a cell phone every day	55%	50%
Send messages every day on social network	41%	37%

M3, Lesson 10, Exercise 5

Speaker 1

I can't stand watching 24/7 news channels. I want to find out what the news is but, in fact, there is too much going on on the TV screen. It requires doing a lot of things at the same time - listening to the speaker's voice, reading the moving text at the bottom of the screen and watching the pictures in the background. You know, scientists say that if we receive information through more than one channel, we actually remember it worse. So is it worth putting all this information on the screen?

Speaker 2

I avoid watching TV. I just don't enjoy sitting in front of the screen for hours. I prefer listening to the radio. One of the advantages is that you can do something else at the same time - I usually manage to clean my room during my favourite discussion programme. My granddad had to give up watching TV because of his eyes and he started listening to the radio instead. He says the radio is much more civilised - journalists don't rush the people they interview and don't interrupt them so much.

Speaker 3

I don't mind watching TV, I watch some soaps and I like comedy shows. I used to watch the BBC news every day but now I usually check the news online. The problem is that there's often too much to choose from. For example, I decide to read something about a hurricane and, two lines into the text, I spot a link to another article. So I click on the link and never finish reading the first text. I think we're now used to scanning websites and papers more than reading them in detail and our idea about what's going on in the world is often really superficial. We have to learn to select the news that may be interesting to us and then follow it in more depth.

M4, Topic Talk, Exercise 1

a Advert for shoes
b Advert for a shampoo
c Advert for an airline company

M6, Lesson 22, Exercise 2

Sherlock Holmes: A Game of Shadows (2011)

Sherlock Holmes is played by Robert Downey Junior. The character is more like James Bond than the original Holmes character, the genius of detection. In the film, this Sherlock Holmes is an action hero who is good at martial arts and clever. But at the same time he is rather childish and ridiculous; he talks too much and wants to be the centre of attention. His jokes are silly and he dresses up in strange disguises. Downey's Sherlock Holmes is brilliant but insecure, unlike the complex and reserved character in Conan Doyle's books.

Dr John Watson is played by Jude Law and is Holmes' loyal friend, a very balanced and practical man. He is an action hero, too, and very witty in his dialogues with Holmes.

Professor Moriarty is an evil genius played by Jared Harris. He is calm and calculating; he looks pleasant but is really a dangerous madman, like the Joker in the Batman films. He is the organiser of an anarchist campaign of terrorist bombings and assassinations to cause a world war.

STUDENT A/B ACTIVITIES MODULES 8-10

M8, Lesson 30, Exercise 9

Khufu Pyramid (the Great Pyramid of Giza)

The pyramid was built around 2560 BC to house the tomb of the Pharaoh Khufu. It was made of 2.3 million blocks of limestone and granite. The pyramid is the last of the seven wonders of the ancient world to survive and for 3800 years it was the highest building in the world. Because of the extremely dry Egyptian climate and the solidity of its construction, the pyramid will last thousands more years. It would actually last longer without humans as the damaging pollution of nearby Cairo would stop immediately.

Derinkuyu Underground City

This underground city in Cappadocia in Turkey was made in prehistoric times, perhaps by the ancient Hittites. The city may have been built by refugees looking for a safe place. It is excavated from soft rock and has eleven storeys, with wide tunnels, houses, churches and mosques. Derinkuyu is still in good condition and could last millions of years as it is resistant to earthquakes and protected from wind and water.

The Panama Canal

In 1914, the Panama Canal was opened for ships to go from the Caribbean to the Pacific. The US government took ten years to build it; millions of tons of soil and rocks were excavated and concrete dams were built to create a huge artificial lake. Despite its huge size and the fact that it is cut into rock, the canal would not last long without human maintenance. The dams would soon overflow and flood the canal, damaging the concrete locks and eventually letting the water out. After twenty years, engineers calculate that the canal would be dry again.

Mount Rushmore

The four giant sculptures at Mount Rushmore in the USA were created by the sculptor Gutzon Borglum. The sculptures, completed in 1941, commemorate four of the greatest US presidents: George Washington, Thomas Jefferson, Abraham Lincoln and Theodore Roosevelt. Because the rock at Mount Rushmore is solid granite, it only erodes 2 or 3 centimetres every thousand years. As a result of this, the faces are likely to last over seven million years and this would be one of the last man-made landmarks on the planet to survive.

M8, Lesson 31, Exercise 1

Tower Bridge in London was finished in 1894. Its objective was to carry traffic from the north to the south bank of the Thames but at the same time to let ships pass under it.

Ponte Vecchio ('Old Bridge' in Italian) was built to carry people and carts across the Arno River in Florence in 1117 but rebuilt in 1345. It has three stone arches with shops on top.

Millau Viaduct in southern France was opened in 2004 and is the second tallest bridge in the world. It carries motorway traffic across the valley of the River Tarn.

M9, Lesson 33, Exercise 1

Name	Business	Started	Why successful
Mark Zuckerberg	Social networking website	When at university. Facebook now worth 17.5 billion dollars.	Produced a social networking site with new features (such as adding friends)
Stella McCartney	Fashion design	Designed first jacket in 1984. Studied fashion and started own label in 2001. Has 16 shops around the world.	Produced original and popular designs
Bill Gates	Computer operating systems	Started programming at school. Dropped out of Harvard and started Microsoft. Was the world's richest person from 1993 to 2007.	Produced the first user-friendly operating system

M10, Lesson 38, Exercise 1

a **EN-V**
The electric network vehicle is a city car with a difference. It has an electric engine for each of its two wheels and a lithium-ion battery. It only has two wheels and uses sophisticated technology to keep its balance.

b **DTV Shredder**
This is a skateboard with an engine and tracks like those of a tank. Its maximum speed is 50 kilometres per hour and the controls are on the Shredder's handle.

c **Electric Super Car**
This prototype, designed by Mark Przeslawski and Hanan Qattan from the University of Coventry, has an electric engine and a special design to make it stable at high speeds.

WORD LIST

Module 1

Page 5

Relationships

cousin — Jamie is the only first cousin I have.
get to know sb — He's very nice when you get to know him.
great-grandfather — Sally's great-grandfather is 91 today.
great-grandmother — His great-grandmother died last week.
have a laugh — Whenever we meet we have a great laugh together.
have a row — He had just had a row with his wife.
have sth in common (with) — I have a lot in common with these people.
put family first — He puts his family first, before the needs of his job.
teammate — He finished just ahead of his Ferrari teammate.
text — Texting while driving can cause an accident.
trust sb — He's very honest and I trust him completely.

Multi-part verbs (1)

be up to sb to do sth — It's up to you to change your life.
get in the way of sth — Nothing should get in the way of your studies.
get in touch with sb — We'll get in touch with you soon.
pay attention to sb/sth — Are you paying attention to what I'm saying?
put sth in place — We've put systems in place to prevent crime.
take sth into account — These figures do not take inflation into account.
empower — The new law empowers minority groups.
face-to-face — Nothing replace face-to-face meetings.
social media — Are the social media important in your life?
athletic — Sarah is athletic and good at netball.
belief — Several members hold similar religious beliefs.
break up — Has Sam broken up with Lucy?
chat up — I spent the evening chatting up Liz.
chat-up line — That's the worst chat-up line I've ever heard!
current — Who is the current President of the USA?
dump — Vicky dumped Neil yesterday.
humorous — The film has some very humorous moments.
magnetic pole — The Earth's magnetic poles are North and South.
opinionated — I found him arrogant and opinionated.
plain — Mrs Cookson was a rather plain woman.
play dumb — 'What is it?' I asked, playing dumb.
put sb off — The restaurant's decor put me off eating there.
speed date — A typical speed date lasts a few minutes.
split up — The band split up two years ago.
uninterested — He was uninterested in politics.
birth parent — He never met his birth parents.
cohabit — Millions of people in America cohabit.
extended family — Some extended families share the same house.
lone parent — She's a lone parent bringing up a child on her own.
remarry — Widowed in 1949, Mrs Hayes never remarried.
separated — We've been separated for six months.
widow — My neighbour is an elderly widow.
widower — He's been a widower for several years.
summarise — Summarise your views in the introduction.
trend — There's a trend towards working from home.
unemployment — The level of unemployment is rising.
conflict — Conflict in the region has led to violence.
hardly any — There were hardly any cars on the road.
parental authority — Parental authority applies to children under 18.
take sb/sth for granted — Bridget was careful not to take him for granted.

Linkers

as you know — As you know, we're trying to reduce costs.
by the way — By the way, have you seen my keys anywhere?
especially — Feedback is especially important in learning skills.
in fact — I know her. In fact, I had dinner with her.
to be honest — To be honest, I don't like Mary.

Module 2

Page 15

Big issues

animal testing — The cosmetics company doesn't use animal testing.
approve — I don't approve of cosmetic surgery.
conservation — The organisation is involved in wildlife conservation.
corruption — Government corruption is a major problem.
cruelty — The children had suffered cruelty and neglect.
cut — Cuts in public spending will affect education.
donate — Last year he donated $1,000 to cancer research.
fundraising — They sent me an Action Pack full of fundraising ideas.
global warming — Scientists are concerned about global warming.
go on — He went on lots of demos when he was younger.
healthcare — The government has promised healthcare for all.
issue — We should raise the issue with the council.
nuclear weapon — The country has no nuclear weapons programme.
petition — I signed a petition against the new law.
public spending — The government vows to control public spending.
vandalism — The lifts were out of order due to vandalism.
break down — The car broke down just north of Paris.
charge — I need to charge the battery in my laptop.
desperate — He was desperate to get a job.
empathy — She had great empathy with people.
fidget — The kids had started to fidget.
forest ranger — My uncle is a forest ranger in Canada.
mysterious — Benson disappeared in mysterious circumstances.
shepherd — The shepherd found his missing lamb.
tension — Exercise is the ideal way to relieve tension.
walking stick — Grandad has to use a walking stick.

Multi-part verbs (2)

bring forward — We'll have to bring forward the date of the meeting.
give up — Why should we give up our right to free speech?
look back on — We often look back on childhood as a happy time.
put down — They had to use troops to put down the riots.
speak out — People were afraid to speak out.
throw off — He was thrown off the train for causing a nuisance.
arrogant — He was unbearably arrogant.
boycott — They are now trying to organise a boycott.
brutally — He was brutally murdered.
challenge — They went to the High Court to challenge the decision.
Constitution — Who wrote the US Constitution?
courageous — He was courageous enough to admit he was wrong.
court case — The court case lasted six weeks.
curfew — There is a night-time curfew in the city.
defiance — They held a protest in defiance of the ban.
defiant — Mark banged a fist on the desk in a defiant gesture.
determined — Gwen is a very determined woman.
infuriate — Her actions infuriated her mother.
inhabitant — The city has six million inhabitants.
key witness — She was the prosecution's key witness in the case.
NGO — She's been working in Africa for an NGO.
outlaw — The bill outlawed several types of gun.
pushchair — She put her child in his pushchair and went out.
second-class citizen — Are women still treated as second-class citizens?
segregation — Racial segregation was made illegal in 1954.
tactics — The team used unfair tactics in the game.
take a stand — We have to take a stand against racism.
tank — The tank took a direct hit.
undemocratic — I think we live in an undemocratic society.
underground — He infiltrated an underground terrorist organisation.
unjust — An unjust law is no law at all.
well-educated — Well-educated people are more likely to find jobs.
wheelbarrow — We need a new wheelbarrow for the garden.

Opinions and reactions

absolutely — 'Shall we go home now?' 'Absolutely.'
definitely — The situation is definitely worse now than a year ago.
exactly — 'So you think we should sell the house?' 'Exactly.'
frankly — Frankly, I think the Internet is overrated.
surely — Surely we can't just let this happen?
airbrush — He airbrushed her out of the picture.
awareness — He works to raise awareness about AIDS.
banner — The onlookers were shouting and waving banners.
computer-manipulated — It's obviously a computer-manipulated photograph.
glossy — All the photographs are printed on glossy paper.
made-up — She was heavily made-up.
self-esteem — Playing a sport can boost your self-esteem.
apart from — Apart from being a coach, he also owns a shop.
for instance — He's very sad. For instance, he's always crying.
furthermore — He is too old; furthermore, he has health problems.
moreover — The rent is low; moreover, the location is perfect.
factory farming — A lot of people are against factory farming.
pesticide — Pesticides are a serious hazard to wildlife.
poultry — The farmer feeds the poultry every morning.

Module 3

PAGE 25

Media use

celebrity — We invited a number of minor celebrities.
chat show — He's been asked to host a chat show.

current affairs — Kate likes to keep up with current affairs.
discussion — Their discussion became very heated.
file sharing — Is file sharing legal or illegal? It depends.
game show — Bob won his car on a game show.
phone-in — The radio phone-in was a great success.
podcast — This programme is also available as a podcast.
quality — I only buy the quality newspapers, not the tabloids.
radio — She works for a local radio station.
reference — The book became a standard work of reference.
search engine — Which search engine do you prefer to use?
sitcom — There have been many successful TV sitcoms.
tabloid — Tabloid reports are often about scandals.
wiki — Ordinary users can edit the content of a wiki.

Idiomatic language (1)

a storm in a teacup — He made a fuss but it was a storm in a teacup!
breathe a sigh of relief — We breathed a sigh of relief afterwards.
dodge a bullet — You dodged a bullet by saying no to that job.
lose your head — He never loses his head in a crisis.
not the end of the world — It's bad, but it's not the end of the world.
run out of steam — I just let her yell until she runs out of steam.
be/get used to — I do the dishes every day, so I'm used to it.
catastrophe — The oil spill caused an ecological catastrophe.
downgrade — The hurricane has been downgraded to a storm.
exaggerate — It's difficult to exaggerate the importance of sleep.
nuclear reactor — How safe are Europe's nuclear reactors?
overreact — Investors overreacted to the stock market news.
panic — Everyone is in a state of panic following the attacks.
puddle — Children splashed through the puddles.
seafront — We stayed in a hotel on the seafront.
update — The report provides an update on recent progress.
ambitious — The bridge is an ambitious engineering project.
avoid — Everyone seemed to be avoiding Nick.
be drowning in sth — The country is drowning in debt.
be not worth (doing sth) — It's not worth worrying about.
coverage — The story received widespread media coverage.
distort — His account was badly distorted by the press.
extensively — The scandal was covered extensively in the media.
financial — It was a good film, but not a financial success.
literally — Dad was literally blazing with anger.
matter — Will it matter if I'm a little late?
minor — They played a minor role in local government.
no news is good news — He hasn't contacted me, but no news is good news.
not mind (sth) — I don't mind the heat; in fact, I quite like it.
pause — He paused for breath, then continued up the hill.
regret — I now regret leaving school so young.
scandal — The college was involved in a drugs scandal.
trashy — I never read trashy novels.
trivial — We were punished for the most trivial offences.
tumour — He died of a brain tumour.
vampire — I don't believe vampires exist.
worthwhile — He wanted to do a worthwhile job.
adapt — The book was adapted for television.
April Fools' Day — People play tricks on each other on April Fools' Day.
at first — At first, Gregory was shy and hardly spoke.
boarding pass — You can't get on a plane without a boarding pass.
crater — The meteorite left a huge crater in Mexico.
deception — She didn't have the courage to admit to her deception.
Halloween — Halloween is on 31st October.
hum — Machines hummed on the factory floor.
impact — A meteorite impact destroyed the dinosaurs.
interruption — We can talk here without interruptions.
in the end — What did you decide in the end?
listener — The radio programme has over a million listeners.
meteorite — A large meteorite collided with Earth years ago.
parody — They performed a funny parody of classical dance.
professor — He's a professor of French literature.
speedy — He made a speedy recovery from injury.
spoof — The play is a spoof on Shakespeare's Julius Caesar.
squash — Do you play squash?
trick — She soon realised she'd been tricked.
update — Did you hear the latest news update?
absurd — It's absurd to waste food when people are starving.
breakthrough — This is a major breakthrough in technology.
broad — The show aims to reach a broad audience.
category — There are five categories of worker.
classify — We'd classify her novels under 'Romance'.
contradictory — The two reports of the incident were contradictory.
convey — What meaning does the poem convey to you?
crucial — Growth is crucial to the country's economy.
dumb down — Complex issues are often dumbed down in the media.
effectively — The poor are effectively excluded from politics.
fascinating — That sounds absolutely fascinating.
graduate — He's a graduate of Edinburgh University.
humanities — Most humanities graduates know little about science.
immense — This is an issue of immense importance.
impression — Arriving late won't create a very good impression.
infidelity — Marital infidelity is one of the main causes of divorce.
methodology — The experiment didn't follow the correct methodology.
objectively — Viewed objectively, the issue is not very important.
over-simplified — The report gave an over-simplified view of the situation.
pointless — Life just seemed pointless to me.
pomegranate — I don't know why people like pomegranate juice.
quote — The statistics he quoted were inaccurate.
reinforce — The film reinforces the idea that lawyers are dishonest.
relevant — We received all the relevant information.
sensational — Sensational stories are what sells newspapers.
simplistic — This is a very simplistic approach to the problem.
study — More studies are needed before this can be proven.
unconfirmed — There are unconfirmed reports of fighting in the region.
wacky — He thinks it's 'wacky', but I think it's just weird.
cabin crew — The plane has a cabin crew of six.
concept — He has an unusual concept for a new drama series.
duo — Do you like the new comedy duo?
racial — This country has a broad range of racial groups.
repetition — The job involves a lot of repetition.
satire — She's a comedian who does political satire.
sexual — 'Boys don't cry' is a common sexual stereotype.
snobbish — Her family seems snobbish.
stewardess — Sharon works as a flight attendant.
voiceover — His job is doing voiceovers on TV.

Module 4

Page 35 — Advertising

aftershave — What aftershave are you wearing?
billboard — Her face appears on billboards around the world.
commercial — He makes a living by acting in commercials.
covert advert — This is a covert advert rather than a message.
direct mail — They advertise by sending out direct mail.
dramatic — The team had a dramatic victory yesterday.
endorsement — A celebrity endorsement can be expensive.
hi-fi (system) — Liam spent a lot of money on a new hi-fi system.
junk mail — All I seem to get is bills and junk mail!
pop-up — You can set your browser to block pop-ups.
product review — I want a new camera, so I'll read the online product reviews.
sexist — A sexist attitude usually offends people.
spam — You can block spam with this software.
sponsor — The competition was sponsored by British Airways.
tasteless — He made a tasteless remark about her.
washing powder — I need to get some more washing powder.
window shopping — She likes window shopping, but she doesn't buy much.
app — I downloaded a great new diary app.
be driven (by) — Driven by jealousy, Phil started spying on his wife.
bombard — I hate being bombarded with advertising.
brand — What brand of detergent do you use?
broadcast — The interview was broadcast live across Europe.
critical — Many parents are strongly critical of the school.
dry-clean — You'll have to dry-clean that jacket - you can't wash it.
exclusive — This offer is exclusive to readers of our paper.
focus — She tried to focus her mind on her work.
fool — I was fooled into believing their promises.
guilty — I feel guilty about forgetting her birthday.
influence — That's not likely to influence his decision.
look up to — I've always looked up to Bill for his courage.
market — If you could market this, you'd make a fortune.
marketer — Lucy works as a marketer with a sales company.
must-have — This is a must-have item for business travellers.
praise — Jane was praised by her teacher.
set up — Can someone set the equipment up?
software — She loaded the new word-processing software.
target — The adverts are targeted at young people.
trolley — I knocked over a pile of tins with my supermarket trolley.
UV radiation — UV radiation from the sun can cause skin problems.

Word pairs

bit by bit — The situation is improving bit by bit.
by and large — Charities, by and large, do not pay tax.
now and then — I just use it now and then, not all the time.
once and for all — Let's settle this matter once and for all.
pick and choose — Come on, you haven't got time to pick and choose.
sick and tired — I'm sick and tired of your excuses.
sooner or later — His wife's bound to find out sooner or later.
antioxidant — Antioxidants may prevent diseases such as cancer.
baldness — All the men in my family suffer from baldness.
comparatively — Comparatively few people have the disease.

connectivity	There's a growing demand for high-speed connectivity.
convince	Her arguments didn't convince anyone.
far and wide	His fame spread far and wide.
at your fingertips	We have all the facts at our fingertips.
follicle	Hair follicles can become infected.
high-definition	The TV channel now offers high-definition broadcasts.
lotion	Don't forget to use suntan lotion on holiday.
pharmaceutical	The pharmaceutical industry makes enormous profits.
price tag	It's difficult to put a price tag on the project.
processor	Should I upgrade the processor in my PC?
property	This herb is said to have healing properties.
rabies	Squirrels may carry rabies.
reversal	We've seen a dramatic reversal in population decline.
reverse	We must reverse this trend.
vaccinate	All children should be vaccinated against measles.
value for money	At only £45 a night, the hotel is great value for money.
blank	The screen suddenly went blank.
calculator	I'll need a calculator to add up these figures.
cursor	Use the cursor to click on the link.
open-source	Linux uses open-source software.
overheat	I think the engine's overheating again.
phishing	This anti-virus program protects you against phishing.
power supply	There seems to be a fault with the power supply.
reboot	You'll have to switch off and reboot.
spyware	Your computer has been infected by spyware.
targeted ad	Targeted ads are often aimed at small children.
agency	The advertising agency is looking for new employees.
creativity	Teachers encourage creativity in their pupils.
dropout	He was a high-school dropout, but he made a fortune.
pessimistic	He's pessimistic about the peace process.
promote	She's in London to promote her new book.
consumer protection	The country has very few consumer protection laws.
fuzzy	All the photos I took with my new camera were fuzzy.
go off	I've set the alarm clock to go off at 7:00.
LCD	My watch has an LCD display.
legal action	She took legal action against the hospital.
satisfactory	None of the solutions was satisfactory.
virtually	He was virtually unknown before running for office.

Module 5

Page 45 — Health

anxious	He was anxious about the results.
appetite	Walking gives me an appetite for dinner.
breast	Breast cancer affects many women.
bruise	She fell off her bike and bruised her knee.
cancer	A lot of cancers can now be treated.
chickenpox	I got chickenpox when I was a child.
cholera	How many people die from cholera every year?
collarbone	He broke his collarbone when he fell off his bike.
constipation	A high-fibre diet helps prevent constipation.
graze	I fell on the gravel and grazed my knee.
heart attack	Ted died of a heart attack last week.
hepatitis	He contracted hepatitis recently.
irritable	Jo was tired, irritable, and depressed.
kidney	She's on the waiting list for a kidney transplant.
ligament	He tore a ligament in his left knee.
liver	Phil may need a liver transplant.
lung	Smoking can cause lung cancer.
measles	Measles is a common childhood disease.
meningitis	He's seriously ill with meningitis.
migraine	I can't go to work - I've got a migraine.
mumps	Most people get mumps when they are little.
on edge	Paul felt on edge about meeting Lisa.
over-tired	When I get over-tired I also get bad-tempered.
pull a muscle	He's pulled a muscle and won't play in the match.
rash	She had a nasty rash on her arm.
rib	She broke six ribs in the accident.
salmonella	Salmonella poisoning is caused by bacteria in food.
sinusitis	The doctor said I had sinusitis.
sprain	I fell down the steps and sprained my ankle.
strain	I've strained a muscle in my leg.
stroke	He had a stroke when he was 50.
tuberculosis (TB)	TB is no longer common in the Western world.
tear	She tore a muscle in her leg.
tendon	Tom has damaged his Achilles tendon.
typhoid	An outbreak of typhoid is likely after the disaster.
under the weather	You look a bit under the weather.

Compounds

anabolic steroid	The cyclist was found guilty of using anabolic steroids.
far-reaching	Tourism had far-reaching effects on the local culture.
first-rate	He's a first-rate surgeon.
full-time	They're looking for full-time staff at the library.
heart attack	Her died of a heart attack.
heart rate	Immediately his heart rate increased.
heart rhythm	He had an irregular heart rhythm.
lactic acid	Exercise produces lactic acid in the muscles.
long-term	The long-term effects of the drug are not yet known.
muscle contraction	Muscle contraction produces movement.
performance-enhancing	Some athletes use performance-enhancing drugs.
speed limit	There's a speed limit of 50kmh on this road.
top-level	Top-level athletes can earn a lot of money.
world-class	He has proved himself a world-class athlete.
world record	He set a new world record for the event.
breakdown	The breakdown of glucose in the body releases energy.
deplete	Salmon populations have been severely depleted.
exhausted	You look absolutely exhausted.
physiology	Sports scientists have to study physiology.
tissue	Training increases the amount of muscle tissue.
check-up	It's important to have regular checkups.
deadline	It has to be in before the deadline of July 1st.
goal	His goal was to set up his own business.
heart disease	Heart disease is a huge health problem.
hedonist	A hedonist lives only for pleasure.
impulse	I bought this on impulse, and now I don't like it.
irresponsible	Dan is completely irresponsible about money.
precisely	He arrived at precisely 4 o'clock.
reckless	He was found guilty of reckless driving.
stable	Children like a stable environment.
curable	Is this form of cancer curable?
inequality	There are inequalities in wealth distribution.
infant mortality	The infant mortality rate in the country is high.
life expectancy	Life expectancy has risen steadily.
mid-income	Mid-income families will feel the effects most.
preventable	Every one of these deaths is preventable.
sanitation	Poor sanitation is a problem in slums.
alcoholism	He suffered from alcoholism in later life.
bond	There is usually a strong bond between twins.
cholesterol	My cholesterol levels are too high.
closely-knit	The village is a closely-knit community.
found	Eton College was founded in 1440.
predictable	The snow had a predictable effect on traffic.
puzzled	Alice had a puzzled expression on her face.
suicide	What makes people commit suicide?
vulnerability	Poor health increases vulnerability to this disease.
acupuncture	Acupuncture is said to help with a range of problems.
alternative medicine	Herbal remedies are popular in alternative medicine.
chronic	Mike suffers from chronic heart disease.
contrast	The film contrasts the lives of rich and poor.
curriculum	Languages are a central part of the school curriculum.
fatigue	He's suffering from physical and mental fatigue.
herbal medicine	The Chinese are very keen on herbal medicine.
holistic	They have great faith in holistic medicine.
homeopath	She went to a homeopath to see if he could help her.
homeopathy	Scientific research disproves the claims of homeopathy.
nevertheless	What you said was true; nevertheless, it was unkind.
practitioner	Lucy is a practitioner of alternative medicine.
prescribe	The doctor prescribed painkillers for my back.
proof	There is no proof that this treatment offers any benefits.
scientific	Their decisions were not based on scientific evidence.
side effect	This medicine has no harmful side effects.
therapist	Bryony is training as a speech therapist.

Module 6

Page 55 — Describing people

absent-minded	Grandad's rather absent-minded.
analytical	This course develops students' analytical skills.
articulate	I teach a class of articulate 17-year-olds.
bite your lip	She paused uncertainly, biting her lip.
blink	I blinked as I came out into the sunlight.
bright	He was an exceptionally bright child.
dedicated	She's a dedicated, thoughtful teacher.
dreamy	He's dreamy and not at all practical.
driven	He claims he is not a driven workaholic.
eccentric	His eccentric behaviour lost him his job.
fearless	These dogs are absolutely fearless.
frown	She frowned as she read the letter.
giggle	Stop giggling or you'll have to leave the room.
grin	She grinned at me, her eyes sparkling.
logical	He took a logical approach to the problem.
meticulous	Their planning and preparation were meticulous.
modest	He's always modest about his achievements.
reclusive	He's reclusive and is seldom seen in public.

reserved	Ellen was a shy, reserved girl.
self-confident	Jan's very self-confident.
shrug your shoulders	I just shrugged my shoulders and ignored him.
single-minded	He worked with single-minded determination.
tap your feet	She tapped her feet in time to the music.
thoughtful	It was thoughtful of you to remember my birthday.
witty	Laura's very witty.
anaesthetic	Most operations are done under anaesthetic.
ancestor	Lions and house cats evolved from a common ancestor.
be descended from	The people here are descended from the Vikings.
beak	A bird's beak shows what sort of food it eats.
characteristic	Violence is a characteristic of people in his family.
disperse	Police used tear gas to disperse the crowd.
distant	We could hear the sound of distant gunfire.
extract	I've only seen short extracts from the film.
joint	The two ministers have issued a joint statement.
mathematician	I was never much of a mathematician.
microbiologist	Microbiologists have studied the disease for years.
natural selection	Darwin proposed the theory of natural selection.
offspring	Most male animals have no contact with their offspring.
outline	The president outlined plans to deal with the problem.
physicist	Physicists don't yet understand the phenomenon.
radical	He has put forward some very radical ideas.
reproduce	The turtles return to the coast to reproduce.
seldom	Karen had seldom seen him so angry.
theology	He studied theology at college.
transform	Industrialisation transformed the landscape.

Word families

beg	She begged us to help her.
exclaim	'No!' she exclaimed in shock.
inquire	'Why are you doing that?' the boy inquired.
observe	The researchers observed the event closely.
snarl	'Shut up,' he snarled.
stare (at)	She stared at me in disbelief.
stride	He strode towards her.
stroll	We were strolling along, laughing and joking.
tiptoe	His mother tiptoed into the room.
whisper	James whispered something to Mike.
agent	Our agent in Rio deals with all our Brazilian business.
brick	Protesters threw stones and bricks.
capture	Government troops have captured the rebel leader.
carriage	She hired an old-fashioned carriage for her wedding.
consulting room	Please knock before entering the consulting room.
(the) Continent	We spent our holiday travelling on the Continent.
curiosity	Margaret looked at him with curiosity.
equal	He treats all his staff as equals.
harmless	He's a bit simple, but he's quite harmless.
investigate	The police are investigating the incident.
midday	I'm meeting him at midday.
pallid	His pallid skin showed he was unwell.
persecution	Celebrities complain of persecution by the press.
philosopher	Ken thinks he's a bit of a philosopher.
shatter	The plate hit the floor and shattered into tiny bits.
shutter	They closed the shutters to keep out the sun.
sinister	He was a handsome man in a sinister sort of way.
spy	He was arrested as a Soviet spy.
sunken	Her eyes looked dull and sunken.
thug	He was beaten up by a gang of young thugs.
clarify	Could you clarify that for me?
day job	He's writing a book but he still has a day job.
folk singer	Bill is a professional folk singer.
pay and conditions	Workers demanded better pay and conditions.
semi-professional	He's a semi-professional boxer.
workload	She's got a heavy workload.
assume	I assume that he knows the facts.
be bound to	An accident was bound to happen on that road.
coincidence	It was a coincidence that we arrived at the same time.
complex	This is a complex issue with no easy answers.
computer terminal	The room was full of computer terminals.
concerto	Who composed this concerto?
diligence	Diligence is necessary for success.
industriousness	Teachers praised their students' industriousness.
peer	Teenagers care greatly about what their peers think.
supposed to	The castle is supposed to be haunted.
tycoon	He made millions of dollars as a property tycoon.
bad-tempered	I'm quite bad-tempered in the morning.
expressive	She has very expressive eyes.
strike (sb)	It struck me that I was the only woman present.

Module 7

Page 65 Communities

abandoned	The inner city has many abandoned buildings.
boarded-up	We passed a few boarded-up shops.
burnt-out	We also saw several burnt-out cars.
cultural diversity	Our country is proud of its cultural diversity.
decent	Don't you have a decent jacket?
gang	Gangs of kids are always hanging around the mall.
hang out	Where do the youngsters hang out?
have a say	The workers had no say in how the factory was run.
heavy traffic	We were stuck in heavy traffic for ages.
housing	We need affordable housing for local people.
keep to yourself	The neighbours are quiet and keep to themselves.
lock	Did you lock the car?
nosy	Don't be so nosy!
privacy	In a large family you don't get much privacy.
riot	His murder triggered vicious race riots.
sense of community	There is a real sense of community in the area.

Multi-part verbs (3)

be off	I must be off now.
be over	I'm so glad the mid-term exams are over.
get on with (sth)	If you're busy, I'll let you get on with your work.
get stuck	Our car got stuck crossing the river.
hang around	I hung around for an hour but he never came.
head on to	We headed on to our next destination.
set up	Let's set up camp here.
stack away	They stacked away the chairs at the back of the hall.
aspect	Alcoholism affects all aspects of family life.
canter	Horses walk, trot, canter or gallop.
centre of attention	Rob loves being the centre of attention.
cynical	He has a cynical view of human nature.
efficient	Ranching is not an efficient use of land.
enviable	He's in the enviable position of not having to work.
existence	Peasants led a miserable existence in those days.
-free	We had a trouble-free journey.
grassland	The grassland stretched as far as the horizon.
hectic	I've had a pretty hectic day.
herd	He keeps a herd of cattle and a few sheep.
horseman	Mongolians are fantastic horsemen.
hospitality	Thanks for your hospitality during my stay.
make camp	It was dark by the time we made camp.
melancholy	The music suited her melancholy mood.
not give a damn	I don't give a damn about her problems.
numerous	Numerous attempts have been made to hide the truth.
pang	She felt a pang of guilt.
pass	The mountain pass was narrow and winding.
pasture	He moved his sheep to their summer pasture.
saddle	She fell off because her saddle slipped.
selfish	How can you be so selfish?
serenity	I love the serenity of these mountain lakes.
steppe	The world's largest steppe region is found in Russia.
stray	The sheepdog rounded up some stray sheep.
track	The track led through dense forest.
treacherous	Loose rocks made climbing treacherous.
assertive	If you aren't assertive, people will take advantage of you.
chronology	The book includes a chronology of his life and works.
establish	They plan to establish a new research centre here.
feminist	She's been an outspoken feminist for over twenty years.
hypothetical	Brennan brought up a hypothetical case to make his point.
matriarchal	The people lived in a matriarchal society.
occur	The explosion occurred at 5:30.
permanent	Make a permanent change in your eating habits.
right	It's on right after the six o'clock news.
separate	At this point the satellite separates from its launcher.
slaughter	All of these animals will be slaughtered for their meat.
table manners	Her children have good table manners.
take a turn	The situation took a turn for the worse.
be fine by (sb)	If he wants to do it, that's fine by me.
be sure about	Are you sure about what to do?
had better	I think you'd better ask Jo first.
liberty	The statue represents the fight for liberty and equality.
see if/whether	I'll see if he wants to join us for a coffee.
would rather	I'd rather have a quiet night in front of the TV.
adopt	Sally was adopted when she was four.
alpha male	The alpha male always got to the food first.
altruism	The work of charities is based on altruism.
be biased	He accused the judges of being biased.
be tempted (to do sth)	I'm tempted to buy that dress.
bonobo	The bonobo is the closest living relative to humans.
deny	It can't be denied that this is an important event.
hierarchy	She's at the top of the corporate hierarchy.

Homo sapiens	Our species is called Homo sapiens.
in disguise	'Tax reform' is just a tax increase in disguise.
orphaned	AIDS in Africa leaves many orphaned children.
self-interest	His offer was motivated by self-interest.
solidarity	They expressed solidarity with the workers.
sympathetic	I'm sympathetic towards her point of view.
yawn	Alan stretched and yawned.
beetroot	Let's get some beetroot to have with the salad.
corridor	Please wait in the corridor until your name is called.
execution	Public executions were common in the past.
head	He headed the ball into the goal.

Module 8

Page 75 Landscape

aqueduct	This Roman aqueduct brought water into the town.
arch	The bridge has three wide arches.
bay	Our house has a view across the bay.
column	The building has four columns supporting the entrance.
coniferous	The larch and pine are both coniferous trees.
deciduous	Most of the trees in my garden are deciduous.
dome	The dome of St Paul's cathedral is a London landmark.
estuary	The Thames estuary has many species of wild bird.
fjord	The Norwegian coast has thousands of fjords.
glacier	Many glaciers in the Arctic appear to be melting.
gorge	Cheddar Gorge is a well-known English beauty spot.
marble	The columns were of white marble.
moorland	Scotland has large areas of open moorland.
pampas	Winters are generally mild on the pampas.
panel	There was a glass panel in the wall facing me.
peak	Snow-capped mountain peaks were all around.
prairie	Once, huge herds of bison roamed the prairies.
savanna	There African savanna is the natural habitat of lions.
shingle	The waves were crashing on the shingle.
spring	There are several hot springs in the area.
stained glass	The stained glass windows were replaced in 2004.
statue	Churchill's statue stands in Parliament Square.
stone circle	The Ring of Brodgar is a stone circle.
tundra	Few species can survive on the Arctic tundra.
ash	Volcanic ash filled the skies.
burial site	Archaeologists learn a lot from ancient burial sites.
claim	The earthquake claimed over 3,000 lives.
destruction	Floods caused widespread destruction.
disrupt	Traffic was disrupted by a bomb hoax.
dormant	Is the volcano dormant or extinct?
duct	Ken developed a problem with his tear ducts.
dust	The wind blew dust over a large area.
eruption	A volcanic eruption is a fantastic sight!
famine	A million people are facing famine.
hemisphere	This is the largest airport in the Northern hemisphere.
insight	We have no insight into the causes of the event.
obscure	The view was obscured by mist.
offering	People leave offerings to the goddess Pele.
preserve	The bodies were preserved by the volcanic ash.
sacrifice	Children were often sacrificed to the Sun god.
tragic	They mourned the tragic death of their son.
widespread	The storm caused widespread damage.

Noun endings

advance	They fought to halt the enemy's advance.
deterioration	The deterioration of the economy is worrying.
exposure	Exposure to the sun can cause skin cancer.
humanity	We want a healthy environment for all humanity.
hypothesis	We haven't yet confirmed our hypothesis.
solidity	This material has the same solidity as concrete.
strength	How do they test the strength of these structures?
thickness	The thickness of the walls is 5 feet.
bronze	The athlete who finishes third wins a bronze medal.
chapter	This chapter discusses how people use power.
coyote	You often see coyotes in this area.
creeper	This creeper turns from green to red in autumn.
decay	Historic buildings are being allowed to decay.
firefighter	Many firefighters lost their lives on 9-11.
fungi	There are some strange fungi growing on the wall.
harbour	The yacht left the harbour and headed out to sea.
humankind	This invention will benefit all humankind.
ice age	The Earth has experienced several Ice Ages.
indicate	Research indicates that global warming is increasing.
indifferent	Sarah was indifferent to him, and it hurt.
pharaoh	Who was the first pharaoh of Ancient Egypt?
principal	Their principal concern was to save human lives.
pump	My bicycle pump was stolen today.
rust	There were large patches of rust on the car.
subway	Boston has the oldest subway system in the USA.
swallow up	New developments are swallowing up the countryside.
tomb	Lenin's tomb is a well-known Moscow landmark.
vault	The bank will keep your valuables in its vault.
worthless	The house was full of worthless junk.
diesel	Our new car has a diesel engine.
discourage (from)	His parents discouraged him from becoming an artist.
dock	Several yachts were tied up at the dock.
hydraulic	A hydraulic pump moves the liquid.
pressurise	They pressurise the water, and that turns the wheel.
stall	Her parents run a market stall in Leeds.
steam	The engines are driven by steam.
walkway	The two buildings are connected by a covered walkway.
be aware of (sth)	They were aware of the company's problems.
drainage	They need to improve the town's drainage system.
insignificant	Our problems are insignificant in comparison.
intact	Only the medieval tower is still intact.
interior	The interior of the church was dark.
project	She projected the slide onto the wall.
striking	I'd call him striking rather than handsome.
sundial	Henry has a sundial in his garden.

Adjectives

breathtaking	The view from my hotel window was breathtaking.
enormous	The house has an enormous garden.
extraordinary	He has extraordinary talent.
eye-catching	We need an eye-catching design for the poster.
good-natured	He's very good-natured, and never loses his temper.
hospitable	The local people were very kind and hospitable.
marvellous	'How was your holiday?' 'Marvellous!'
picturesque	We spent our holiday in a picturesque fishing village.
welcoming	Everyone was very welcoming.
slum	The slums have been replaced with low-cost housing.

Module 9

Page 85 Business and work

ambition	Her ambition was to run in the Olympics.
chain store	I prefer local shops to chain stores.
civil servant	They plan to reduce the number of civil servants.
community service	He was sentenced to community service.
corner shop	I'm going to the corner shop to get a pint of milk.
department store	There's a large department store in town.
hypermarket	The huge hypermarket sells absolutely everything.
inefficient	Local government was inefficient.
inexpensive	Painting is an inexpensive hobby.
multinational (company)	Multinationals have made large investments in Thailand.
overpriced	I'm not buying that overpriced rubbish!
programmer	My brother's a computer programmer.
provider	Who's your internet provider?
punctual	She's always very punctual.
self-employed	My dad's a self-employed plumber.
service	We offer a wide range of financial services.

Idiomatic language (2)

by word of mouth	A lot of information is passed on by word of mouth.
clock up	I clocked up 90,000 miles in my Ford.
cloud sb's vision	Fear had clouded his vision.
in the long run	Moving to Spain will pay off in the long run.
pay off	Teamwork paid off when they won the match.
take matters into your own hands	Don't take matters into your own hands – leave it to the police.
backstage	Can we go backstage after the concert?
conference	Experts from around the world attended the conference.
controversial	This is a highly controversial issue.
entrepreneur	He started off as a teenage entrepreneur.
exaggeration	It's an exaggeration to say that we're close friends.
generate	Tourism generates income for local communities.
gig	The band are doing a gig here tonight.
grounding	I got lots of groundings for coming home late.
hybrid	This music is a hybrid of different kinds of music.
improvise	Jazz musicians often improvise.
input	Farmers contributed most of the input into the survey.
label	Their new release is on the Ace Sounds label.
mainstream	Deaf children can be included in mainstream education.
perspective	The novel is written from a child's perspective.
quirky	I like his quirky sense of humour.
reach	Cable TV reaches a huge audience.
restrict	I'm restricting myself to two cigarettes a day.
revenue	Strikes have cost £20 million in lost revenue.
sponsored	And now for another sponsored ad break.
spot	Can you spot the differences between these pictures?

accuse	Smith accused her of lying.
applicant	Applicants will be interviewed today.
apprenticeship	He did an apprenticeship as a printer.
chairman	Who's the chairman of the committee?
ease	This will ease the burden on taxpayers.
expectations	The album didn't live up to our expectations.
fire	The airline fired several pilots.
GCSE	Adam took his GCSEs last year.
inflation	Inflation is now running at over 16%.
in (good/perfect/	The economy is in worse shape now than it was last
year.	bad, etc.) shape
loan	The bank makes loans to private businesses.
public relations	He works for a public relations company.
salon	How often do you go to a hair salon?
sceptical	I'm sceptical about what I read in the press.
union	Are you planning to join the union?
unpaid	James does a lot of unpaid work for charity.
unsuitable	The book is unsuitable for children.

Business

brainstorm ideas	Employees get together and brainstorm ideas.
find a gap in the market	She found a gap in the market, and made a fortune with her new products.
identify potential users	How can we identify potential customers?
produce a prototype	He wants to produce a prototype of the new car.
do market research	They did market research, then advertised the product.
unique selling points	Please list the unique selling points of your idea.
study the competition	I went to the trade fair to study the competition.
facility	Is there a call-back facility on this phone?
in a hurry	Sorry, I can't stop, I'm in a hurry.
translation	She read the letter and gave us a translation.
up-to-date	I need up-to-date information.
acquire	We acquired this property very cheaply.
conscious	Without conscious thought, she took his hand.
disadvantage	Both methods have their advantages and disadvantages.
first impression	Always make a good first impression.
guideline	Please follow these general guidelines.
intuition	Intuition told her it was unwise to argue.
investment	We bought the property as an investment.
judgment	In my judgment, we should accept his offer.
relatively	The system is relatively easy to use.
snap decision	Don't make a snap decision that you'll regret later.
stockbroker	Tim's dad works as a stockbroker in London.
straightforward	Installing the program is straightforward.
strategy	What's their long-term economic strategy?
arts and crafts	There's an arts and crafts fair here next month.
essential	A good diet is essential for everyone.
grape	Dave ate a whole bunch of grapes.
instructor	My driving instructor thinks I'll pass my test.
providing/provided	You can use the car, provided you're back by 6:00.
vital	It's vital to keep accurate records.

Module 10

Page 95 — Style

appealing	He has an appealing combination of wit and good looks.
beige	Early computers were all beige.
bizarre	Her appearance is always rather bizarre.
burgundy	That burgundy skirt goes well with your hair.
checked	Have you got a checked blouse that I can borrow?
close-fitting	His close-fitting shirt showed off his muscles.
corduroy	He wore a corduroy jacket and flannel trousers.
cream	A cream carpet is very difficult to keep clean.
crimson	She looked stunning in a crimson dress.
dated	That dress looks a bit dated now.
durable	Wool is a durable material.
environmentally friendly	Are these products environmentally friendly?
feminine	Dianne loved pretty, feminine things.
functional	Her clothes are pretty, but not very functional.
impractical	James was full of impractical plans.
innovative	He has an innovative approach to teaching.
linen	That linen jacket is very expensive.
masculine	The décor in his flat is very masculine.
ostentatious	She wore ostentatious gold jewellery.
outrageous	That's such an outrageous hairstyle!
scarlet	That scarlet lipstick doesn't suit her.
sophisticated	She designs very sophisticated clothes.
striped	I got a striped shirt for my birthday.
stylish	She's a stylish woman in her forties.
tacky	The room was full of tacky ornaments.
trendy	Mike likes to eat at trendy restaurants.
turquoise	Turquoise is a mixture of blue and green.
unoriginal	That's a pretty unoriginal suggestion.
user-friendly	I need a user-friendly guide to this software.
V-necked	Marie doesn't like V-necked sweaters.
velvet	Do you like these velvet curtains?
wool	She was wearing a pure wool skirt.
architect	A famous architect designed this building.
canteen	The workers eat meals in the factory canteen.
citrus fruit	Citrus fruit is good for you.
classic	This is one of the classic designs of the last century.
freak	He's a bit of a fitness freak.
futuristic	The futuristic building is the pride of the city.
icon	Bob Dylan was a cultural icon in the 1960s.
lamppost	He crashed into a lamppost.
Nobel Prize	Marie Curie won the Nobel Prize twice.
pay tribute (to)	He paid tribute to all who had died in the struggle.
universal	These stories have universal appeal.

Prefixes

automated	The production process is now fully automated.
automobile	The automobile industry is facing many challenges.
autopilot	The plane was on autopilot for much of the flight.
insecure	She's very insecure about her appearance.
overambitious	His plan was overambitious.
overcrowded	Staff had to work in overcrowded conditions.
pre-charged	The batteries in this camera don't come pre-charged.
preview	They showed a short preview of the film.
recharge	I need to recharge my phone – the battery's dead.
reinvent	The politician reinvented his public image.
underestimate	We underestimated how hard it would be.
underused	We bought an iPad, but it's pretty underused.
unsure	If you are unsure about anything, just ask.
butler	They were so wealthy that they even had a butler!
cargo	A ship carrying a cargo of oil has run aground.
compliment	Bob complimented me on my new hairstyle.
en route	We stayed there en route to London.
hire (sth) out	The company hires out boats to tourists.
internal combustion engine	The internal combustion engine creates pollution.
mobility	The army's effectiveness depends on its mobility.
mode	I normally use the 'auto' mode on my camera.
neatly	Can't you write more neatly?
pedal	She put her foot down on the accelerator pedal.
sensor	The sensor detects any movement.
vehicle	Have you locked your vehicle?
aerial	Do I need a new TV aerial to get HD broadcasts?
chronologically	The paintings are displayed chronologically.
crash	The system crashed and I lost my work.
gear	His mountain bike had 18 gears.
glitch	A software glitch delayed the project.
interference	Do mobile phones cause interference on TVs?
shares	They sold their shares for a good price.
sub-topic	Split your outline into topics and sub-topics.
technical	Technical problems caused a delay.
auction	They held an art auction to raise money.
bare	She felt the sun warm on her bare arms.
breeze	There were flowers waving in the breeze.
flash	Did the flash go off?
flesh	His flesh was red and covered in sores.
flutter	Dead leaves fluttered slowly to the ground.
glamour	Designer clothes are all about glamour.
grate	Leaves clogged the grate over the drain.
halter dress	Jen was wearing a black halter dress.
innocence	In our innocence we believed what we were told.
lightweight	Take a lightweight jacket in case it gets cool.
onlooker	Some onlookers gathered at the scene of the crash.
permit	You are not permitted to leave until the exam is over.
pleated	She wore a classic pleated skirt.
portray	Religion was portrayed in a negative way.
possibility	There's a possibility that he'll leave.
prohibition	They want prohibition of the sale of firearms.
timeless	I love the timeless beauty of Venice.
waistband	This waistband is cutting into my stomach.
A level	She decided to do her A levels.
excursion	We went on a school excursion to London Zoo.
fine art	Can photography be considered fine art?
graphic design	He was trained in graphic design.
individual	Some students need more individual attention.
interior design	He has an MA in interior design.
residence	We stayed in a student residence.
studio	This is the photographer's studio.
vegan	She used to be a vegan.

Language Choice

Contents

MODULE 1: LANGUAGE CHOICE

PRACTICE

1 Talking about relationships **Complete the description.**

My name's Jason and I suppose I'm quite shy - I've got a few very close friends. My girlfriend is called Mary. We met each [1]*other* at a club about a year ago. I suppose we get [2]________ well together because we have similar [3]________ and tastes. We go [4]________ together two or three times a week and use NetFriends to [5]________ in touch the rest of the time. I've got a small family with only two cousins and one [6]________ - my dad's sister. We are not very [7]________ as a family and we hardly ever see each other because they live in Australia. I get on especially well [8]________ my mum although we sometimes argue a bit. My mum and I [9]________ a lot in common and we have a similar [10]________ of humour. She can be very funny, you know!

2 Multi-part verbs (1) **Order the words to make sentences.**

1 finish / to / is / it / up to / you / that project

It is up to you to finish that project.

2 got / in touch / with / last / old friend / an / me / week

3 computers / the time / take / we / into / account / we spend / should / on

4 parking system / they / a new / put / have / in place / in the town centre

5 pay / you / attention to / should / the safety instructions

6 get / communication / of / modern technology / in the way / can

3 Result linkers **Rewrite the sentences using the words in brackets.**

1 I got bored in the film because it was so long. (such)

It was such a long film that I got bored.

2 He plays football really well and he'll probably be a professional. (so)

3 She was very tired and slept for twelve hours. (so)

4 The party was brilliant and everyone had a great time. (such)

5 The exam was really difficult and most of the class failed. (such)

6 We arrived very late and missed most of the game. (so)

REFERENCE

Talking about relationships

*I've got a big family with lots of **aunts, uncles** and fifteen **cousins**. At home, I've got two **sisters, a half-brother** and a **stepbrother**. We are very **close as a family** and we **get on well together** but of course we sometimes have rows. I get on especially well with my cousin Fred and we **have a lot in common** and **a similar sense of humour**. We always have **a real laugh together** and **help each other out** when we've got problems. My **best friend** is called Tom and we **got to know each other** when we were teammates in the village football team. I suppose we **get on well together** because we **have similar interests and tastes** and we **trust each other**. We **go out together** every weekend and use Facebook to **keep in touch** during the week.*

Multi-part verbs (1)

These verbs are different from typical multi-part verbs (e.g. *get up, get on with*) because they have nouns and pronouns in them.

*You should **take into account** the battery life when you buy a new mobile.* (think about)
*He spent so much time playing computer games that it **got in the way of** his relationship with his girlfriend.* (negatively affected)
*I didn't **pay attention to** my science teacher and I revised the wrong things for the exam.* (listen to)
*I need to **get in touch with** the trainer of my football team to ask about the game on Saturday.* (contact)
*The school is going to **put in place** a new wi-fi system throughout the whole school.* (install)
***It is up to you** to study for the exam. Nobody else can do it for you.* (your responsibility)

Result linkers

These linkers are used to explain the result of an action or situation.

so + adjective/adverb + that
*I'm **so** tired **that** I can hardly keep my eyes open.*
*He arrived **so** late **that** he missed most of the game.*

such + a/an (adjective) + noun/pronoun + that
*It was **such** an exciting game **that** I forgot to ring my girlfriend.*
*The film was **such** a long one **that** I fell asleep towards the end.*

MODULE 1: LANGUAGE CHOICE

PRACTICE

4 Present and past tenses **Complete the sentences with the correct form of the verbs in brackets.**

1 I *don't understand* (not understand) people who ________ (fall) in love at first sight.
2 When I ________ (see) Lucy for the first time in summer, she ________ (practise) yoga in the park.
3 When my grandparents ________ (meet), my granddad ________ (be) in the army for a few years.
4 It's strange. Brian ________ (always / prefer) blondes but now he ________ (go out) with Mary for a few weeks and her hair ________ (be) really black.
5 ________ (you / wait) for Julia? I ________ (just / see) her with Nick. I think they ________ (be) in love.
6 Mark ________ (never / have) a girlfriend but now I think he ________ (think) of asking Martha out.
7 Yesterday I ________ (realise) that my brother (not meet) my girlfriend.
8 What ________ (you / do) when I ________ (call) you last night?

5 Present and past tenses **Complete the sentences with the correct form of the verbs in brackets. Use the context to help you decide.**

1 You're bored with your boyfriend: I *have been going out* (go out) with him for eight months.
2 You're very active on social networking sites: I ________ (use) Facebook a lot.
3 You want to explain what you're busy with at the moment: I ________ (write) an email to Lena.
4 You want to explain why you broke up with your boyfriend: I dumped him when I found out he ________ (cheat) on me for ages.
5 You're describing the situation in the past: It ________ (rain) when I met Carol.
6 You're talking about your romantic experiences so far: I ________ (have) three boyfriends.
7 You're talking about your actions last night: I ________ (come) home at 6 p.m. and ________ (go) to bed.
8 You're talking about your current girlfriend: I ________ (be) in love with her for three months.

6 Quantity **Rewrite the sentences using the words in brackets.**

1 We've got no time left. (any)
We haven't got any time left.
2 Both my parents are tall. (neither)
____
3 All my friends are rich. (none)
____
4 I haven't got a lot of money. (little)
____
5 There are very few people in the shop. (hardly)
____
6 Peter has more friends than David. (fewer)
____
7 Jane spent more than half of her money. (most)
____
8 There aren't many teenagers in my family. (few)
____

REFERENCE

Present and past tenses

Present Simple

We use the Present Simple to talk about:

- **activities that happen regularly, habits and routines.**
  *I usually **go** out on Saturdays.*
- **feelings, opinions, permanent situations.**
  *We **like** people similar to us.*

Present Continuous

We use the Present Continuous to talk about:

- **things happening exactly at the time of speaking.**
  *Look, that girl **is trying** to chat up your boyfriend.*
- **things happening around now, not necessarily at the time of speaking.**
  *She **is looking** for a new flatmate.*

Present Perfect

We use the Present Perfect to talk about:

- **past events that have consequences in the present.**
  ***I've met** the most gorgeous man in the world. (I'm in love)*
- **past events, when it doesn't matter when exactly they happened.**
  *They**'ve been** to most clubs in our city.*
- **situations that started in the past and are still going on.**
  ***I've** always **believed** in love at first sight.*

Present Perfect Continuous

We use the Present Perfect Continuous to talk about:

- **activities that started in the past and are still going on.**
  ***I've been dating** a law student for some time.*
- **activities (finished or not) which have some consequences in the present.**
  *You look slimmer. **Have** you **been exercising** recently?*

Past tenses

See page 7.

Quantity

	uncountable nouns	plural countable nouns
all	all music	all homes
most = more than half	most food	most teens
a lot of / plenty of	a lot of time / plenty of money	a lot of shops / plenty of friends
many	–	many people
much	much freedom	–
some	some respect	some kids
several = some	–	several families
little = not much	little discipline	–
a little = some	a little time	–
less	less understanding	–
few = not many	–	few emails
a few = some	–	a few boys
fewer	–	fewer problems
(hardly) any = (almost) no	hardly any support	hardly any students
no	no love	no children
none of = not any of	–	none of the parents

We use *all, most, many, much, some, (a) few, (a) little and none + of* in front of pronouns, possessive adjectives and *the* ... when we refer to a specific group or category:
*Mike has read **all of his** books.*

We do not use *none* with a verb in the negative form.
We use *both (of)* and *neither of* to talk about two people or things. *Both* is always plural:
***Both** students come from large families.*

We can use *both* or *both of* in front of possessive adjectives and *the* + plural noun:
***Both (of) my** parents are strict. **Both (of) the** boys love games.*
We use *both of* in front of pronouns:
***Both of** us are learning to drive.*

We use *neither of* in front of plural pronouns, possessive adjectives and *the* + plural nouns. The verb can be singular or plural:
***Neither of them** could win the competition.*

We do not use *neither* with a verb in the negative form.

MODULE 2: LANGUAGE CHOICE

PRACTICE

7 Past Perfect Continuous **Complete the sentences with the Past Perfect Continuous form of the verbs in brackets.**

1 A charity funded prizes for the international science competition that the children *had been preparing* (prepare) for.
2 I didn't know what my brother ________ (save) money for.
3 My mother ________ (use) these cosmetics for years when it turned out they contained heavy metals.
4 I realised that my classmates ________ (work) in an animal shelter since the beginning of the school year.
5 We felt exhausted because we ________ (walk) with heavy backpacks for five hours.
6 I ________ (look for) a job for weeks when I saw an advert for a job with an NGO.

8 Past Perfect or Past Perfect Continuous **Complete the sentences with the correct form, Past Perfect or Past Perfect Continuous, of the verbs in brackets.**

1 We *had been waiting* (wait) for the bus for a long time when a man offered us a lift.
2 We found out that our school ________ (be) the best school in our city 20 years earlier.
3 I helped the woman carry her shopping because she ________ (push) her shopping trolley with difficulty.
4 I couldn't fall asleep because I ________ (watch) horror films all evening.
5 I didn't know that my father ________ (travel) to Africa as a student.
6 I failed the exam because I ________ (not read) the most important book.

9 Emphasis **Order the words to make sentences.**

1 I / my grandmother's house / is / a place / love / really
A place I really love is my grandmother's house.
2 I admire / animals / the ones / are / the people / who help
____
3 tennis player / I like most / is / the / Novak Djokovic
____
4 for the environment / I / like / the ones that / the organisations / are / fight
____
5 to animals / are / I / those who / the people / dislike / are cruel
____
6 of whales / is / I / the hunting / the thing / hate
____

10 Linking prepositions **Choose the correct linking prepositions to complete the sentences.**

1 My sister works as a volunteer in hospital *because of*/*in spite of* her very busy timetable.
2 He was really helpful *because of*/*in addition to* being very nice.
3 As a *result of*/*except for* the pressure from the local youth, the school organised a film festival.
4 I try to be nice to people *instead of*/*in addition to* treating everyone like an enemy.
5 *Apart from*/*In spite of* reading a lot about ecology, we're doing research on water pollution.
6 I like all animals *because of*/*except for* snakes.

REFERENCE

Past tenses

Past Simple

We use the Past Simple to talk about past events, situations or habits when we know when they happened:

*We **met** during the demonstration.*
*I **didn't know** Mary as a child.*
*I **went** to the cinema a lot when I was at university.*

Past Continuous

We use the Past Continuous to talk about activities that continued for some time in the past or formed a background to past events:

*It **was raining** all night.*
*We **were doing** shopping when we heard the news.*

Past Perfect

We use the Past Perfect to talk about an event or situation in the past which happened before other past events:

*We couldn't enter go in because someone **had locked** the door.*

When we use the Past Simple and the Past Perfect in one sentence, the Past Perfect refers to an earlier event:

*She **went** to the demonstration although she **had heard about possible violence.***

Past Perfect Continuous

We use the Past Perfect Continuous to talk about longer activities in the past that happened before another past event:

*The police arrested him because he **had been running** an illegal casino.*

would / used to

We use *would* or *used to* to talk about past habits and states that do not happen anymore.

- ***Used to* can be used for both states and repeated actions:**
  *He **used to be** slim.*
  *He **used to buy** a lot of fast food.*
- ***Would* can be used for actions only:**
  ***When he was a student, he** would go **to every protest march**.*

Emphasis

To add more emphasis we can change the word order of a sentence and put the object at the beginning:

I really hate cruelty to animals.
***The thing I really hate** is cruelty to animals.*

Singular object:

***The thing I really dislike** is whale hunting.*
***Someone I really admire** is Nelson Mandela.*
***The football team I love** is Spurs.*

Plural object:

***The people I really admire** are those who/the ones who campaign for what they believe in.*
***The issues I think are really important** are those which/the ones which are related to the environment.*
***The animals I am afraid of** are those with/the ones with no legs!*

Linking prepositions

We use these prepositions to link ideas. They can be followed by a noun or the *-ing* form of a verb.

*The picnic was cancelled **because** of the weather.* (= as a consequence of)
*People put on weight **as a result** of eating too much fast food.* (= as a consequence of)
*We are planning to prepare a short film **in addition to** the posters.* (= as well as)
***Apart from** working in a zoo, he runs an animal charity.* (= not including)
***Except for** my sister, we all work for different NGOs.* (= not including)
*I preferred to eat something vegetarian **instead of** a steak.* (= rather than)
*They are building a new skyscraper **in spite of** the protests.* (= although)

MODULE 2: LANGUAGE CHOICE

PRACTICE

11 Talking about big issues **Complete the dialogue.**

A: What issues do you really care [1] *about* ? I support campaigns [2] ________ the environment and I support those [3] ________ cruelty to animals, too.

B: I think other [4] ________ are more important. I don't really [5] ________ of campaigns against animal testing. In my opinion, we should really do something [6] ________ homelessness.

A: But you can't do everything, can you? I'm in an [7] ________ that defends the environment.

B: Well, I'm not in an organisation and I've never worked [8] ________ a volunteer, but I often donate money.

A: I haven't got much money but I've been [9] ________ lots of demonstrations. There's one on Saturday against [10] ________ power. Do you want to come?

12 Multi-part verbs (2) **Rewrite the sentences using multi-part verbs.**

1 George Clooney has publicly protested about the situation in Sudan.

George Clooney has spoken out about the situation in Sudan.

2 I let my friend take my place on the bus.
3 I often remember my time at primary school.
4 I think we should go on that walk earlier.
5 Two young girls were told to get off the bus.
6 The army tried to stop the protest movement.

13 *as* **Rewrite the sentences using *as*.**

1 I am a student and I that think we should have fewer exams.

As a student I think that we should have fewer exams. [example]

2 I realised that I was in love with her while she was talking to me.
3 I bought some things at the market and also went to the bank.
4 She is less punctual than her brother.
5 I'd like to join an NGO like Amnesty International.
6 I would like to study Chinese because I am interested in the culture.

REFERENCE

Talking about big issues

*There are **a lot of issues that I care about. I support campaigns for** human rights, wildlife conservation and **I support those against** child poverty. However, **I don't really approve of campaigns against** animal testing and nuclear power. I think **other issues are more important, like** freedom of speech and corruption. In my opinion, **we should really do something about** child poverty. I am not in any NGOs and I have never **been on a demonstration or protest march** but I have **donated money, signed a petition** and **worked as a volunteer**.*

Multi-part verbs (2)

*When I **look back on** the last year, I can remember lots of great experiences.* (remember)
*Martin Luther King **spoke out** inequality.* (said something publicly in protest)
*The man **was thrown off** the train.* (was forced to leave)
*They **brought forward** the time of the game.* (was moved to an earlier time)
*A man **gave up** his seat to me because I was looking so tired.* (gave to someone else)
*The government tried to **put down** the movement for more human rights.* (stop by force)

as

Addition linker:
***As well as** arriving late for the exam she forgot her pen.*

Giving examples:
*There are lots of things you can do for the environment, **such as** saving energy and feeding the birds in the winter.*

Time linker (at the same time as):
***As** I was coming into the room, I saw my friend Alan.*

Reason linker:
*I arrived late **as** there was a terrible traffic jam.*

Comparison:
*Alice is nearly **as** tall **as** her brother Tom.*
*I played **as** well **as** Colin but he was very lucky and beat me.*

Describing a role:
***As** a user of the buses, I think they should be more punctual.*

MODULE 3: LANGUAGE CHOICE

PRACTICE

14 Talking about media use **Complete the interview.**

A: Where do you get your news?
B: Whenever I want to keep [1]________ with the latest news, I read a national tabloid [2]________.
A: Where do you get information about your interests?
B: I often [3]________ out online film magazines like Empire. And when I'm tired, to [4]________ out, I read fashion magazines.
A: Do you use social media?
B: Yes, when I want to express my own opinions, I [5]________ comments on Twitter. And to [6]________ up with my friends' news, I use Facebook.

15 Idiomatic language (1) **Complete the expressions in the sentences.**

1 When the bus crashed, everybody ___lost___ their ___heads___ and screamed.
2 Don't worry about the exam. It's not the ________ of the ________ if you've failed.
3 There was an argument about the team but it was all a ________ in a ________ because we won easily.
4 My mum ________ a ________ of ________ when I passed my exams.

16 *Used to* **Rewrite the sentences using different forms of *used to*.**

1 When I was young, I always got up early.
I ___used to get up early___ when I was young.
2 He usually gets up early in the summer.
He is ________ in the summer.
3 When I was in France, I got into eating snails.
I ________ eating snails when I was in France.
4 When I lived in London, I did not usually go out on my own.
I did not ________ when I lived in London.
5 I hardly ever go to the cinema these days.
I ________ going to the cinema these days.

REFERENCE

Talking about media use

To get information about my interests, I ***often check out*** *online sports magazines like www.tennis.com.* ***Whenever I want to keep up with the latest news,*** *I read national newspapers like The Guardian.* ***To chill out,*** *I read celebrity websites like www.hellomagazine.com.* ***My favourite TV programmes are*** *Mad Men and The Tudors. When I want to express my own opinions,* ***I post comments on*** *the school website. When I am* ***doing research for school work,*** *I use www.refdesk.com. To* ***catch up with my friends' news and give my own,*** *I use Facebook.*

Idiomatic language (1)

Everyone was worried about changing the school timetable but it was all ***a storm in a teacup*** *and it was fine.* (an event whose importance was exaggerated)
We have worked very hard on that project but we ***are running out of steam.*** (are losing momentum)
It would be good to take notes in the talk but it's ***not the end of the world*** *if you don't.* (not so bad)
I ***breathed a sigh of relief*** *when I passed my exam.* (was no longer worried)
When the fire alarm went on the train, a lot of people ***lost their heads.*** (panicked)
We all thought the tornado would hit our house but luckily we ***dodged the bullet.*** (escaped danger)

Used to

We use *used to* talk about a past habit:
When I was at primary school, I ***used to*** *finish at 3.00 pm and I* ***didn't use to*** *have so much homework!*
We use *to be used to* to describe being familiar with something:
I am used to *getting up early but* ***I'm not used to*** *leaving home before half-past eight.*
We use *get used to* to describe becoming familiar with something.
When I was on holiday in Spain, ***I got used to*** *eating the food but* ***I didn't get used to*** *having dinner at 10pm!*

MODULE 3: LANGUAGE CHOICE

PRACTICE

17 Verb patterns **Choose the infinitive or the *-ing* form of the verb to complete the sentences.**

1 Football games are boring. I stopped to *watch/watching* them a long time ago.
2 If your computer freezes, try to *talk/talking* to it.
3 I didn't remember to *pay/paying* for my mobile phone so I was cut off.
4 I never regret to *go/going* to the cinema, I love all films.
5 I forgot to *save/saving* that file and all my work was lost.
6 I regret to *announce/announcing* that the competition has been cancelled.
7 On the way home, I stopped to *look/looking* at the newest netbooks.
8 Sorry, I forgot to *bring/bringing* your book.
9 I remember to *read/reading* this article. It must be an old text.
10 I speak very fast. I try to *slow/slowing* down but it's hard.

18 Verb patterns **Complete the dialogue with the infinitive or the *-ing* form of the verbs in brackets.**

A: Let's hurry! I want [1] *to watch* (watch) the evening news.
B: The news? I gave up [2] ________ (watch) TV news a long time ago. I've got used to [3] ________ (check) the news regularly on the internet. It's faster.
A: Maybe. But it requires [4] ________ (be) online all the time. And I'm trying [5] ________ (cut down) my time online. I used [6] ________ (spend) a lot of time on the internet but it's bad for your concentration. I start [7] ________ (read) a news item, then I notice another one so I stop [8] ________ (read) the previous one and so on. I don't mind [9] ________ (watch) films online but I avoid [10] ________ (go) to news websites. They are horrible
B: And I can't stand [11] ________ (listen) to people complaining about the internet. If you can't learn [12] ________ (use) it wisely, just don't use it at all.

19 Negation **Complete the sentences with words from the box.**

any	few	hardly (~~x2~~)	little
no	no one	nothing	

1 I read *hardly* any political articles.
2 I looked out but saw ________ in the darkness.
3 ________ enjoys visits to the dentist.
4 They left me without ________ help.
5 Very ________ people understand nuclear physics.
6 They ________ ever went to parties.
7 They had ________ idea how difficult the experiment was.
8 I wanted to buy that book but had very ________ money.

REFERENCE

Verb patterns

1 Verb + *to* + infinitive

We decided to go home.

These verbs take this pattern:
afford, agree, choose, decide, expect, help, learn, manage, need, offer, plan, promise, refuse, start, want, would like/love/prefer, used to

These verbs take the pattern: verb + *someone* + *to* + infinitive
advise, allow, beg, help, invite, order, tell, want, would like/love/prefer
I want you to stay.

2 Verb/expression + *-ing* form

He finished writing his book.

These verbs take this pattern:
adore, avoid, be used to, can't stand, consider, enjoy, finish, give up, hate, it's worth, like, love, not mind, prefer, require, risk, start, suggest

***Hate, like* and *love* can also be followed by 'to' infinitive.**

3 Verb + *-ing* form or infinitive

Some verbs can take both patterns but there is a difference in meaning.
*I **stopped to buy** The Times.*
(I interrupted my walk in order to buy *The Times.*)
*I **stopped buying** The Times.*
(I don't buy *The Times* anymore.)

*We **regret to inform** you that you failed the test.*
(We feel sorry before we inform you.)
*I **regret informing** him that he failed the test.*
(I feel sorry after I informed him.)

*I **forgot to lock** the door.*
(I didn't lock the door because I forgot.)
*I **forgot locking** the door.*
(I locked the door and later forgot that I had done it.)

*I **remembered to watch** the news.*
(I watched the news, I didn't forget about this obligation.)
*I **remember watching** the news but don't know what happened later.*
(I recall that I watched the news.)

***Try to run** faster!*
(See if you can run faster, test yourself.)
***Try watching** it with the sound off.*
(Watch with the sound off as an experiment.)

Negation

In English, negative meanings can be expressed in different ways:
*They do**n't** do **any** useful work.*
(They do **no** useful work.)
*There are students **without any** money.*
(There are students with **no** money.)
*They gave **no** explanation.*
(They did**n't** give **any** explanation.)
*Very **few** students are interested in science.*
(**Not many** students are interested in science.)
*We have very **little** time.*
(We do**n't** have **much** time.)
***No one** likes him.*
(People do**n't** like him.)
*We know **nothing** about it.*
(We do**n't** know **anything** about it.)
*We have **nowhere** to go.*
(We do**n't** have **anywhere** to go.)
*We **never** work at night.* (We do**n't ever** work at night.)
*They **hardly** speak English.*
(They **almost** do**n't** speak English.)
*People **hardly ever** read science articles.*
(People **almost never** read science articles.)
*We had **hardly any** information about the new drug.*
(We have **almost no** information about the new drug.)

MODULE 4: LANGUAGE CHOICE

PRACTICE

20 The Passive **Use the beginnings to rewrite the sentences using the Passive. Use a 'by phrase' when necessary.**

1 I hope someone can repair my bike for tomorrow.
I hope my bike _can be repaired for tomorrow_ .

2 They are not going to sell the new car in the USA.
The new car ______________________________
______________________________ .

3 People were talking about Nike's latest advertising campaign everywhere.
Nike's latest advertising campaign ______________
______________________________ .

4 We didn't know that all our teachers had seen our documentary about the school.
We didn't know that our documentary about the school ______________________________
______________________________ .

5 They are designing a new drug against acne.
A new drug against acne ______________________
______________________________ .

6 They shouldn't broadcast some commercials before 10 p.m.
Some commercials ______________________________
______________________________ .

7 Film stars often advertise expensive goods.
Expensive goods ______________________________
______________________________ .

8 Someone has damaged my laptop.
My laptop ______________________________
______________________________ .

21 The Passive **Complete the dialogue with the correct passive form of the verbs in brackets.**

A: I hate adverts, they 1 _should be forbidden_ (should / forbid). I hate 2 ________ (tell) what to buy.

B: But they 3 ________ (need). Thanks to ads, people 4 ________ (inform) about new products.

A: I don't need 5 ________ (inform) about a new mobile phone by a huge billboard. Last year, a new Nokia mobile phone 6 ________ (advertise) on TV, radio, the internet, everywhere. Imagine how much money 7 ________ (spend) on these ads!

B: I agree advertising money 8 ________ (could / use) in a more sensible way. But ads 9 ________ (produce) for centuries and I don't think they 10 ________ (can / ban).

22 Nouns **Complete the table with the nouns below. Use a dictionary if necessary.**

~~colour~~ women billboard news feet people police euro tights information box newspaper men furniture parents chess language jeans tomato flu clothes drink goods

uncountable nouns	
countable nouns with regular plural	*colour*
countable nouns with irregular plural	
plural nouns with no singular form	

REFERENCE

The Passive

We use the Passive

- **to focus on the action when we don't know or it's not important who does it.**
  *These computers **are made in** China.*
  *The window **has been broken**.*
- **to focus on the action when it is obvious who does it.**
  *He **was operated on** this morning.*
  *The robbers **will be found**.*
- **to put emphasis on who does the action (we use a 'by phrase' at the end of the sentence).**
  *This ad **has been produced by** my uncle's company.*
  *This cake **was made** by Susan.*

Present Simple	*The door **is** always **locked**.*
Present Continuous	*The kitchen **is being redecorated**.*
Present Perfect	*The car **has been stolen**.*
Past Simple	*The campaign **was stopped**.*
Past Continuous	*The shop **was being burgled** when we arrived.*
Past Perfect	*The shampoo **hadn't been sold** in the USA before.*
***be going to* + infinitive**	The slogan **is going to be used** in all the ads.
***will* + infinitive**	*They **will be rejected** by their friends.*
***modal* + infinitive**	*Drugs **can't be sold** in shops.* *The bill **should be paid** at once.* *They **have to be told** what to do.*
passive infinitive	*I want **to be liked** by everybody.* *The film must **be advertised** online.*
passive *-ing* form	*No one likes **being criticised** in public.* *Avoid **being seen** by the head teacher.*

Nouns

In English there are different types of nouns:

- **Uncountable nouns**
  e.g.: history, news, information, time
  *There is no further **information** about the survivors.*
- **Countable nouns**
  with a regular plural: agency ➜ agencies, girl ➜ girls
  *There are twelve **girls** and fifteen **boys** in my class.*
  *with an irregular plural: man ➜ men, foot ➜ feet, tooth ➜ **teeth***
  I broke two teeth when I fell off the ladder.
- **Plural nouns with no singular form**
  e.g.: people, police, media, scissors, stairs, clothes

Some nouns refer to groups of people (group, crew, team, staff, etc.). They are used with singular verbs when we see the group as one unit:

*Our team **was** the best.* (the team as a unit, as one body)
*My family **is** very big.* (the family is a unit)

They are used with plural verbs when we see the group as individuals:

*The team **are discussing** the tactics for today's game.* (every member of the team has an individual opinion)
*When I was having an operation, my family **were waiting** outside.* (we think about the family members as individuals)

MODULE 4: LANGUAGE CHOICE

PRACTICE

23 Talking about advertising **Complete the dialogue.**

A: Do you think advertising ___*affects*___ everyone?
B: Yes, I do. What sort of ads do you like?
A: The adverts I like the 2__________ are some TV ads because they can be very clever and funny.
B: I like those too but I can't 3__________ sexist or tasteless adverts.
A: I agree completely, but the ads that 4__________ me most are the 5__________ that come up on your screen when you're on the Net. I hate them!

24 Word pairs **Complete the sentences with word pairs.**

1 I think that ___*sooner*___ or ___*later*___ people will use more electric cars - it is inevitable.
2 __________ and __________ phones these days have internet connections.
3 I am __________ and __________ of this weather - it's been raining for months!
4 I don't go skiing very often but __________ and __________ we go to a nearby resort.
5 This city is changing slowly - __________ by __________ it's becoming a better place to live.

25 *need* **Choose the best option, a) or b).**

1 My shirt needs *a) to be washed (b)washing)* immediately - I spilt milk over it.
2 That cough medicine needs *a) to be taken b) taking* twice a day.
3 Your hair needs *a) to be cut b) cutting* - it's really long!
4 Our dog needs *a) to be taken out b) taking out* three times a day.
5 That tennis racquet is broken and needs *a) to be repaired b) repairing* now.

26 Preferences **Rewrite the sentences using the words in brackets.**

1 They don't want you to tell anybody. (rather)
They'd rather you didn't tell anybody.
2 We want you to come early. (prefer)
3 I don't want to go to the cinema tonight. (rather)
4 She would like to have dinner at home. (prefer)

REFERENCE

Talking about advertising

I think **advertising affects everyone. The adverts I like the most are** magazine ads. **The ones that annoy me most are** pop-up ads. **For me, the best adverts are those that are** humorous, but I **can't stand ads that are** dull. **My least favourite ones are those for** gadgets. **Whenever I buy something important, I shop around a lot.**

Word pairs

Word pairs are fixed expressions. You cannot change the order *(e.g.* **black and white** *- not ~~white and black~~).*

- **Repeated words**
  More and more *people are using tablet computers.*
  My hair got better ***bit by bit*** *with that shampoo.*
  I speak ***face to face*** *with friends in the café.*
- **Opposites**
  Sooner or later*, printed books will disappear.*
  I go out ***now and then****, but I usually stay at home.*
- **Synonyms**
  I'm ***sick and tired*** *of waiting for buses that are late.*
  You can ***pick and choose*** *any app you want.*

need

We use ***need*** **+** ***-ing*** **when it is clear that something should be done now:**
My car ***needs repairing****, it's making a terrible noise.*
Your bedroom ***needs tidying****, it's in a terrible mess.*
We use ***need*** **+ passive infinitive when something has to be done regularly:**
The oil ***needs to be changed*** *after 20,000 kilometres.*
Your passport ***needs to be renewed*** *every 10 years.*

Preferences

Expressing what someone wants to do:
She'd prefer not to *go out.*
We'd rather *stay at home.*
Expressing what someone wants someone else to do:
I'd prefer you to *come to my house.*
They'd rather you *didn't come earlier.*

MODULE 5: LANGUAGE CHOICE

PRACTICE

27 Talking about health **Complete the dialogue.**

A: Have you ever [1] *broken* a bone?
B: No, but I [2]________ a muscle once when I was playing football. What about you?
A: I broke [3]________ arm once when I was skiing.
B: Really? Well, I usually have hay [4]________ when we've got exams.
A: I always feel stressed [5]________ during exams.
B: To [6]________ healthy, I have a good diet and do lots of exercise.

28 Compounds **Match the compound words below with the definitions.**

world-class heart attack far-reaching
hi-tech full-time performance-enhancing

1 for all the hours of a week during which people usually study or work *full-time*
2 having a great influence or effect
3 when someone's heart stops working normally
4 using advanced technology
5 improving an athlete's speed or strength
6 among the best in the world

29 Comparatives **Complete the sentences with the comparatives below.**

more stressful more (x3) ~~faster~~ longer
healthier more nervous better bigger

1 The *faster* he drives, the ________ I get.
2 The ________ you practise playing the guitar, the ________ you get.
3 The ________ I live here, the ________ I like it.
4 The ________ exercise you do, the ________ you become.
5 The ________ this city gets, the ________ it becomes.

REFERENCE

Talking about health

*I have **broken my finger** once and **bruised and grazed myself** several times but I've never **pulled a muscle or a tendon.** I sometimes **have headaches** and hay fever but **I've never had anything more serious, like** asthma or hepatitis. I never have problems sleeping but I do occasionally **feel over-tired** and **stressed out. To keep healthy**, I do regular exercise and have a good diet.*
***In my opinion, the most dangerous diseases in my country are probably** cancer and lung disease because a lot of people smoke.*

Compounds

Compound nouns (Two words):
anabolic steroids, heart attack, heart rate, heart rhythm, lactic acid, muscle contraction, speed limit, world record

Compound adjectives (Two words with hyphen):
far-reaching, first-rate, full-time, health-related, hi-tech, long-term, performance-enhancing, top-level, well-known, world-class

Comparatives

We use *the* ... *the* ... with comparatives to show that two things change together:

***The faster** you run, **the quicker** your heart rate gets.*
***The older** I get, **the happier** I am.*
***The more** you practise the piano, **the better** you become.*
***The more** he sleeps, **the more** tired he gets.*
***The more** money she has, **the more** she wants.*

MODULE 5: LANGUAGE CHOICE

PRACTICE

30 *will have* + third form **Use the cues to write sentences with *will have* + third form.**

1 I / pass my driving test / by next month.
I will have passed my driving test by next month.

2 you / complete your studies / before 2018
____

3 my family / move three times / by the end of this year
____

4 she / finish writing her essay / by the time the party starts
____

5 my brother / visit twenty countries / by the end of this month
____

6 we / eat all these chocolates / before the guests arrive
____

7 you / do all the work / by midnight
____

8 the house / be built / by the summer
____

31 Time clauses **Complete the sentences with the correct forms of the verbs in brackets.**

1 You *will feel* (feel) relaxed after you *have had* (have) an afternoon nap.
2 When I ________ (earn) enough money, I ________ (buy) a new computer.
3 We ________ (have) a party as soon as we ________ (finish) the school year.
4 We ________ (finish) the meeting when we ________ (discuss) all the problems.
5 As soon as I ________ (pass) my driving test, I ________ (start) driving to school.
6 You ________ (sleep) well after you ________ (drink) this herbal tea.
7 She ________ (go) jogging when she ________ (do) her homework.
8 After he ________ (find) a good job, he ________ (look) for a nice flat.

32 Time reference in the past **Use the cues and *would* or *was going to* to finish the sentence in two different ways.**

When my grandmother was ten, she didn't know that

1 war / break out soon
war would break out soon
war was going to break out soon.

2 she / have an accident that summer
____

3 her sister / be born the next year
____

4 her brother / run away from home
____

5 she / get a book of short stories for her birthday
____

6 her family / move to a big city
____

7 she / become a writer
____

8 she / write a book about her childhood
____

REFERENCE

Future

We use several verb forms to talk about future events:

Present Simple

- **to talk about fixed events in the future that we can't move (future facts):**
  *My train **leaves** in twenty minutes and **arrives** in Paris at 10.30 a.m.*
  *I **have** an exam in two weeks.*

Present Continuous

- **to talk about future events that we have arranged:**
  *I'**m leaving** tonight.*
  ***Are** you **going** to school tomorrow?*

be going to + infinitive

- **to express an intention:**
  *I'**m going to relax** more this year.*
- **to express a prediction based on something we can observe:**
  *The journey **is going to take** more time than we expected.*

will + infinitive

- **to express a prediction based on our opinions, knowledge or beliefs:**
  *They'**ll** probably **forget** to bring the food.*
  *She'**ll** certainly **come** on time.*
  We often use adverbs like *probably, maybe, certainly* in these sentences.

may/might + infinitive

- **to express a weak prediction:**
  *We **may lose** a lot of money.*
  *She **might change** her mind.*

will be + -ing

- **to talk about activities that will be in progress at a certain time in the future:**
  *At this time on Saturday, I'**ll be dancing** at your wedding.*
  *We'**ll be decorating** the Christmas tree in the morning.*

will have + third form of the verb

- **to talk about actions that will be finished before a certain time in the future:**
  *By the end the month I **will have done** seven exams.*
  ***Will** you **have achieved** anything by the time you are thirty?*

Time clauses

In time clauses referring to the future, *after when, as soon as, until, before and after,* we do not use *will.*

- **We use the Present Simple:**
  ***When** you **meet** her, you'll see how nice she is.*
- **or the Present Perfect, if we want to emphasise the fact that this action will be finished before the other one happens:**
  ***When** you'**ve finished**, I'll show you something.*
  *I'll call you **as soon as** I'**ve checked** my emails.*

Time reference in the past

When we talk about the past, we sometimes also talk about events which were in the future or past at that time. Then we use the following verb forms:

- **To talk about something that was in the future at that time:**
  *I **was** sure he **would help** me.*
  *When I last **saw** him, he was **going to get married**.*
  *I **didn't know** he **was leaving** the country the next day.*
- **We also use the conditional and time clauses to talk about events that were in the future at that time:**
  *I **realised** that if I **moved** the snake **would bite** me.*
  *Everyone **knew** that when the game **was** over, the fans **would start celebrating**.*
- **To talk about something that was already in the past at that time:**
  *I **noticed** that he **had been eating** chocolate.*
  When we met, they had lived in Italy for fifteen years.
- **To talk about events that happened at the same time as other events:**
  *It **was** obvious that he **didn't like** big parties.*
  *Then I **saw** Harry. He **was** cycling up the hill.*

MODULE 6: LANGUAGE CHOICE

PRACTICE

33 Reference **Complete the text with the words below.**

there others a ~~then~~ some this an

Einstein received a Nobel Prize in 1921. He was 42 years old [1] *then* . In 1933 he emigrated from Germany to the USA. He worked [2]_________ until his death. He became [3]_________ US citizen in 1940. Einstein published hundreds of papers. [4]_________ were on theoretical physics, [5]_________ were non-scientific works. He was [6]_________ exceptionally bright and eccentric person. [7]_________ made him a popular figure.

34 Reference **Choose the correct words to complete the dialogue.**

A: Listen! Steven Spielberg is going to make a film about Einstein.

B: I'd prefer a film about [2]_________ scientist, like Steve Jobs or Bill Gates. [3]_________ started their careers in similar ways. In addition, [4]_________ was the most creative businessman ever and [5]_________ is one of the richest people in [6]_________ world.

1 a a b some c the
2 a another b a c other
3 a all b some c both
4 a one b that c another
5 a another b the other c this
6 a the b other c a

35 Uncertainty **Rewrite the sentences using the words in brackets to make them less certain.**

1 Millionaires spend their holidays in fashionable resorts. (tend)
Millionaires tend to spend their holidays in fashionable resorts.

2 Copernicus was more interested in mathematics than astronomy. (may)
____

3 Some countries are more successful than others. (seem)
____

4 Darwin wasn't lazy. (can't)
____

5 Great actors know a lot about the way people think. (be bound to)
____

6 Leonardo da Vinci was an expert in anatomy. (clearly)
____

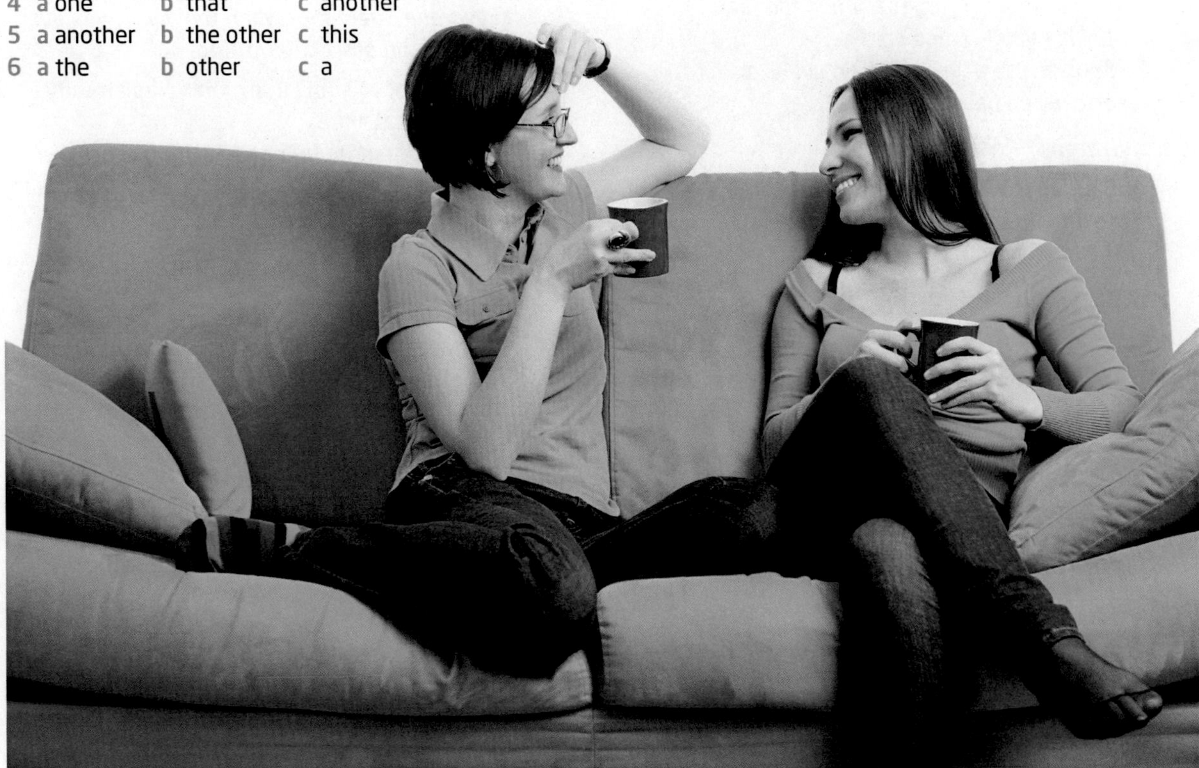

REFERENCE

Reference

There are different ways to refer to people, things, facts and actions:

- ***a/an***
  *We need **a** new car.* (we don't identify which car)
- ***the***
  ***The** school has burnt down!* (we don't know which school)
  *I read **the** book you gave me.* (we identify which book)
  ***The** sun is beautiful.* (the sun is unique)
- ***another*** (in front of singular countable nouns)
  *Would you like **another** book?* (one more)
- ***other*** (in front of plural nouns)
  *I saw him but the **other** people didn't.* (additional people)
- ***the other*** (in front of countable nouns)
  *One boy is ill, **the other** is fine.* (the remaining one)

We also use these words to refer to people, things, etc. that have been mentioned before:

- ***this/that*** **= this/that fact/event**
  *He failed his exam. **That** affected the rest of his life.*
- ***there*** **= in that place**
  I went to Paris and started a new life ***there***.
- ***then*** **= at that time**
  *They met in 1998. They were still teenagers **then**.*
- ***both*** **= two people/things**
  *Bill and Steve went out. **Both** had fun.*
- ***one*** **= a person/thing clear from the context**
  *Give me the red **one**.*
- **all/some = all/some people or things**
  *They **all** like rock music but **some** like jazz, too.*
- **others = not the people/things mentioned earlier**
  *Some people supported Darwin, **others** opposed him.*

Uncertainty

When we don't want our sentences to sound like facts, we can use different means to signal that our knowledge is not full and express doubt.

- **Modal verbs**
  *Being a genius **must** be difficult.* (= I'm **almost certain** that being a genius is difficult.)
  *He **can't** be a genius.* (= I'm **almost certain** that he is not a genius.)
  *He **may** be working on a new invention.* (= **It's possible that** he is working on a new invention.)
- **Certain verbs and expressions**
  *We **tend to** like successful people.* (statement of fact: We **like** successful people.)
  *Asian people **are supposed to** be the most hard-working in the world.* (statement of fact: Asian people **are** the most hard-working in the world.)
  *Poor people **seem** to be as happy as rich people.* (statement of fact: Poor people **are** as happy as rich people.)
  *Successful people **are bound** to work hard.* (statement of fact: Successful people **work** hard.)
- **Adverbs of probability**
  ***Perhaps/Maybe** they have inherited their money.* (= They have **probably** inherited their money. (we are very uncertain, we are guessing)
  *They have **most probably** won the lottery.* (we make a justified guess)
  *They have **clearly/obviously/certainly** earned their fortune by working hard.* (we draw a logical conclusion)

MODULE 6: LANGUAGE CHOICE

PRACTICE

36 Describing people **Complete the dialogue.**

A: So what's Alan's new girlfriend like?
B: She's very good [1] *at* getting on [2] ________ other people.
A: So you like her?
B: Well, at [3] ________ I thought she was a bit too serious. When you meet her she [4] ________ rather reserved but when you get to know her she is really good fun.
A: She sounds perfect.
B: Well, sometimes she [5] ________ to be [6] ________ competitive, but she is usually pretty relaxed.

37 Word families **Choose the correct words to complete the sentences.**

1 After lunch, we *strolled/tiptoed* along the beach.
2 He *strode/tiptoed* quietly up the stairs.
3 I rang up and *begged/inquired* what time the restaurant opened.
4 She *snarled/whispered* the answer to her friend in the exam.

38 *by/for + -ing* **Complete the sentences with the *by/for + the -ing* form of the verbs in brackets.**

1 I got here *by taking* (take) a taxi.
2 That program is ________ (design) posters and brochures.
3 I found the answer ________ (look) on the internet.
4 That phone is great ________ (take) photos.
5 I got money for my new camera ________ (sell) my old computer on eBay.

39 Emphasis **Complete the dialogue with the correct auxiliaries.**

A: Hi there, Lucy.
B: Hi, Amanda. You [1] ________ look great today!
A: Thanks. Well I [2] ________ spend a couple of hours on my hair. I'm meeting that guy Paul this evening.
B: Paul? You [3] ________ choose the good-looking ones, don't you? He's not very tall but he [4] ________ look a bit like Robert Pattinson.
A: I don't know about that but I [5] ________ love his blue eyes when I first saw him. And he [6] ________ have a lovely voice, too!

REFERENCE

Describing people

At first, she seems arrogant **but when you get to know her, you realise she's really quite** shy. **Sometimes, she tends to be slightly too** relaxed. **She is good at** debating **but she is not so good at** getting on with people.

Word families

There are often specific ways of describing things which make descriptions much more interesting.

Say/speak: ***Exclaim:*** to say something suddenly when you are surprised or angry / ***Snarl:*** to say something aggressively / ***Whisper:*** to say something very quietly
Ask: ***Beg:*** to ask for something in a way that shows you need it badly / ***Inquire:*** to ask someone for information formally
Look at: ***Observe:*** to watch someone carefully. ***Stare at:*** to look at something for a long time without moving your eyes.
Walk: ***Stride:*** to walk quickly with long steps /***Stroll:*** to walk slowly for pleasure / ***Tiptoe:*** to walk on your toes.

by/for + -ing

- **We use *by + -ing* to describe *how* something is done:**
  *He found the answer to the crossword **by using** a dictionary.*
- **We use *for + -ing* to describe *the reason* for something:**
  *I gave him directions **for getting** to my house.*

Emphasis

We use auxiliaries (*do/does/did*) in affirmative sentences to express emphasis or surprise:
*She is a great person but she **does irritate** me sometimes.*
*I was very tired towards the end of the race but **I did finish**.*

MODULE 7: LANGUAGE CHOICE

PRACTICE

40 Talking about communities **Complete the dialogue.**

A: Where do you live?
B: I've lived in a small town in the North [1] __for__ ten years.
A: What's the [2] ______ thing about living there?
B: People help each other out - there is a real [3] ______ of community. Another [4] ______ thing is that there are good sports [5] ______.
A: And what is the worst [6] ______ about it?
B: Well, there is a lot of [7] ______ traffic.

41 Multi-part verbs (3) **Replace the words in *italics* with multi-part verbs.**

1 I've got an exam tomorrow so I need to *do* my revision.
I've got an exam tomorrow so I need to get on with my revision.
2 Our car *stopped* in the snow.
3 We *waited* for ages before the concert started.
4 Goodbye, I'*m leaving*.
5 The summer *has finished* and it is getting colder.
6 We *went in the direction of* the hotel.
7 After the party we washed the plates and glasses and *put* them *away* in the cupboards.
8 They *put up* their tents under the trees.

42 Verbs of perception + infinitive/*-ing* form **Choose the best sentence, a or b, to follow the first.**

1 I heard him getting back home last night.
(a) But I went back to sleep immediately.
b He opened the door and tiptoed upstairs.
2 I saw a woman steal some earrings.
a She put them into her bag.
b She was looking nervous.
3 I smelt something burning.
a It took ten minutes to burn.
b So I turned off the toaster.
4 I watched him play football.
a He was scoring a goal.
b He scored three goals.
5 I felt something crawling up my leg.
a I looked down and saw a spider.
b It went from my ankle to my knee.

REFERENCE

Talking about communities

***I've lived here for** fifteen years and I know a lot of people. **The best thing about living here is that** people help each other out and you can trust people. I suppose you could say there is a sense of community. **Another positive thing is that** there are lots of local clubs and volunteer groups. There is always something happening. **The worst thing about my area is that** there is a lot of heavy traffic and pollution and there aren't any good shops. But it is much better than other areas where there is a lot of vandalism and crime. **My area would be better for young people if there were** better sports facilities and if young people could take part in making decisions about local issues.*

Multi-part verbs (3)

*We had to **hang around** for hours at the airport.* (wait with no particular purpose)
*When we visited the village, the people just **got on with** their daily life.* (continued)
*After the end of the rock festival, all the temporary buildings **came down**.* (were taken down)
*After the concert **was over** we **stacked away** the chairs.* (was finished; put in a pile)
*We packed everything into the car and at ten o'clock we **were off**.* (were leaving)
*The land Rover **got stuck** when they were crossing the river.* (was unable to move)
*After having lunch, we **headed on to** nature reserve.* (moved towards)
*We **set up** our tents next to the river.* (put up)

Verbs of perception + infinitive/*-ing* form

- **We use an *-ing* form to describe seeing/hearing etc. an activity happening.**
  *We **watched** them **playing** tennis.*
  *I **saw** her **crossing** the road.*
- **We use an infinitive to describe seeing/hearing etc. completed actions.**
  *I **watched** them **play** tennis. Paul won easily.*
  *We **saw** him **cross** the road and get into his car.*

MODULE 7: LANGUAGE CHOICE

PRACTICE

43 Unreal and past conditionals **Use the cues to write unreal and past conditional sentences.**

1 If I were a politician, / campaign / for peace in the world.

If I were a politician, I would campaign for peace in the world.

2 My parents wouldn't have got married if / not study / together.

____

3 If my grandmother hadn't looked after me, / have to / go to nursery school.

____

4 People would be happier if / live / in friendly communities.

____

5 If I had taken that summer job, / earn / enough to pay for my holiday.

____

6 My grandfather would've become a soldier if / not have / an accident as a child.

____

44 Mixed conditionals **Complete the mixed conditional sentences with the correct form of the verbs in brackets.**

1 If children *ran* (run) the world, corporal punishment *wouldn't have been used* (not used) in schools in the past.
2 If I________ (lock) the front door every time I come home, I________ (not be) robbed last night.
3 If our neighbourhood________ (be) safer, my parents ________ (let) me play in the street when I was a child.
4 If my neighbours________ (not be) so nosey, they ________ (not find out) about my new boyfriend.
5 If my brother ________ (not witness) a mugging last night, he ________ (not be) questioned by the police now.
6 If that new club ________ (not open) in my street last month, we ________ (not have) a place to meet.

45 *It* and *There* **Complete the text with *it is* or *there is/are*.**

I live in a small village. [1] *There are* only about fifty houses and [2]________ difficult to get there. The village is in the middle of the forest and [3]________ no buses or trains that go there. I love my village because the air is clean and [4]________ a small lake nearby. However, most young people have moved to the cities because [5]________ easier to find jobs there. But [6]________ clear that the people are happier than in crowded cities.

REFERENCE

Conditionals

We use the Present (Zero) Conditional:

- **to describe rules and situations where one event always leads to another event. In these sentences *if* means *when*.**
  *If the parents **are** happy, the children **are** happy too.*
- **to give advice or orders and to make suggestions or requests.**
  *If you **want** to make a good impression, **remember** to smile and make eye contact.*

We use the Future (First) Conditional:

- **to talk about possible future events which depend on other future events.**
  *If you **read** this report, you **will understand** our situation much better.*

We use the Unreal (Second) Conditional:

- **to talk about imagined events in the future, which are impossible or unlikely.**
  *If I studied really hard, I **could/would/might** be the best student in my school.*
- **to talk about impossible present situations.**
  *If people **had** more common sense, there **wouldn't be** any wars in the world.*
  *If I **was/were** taller, **I'd play** basketball.* (were is more formal than was)

We use the Past (Third) Conditional:

- **to talk about unreal situations in the past and their consequences that did not happen.**
  *If we **hadn't left**, we **could've/would've** seen the end of the film.* (We left so we didn't see the end.)

We use 'mixed conditionals' to talk about:

- **Imaginary past events and their hypothetical consequences in the present.**
  *If the rescue team **hadn't found** him, he **would be** dead.* (but they found him so he's alive)

In such sentences we use the pattern:

if clause main clause
If + Past Perfect, *could/would* + infinitive.

- **imaginary present situations, usually imaginary permanent states, and their hypothetical consequences in the past.**
  *If I **was** more confident, I **would've complained** about the poor service.* (I'm not confident so I didn't complain)

In such sentences we use the pattern:

if clause main clause
If + Past Simple, *would/could* + perfect infinitive

It and *There*

We use *it* as the subject of the sentence:
• to refer to something.
***The forest** was beautiful. **It** was dark green and very silky.*
• as an empty subject with no particular meaning (all sentences in English have to have a subject):
***It**'s very late.*
***It**'s time to do something.*
***It**'s possible that traditional communities will disappear.*

We use *there* as an empty subject to say that something exists or existed.
***There** was an interesting custom among the bonobos.*
***There** weren't any young people in the village.*
***There** aren't many chimpanzees here today.*

MODULE 8: LANGUAGE CHOICE

PRACTICE

46 Relative clauses **Underline the relative clauses in the sentences below and decide which are defining (D) and which are non-defining (ND). Cross out unnecessary relative pronouns and add commas where needed.**

1 I've just returned from Croatia, where I ate the most delicious seafood in the world. *ND*
2 I like to spend my holidays in a place that tourists don't go to.
3 The Eiffel Tower which was built in 1889 is the most famous tourist attraction in Paris.
4 I've always wanted to visit Milan which is the fashion capital of Italy.
5 There are some villages in Africa where people live like they did a hundred of years ago.
6 Tibet is full of tourists whose main aim is to find spiritual inspiration.

47 Sentential relatives **Rewrite each pair of sentences as one sentence.**

1 London is always crowded and noisy. This fact annoys me.
London is always crowded and noisy, which annoys me.
2 It rained throughout our holidays in Wales. The weather wasn't very enjoyable.
____
3 There are a lot of pickpockets in Barcelona. This discourages some tourists.
____
4 Thousands of tourists visit Stonehenge every year. The crowds caused the authorities to restrict access to the stones.
____
5 Most London museums are free. This is great for art lovers.
____
6 Not many people spend their holidays in Alaska. Lack of tourists makes Alaska attractive for adventurers.
____

48 Nominal relatives **Use *what* or *whatever* to rewrite the sentences in *italics*.**

A: So now we've got two hours' free time. [1] *We can do anything we want.*
We can do whatever we want.
B: [2] *I'd like to go shopping.*
A: [3] *And I'm going to sit down in a café.* I've had enough of sightseeing.
B: *Come with me!* [4] *You can help me choose the things to buy.*
A: I'm not going anywhere. [5] *I need rest.*
B: Please! [6] *I'll buy you any drink you want afterwards.*

REFERENCE

Relative clauses

We use defining relative clauses to identify the person or thing we are talking about.

I've got a friend ***who*** *has been to every continent.*
I found an old photograph ***which/that was taken in Monte Carlo.***
We have a teacher ***whose travel book has just been published.***
Do you know a place ***where we could have a cheap meal?***
I remember the moment ***when I saw the Pantheon.***

In defining relative clauses:

- we do not use commas.
- we can omit the relative pronoun *who, which* or *that* if the pronoun is not the subject of the relative clause.
  We all agreed that the museum ***(that)*** *we visited wasn't very interesting.*
- we can put a preposition at the end of the clause.
  This is the hotel ***(that)*** *we talked* ***about.***

We use non-defining relative clauses to give extra information about a person or thing which has already been identified.
We visited the Tate Modern, ***which is the most interesting museum in London.***
Daniel Libeskind, ***who has designed a lot of famous buildings,*** *is working on a new skyscraper in New York.*

In non-defining relative clauses:

- we always use commas.
- we do not use that.
  My flat, ***which*** */ ~~**that**~~ I only bought last month, is spacious and full of light.*
- we cannot omit the relative pronoun.
  The Pantheon, ***which*** *is one of the oldest buildings in Rome, is in excellent condition.*

Sentential relatives

We use sentential relatives to add more information or a comment to what was said before.
A lot of museums are free, ***which allows everybody to visit them.***
I learned three foreign languages at school, ***which has helped me a lot while travelling.***

In sentential relative clauses:

- we always use a comma.
- we use the relative pronoun *which* (not *what*).

Nominal relatives

- **We can use clauses with *what* instead of nouns (*what* = the thing that).**
  I bought ***what I wanted.***
  We are talking about ***what we could do now.***
- **To emphasise choice, we sometimes use *whatever* (= everything/anything).**
  After you've paid 15 dollars, you can eat ***whatever you want.*** (you can eat anything you want)
  They are happy with ***whatever life brings them.*** (they are happy with everything life brings them)
- **We also use nominal relatives to emphasise something.**
  What makes me happy *is my friends.* (emphasis is on *my friends*)
  What I would really like to visit *is Machu Picchu.* (emphasis on Machu Picchu)

MODULE 8: LANGUAGE CHOICE

PRACTICE

49 Talking about landscapes **Complete the sentences with the words below.**

stained tower fjords ~~area~~
landmark man-made

1 The *area* I like most is the coast of Norway because of the beautiful ________.
2 My favourite ________ landmark is the Eiffel ________ in Paris.
3 My favourite natural ________ is the Perito Moreno glacier.
4 The cathedral of Chartres in France has got beautiful ________ glass windows

50 Noun endings **Complete the description with the correct form of the words below.**

found maintain grow
~~hypothesise~~ disappear

My [1] *hypothesis* is that my town would soon disappear without humans. With the [2]________ of people, the [3]________ of plants and trees in the streets would happen quickly. With no [4]________ the buildings without strong [5]________ would collapse.

51 Conditionals **Use the cues to write sentences with *were to*.**

1 I / win the lottery / buy / a car
If I were to win the lottery, I would buy a car.
2 humans / disappear / more whales / survive
3 they / invent / time travel / I / go back 50 years
4 I / become rich / give money / to charity
5 a world war / start / millions of people / die

52 Expressions + infinitive/*-ing* form **Rewrite the sentences using the words in brackets.**

1 You must take warm clothes. (important)
It's important to take warm clothes.
2 You really should visit the gallery. (worth)
3 There's no need to take a coat. (no point)
4 I'd recommend that you take your camera. (good idea)

REFERENCE

Talking about landscape

In my country, there are *mainly mountains* ***in the west*** *although there are river valleys* ***in the east and north. Where I live there are also*** *some desert areas.* ***The area I like most is that*** *around Lake Titicaca.* ***My favourite natural landmark*** *in Bolivia is Fish Island which is an oasis in the Salar de Uyuni, the world's biggest salt lake.* ***One of my favourite man-made landmarks*** *is the cathedral in Santa Cruz.*

Noun endings

These are some common noun suffixes.
-sis: hypothesis (v. hypothesise), analysis (v. analyse)
-ity: humanity (adj. human), solidity (adj. solid), vulnerability (adj. vulnerable)
-al: arrival (v. arrive), mineral (v. mine), survival (v. survive)
-ance: disappearance (v. disappear), importance (adj. important), maintenance (v. maintain)
-th: growth (v. grow), length (adj. long), depth (adj. deep), strength (adj. strong), width (adj. wide)
-ation: foundation (v. found), imagination (v. imagine), colonisation (v. colonise), deterioration (v. deteriorate)
-ure: exposure (v. expose)
-ness: happiness (adj. happy), thickness (adj. thick), weakness (adj. weak)

Conditionals

We use *were* to to emphasise the unlikely nature of a future or hypothetical situation.
What would you do if I ***were to*** *become famous?*
If I ***were to*** *win the lottery, I would go on holiday.*

Expressions + infinitive/*-ing* form

Expressions + infinitive
It's a good idea to *put on sun cream.*
It's important to *buy a guidebook.*

Expressions + *-ing* form
There's no point *taking an umbrella.*
It's worth *going to that museum.*

MODULE 9: LANGUAGE CHOICE

PRACTICE

53 Talking about business and work **Complete the dialogue.**

A: I've got problems with my mobile again. *Lemon* [1] *offer* really poor service.
B: I agree that they're not very good [2] _______ for money. Beta are a bit better, but my favourite [3] _______ is Banana. They make great mobiles and their products are always very good [4] _______ .
A: My favourite is Aubergine, the clothes chain store. I did some [5] _______ -time work there.
B: Lucky you! I would like to get a job [6] _______ a waitress but there's nothing at the moment.
A: Well, my [7] _______ is to work to be a model.
B: I'd like to [8] _______ up my own company.

54 Idiomatic Language (2) **Rewrite the sentences using idiomatic language.**

1 My parents said to me 'you can't go out for a month!'

My parents said to me 'you're grounded for a month!'

2 In the future your smoking will be very bad for your health.
3 All her hard work has had an effect and she has got into the best university.
4 We've done a lot of driving and have done 50,000 kilometres so far this year.
5 There was no publicity for the concert but we heard about it from our friends.
6 There are a lot of problems with the film club and I'm going to solve them myself.

55 Reference **Complete the sentences.**

1 I did a clothing design course. That *'s what* started me making clothes.
2 I was out shopping. That _______ I decided to make hats.
3 I went online and asked for advice. That _______ I learnt how to make hats.
4 There's a market in my town. That _______ I sold my first hats.
5 My hats are cool. That _______ they are so successful.
6 I get a lot of support from my sister. That _______ helps me when I'm busy.

REFERENCE

Talking about business and work

I think most phone manufacturers give ***good value for money*** *but a lot of mobile phone network providers* ***offer poor services. My favourite company is*** *TopShop because its products are* ***attractive and good quality****. I dislike the local buses because the service is* ***unpunctual and unreliable as well as being over-priced****. There are few job opportunities for young people now because of the economy.* ***I have done part-time*** *work as a waitress and as a shop assistant and* ***I would like to do work experience*** *in a computer company.* ***My ambition is to*** *work for a big multinational company because I want to travel.*

Idiomatic language (2)

You're ***grounded*** *for coming home late. You can't go to that party on Saturday!*
I ***took matters into my own hands*** *and rang a taxi when nobody came to collect me.*
That new book has had no publicity but it has sold ***by word of mouth****.*
There are a lot of opportunities in computer games – ***the door is wide open*** *for a bestseller.*
Practising the piano every day ***has paid off****. He's won the school prize.*
My blog has ***clocked up*** *50,000 visitors.*
All the wealth and fame ***clouded his vision*** *and he lost many friends.*
In the long run*, the best thing to do is to study abroad and then get a job in a multinational company.*

Reference

I met her on New Year's Day. ***That's when*** *I fell in love.*
We went to Cornwall. ***That's where*** *I learn to surf.*
I forgot to buy a map. ***That's how*** *I got lost.*
It was very hot. ***That's why*** *we decided to go to the beach.*
He was given a guitar. ***That's what*** *started his career as a musician.*
She had a great teacher at school. ***That's who*** *helped her write her first poems.*

MODULE 9: LANGUAGE CHOICE

PRACTICE

56 Reporting verbs **Use the verbs in brackets to report the mini dialogues.**

1 (inquire / offer / explain)
Candidate: How much can you pay me for this job?
Manager: We can pay you £200 a week. Business is not great at the moment.
The candidate inquired how much they could pay him for that job. The manager ...

2 (advise / warn / admit)
Careers officer: You should look for a job in a restaurant. It may take weeks to find an office job.
Student: You're right, I don't want to be unemployed any longer.

____

____

3 (threaten / suggest / refuse / accuse)
Workers: We will go on strike if you don't pay us twenty percent more.
Manager: Maybe we could negotiate it.
Workers: Sorry, but no. You cheated us last time we negotiated with you.

____

____

57 Reporting **Use the beginnings to rewrite the sentences.**

1 'Rich people have to pay higher taxes', the new Prime Minister said.
The new Prime Minister said that *rich people had to pay higher taxes* .

2 It is said that smaller companies are more effective.
Smaller companies ____________________ .

3 'We're going to spend more money on education,' said the minister.
The minister said ____________________ .

4 Everyone knows that last year's economic crisis has led to very high unemployment.
Last year's crisis ____________________ .

5 It is expected that teachers will go on strike next month.
Teachers ____________________ .

6 'We will reduce youth unemployment by thirty percent next year', said the minister.
The minister said that ____________________ .

58 Infinitives **Are the infinitives in bold in the text simple (S), continuous (C), perfect (PR), passive (PS) or passive perfect (PS/PR)?**

I got my first business experience when I was fifteen. My uncle Jack, who owned a stand at a seaside resort, asked me **to sell** *(S)* sea shells while he went away for two days. On the first day I seemed **to be doing** okay but I wanted **to impress** my uncle so the next day decided **to change** my sales technique. I prepared a large advertisement saying 'Shells **to die** for! Allow yourself **to be charmed** by wonders from all over the world. Only 50p each!' My new strategy appeared **to be working** perfectly: within the first two hours I must **have had** well over a hundred customers and I seemed **to have sold** most of my uncle's stock. 'It will be great **to be praised** by Uncle Jack when he's back', I thought.
The next day, at dinner, Uncle Jack wanted **to be informed** about the shell sales. When I described my revolutionary strategy and mentioned the price of the shells, he said: 'You must **be joking**.' When I told him the whole story and very proudly showed him the £50 I had earned, he seemed **to be choking** on his potatoes. Then my aunt told me that quite a few of the shells must **have been** worth more than £10 each. I must **have been given** the price list of the most valuable shells before he left but I lost it somewhere. And my customers were too clever **to point out** that the prices were more than generous.

REFERENCE

Reporting

When we report something that was said in the past, we change the tense in the reported sentence.
'I'm thirsty.' ➜ *He said he* ***was*** *thirsty.*

We don't change the original tense if:

- **the reporting verb is in the present tense.**
  'He's nice' ➜ *Everyone says he's nice.*
- **we report a general truth.**
  'The earth is round' ➜ *Galileo said that the earth is round.*
- **we report something that is still true because the context hasn't changed.**
  'The euro is not very strong.' ➜ *The minister admitted that the euro is not very strong.*
- **we report a future event that hasn't yet happened at the moment of reporting.**
  'We're meeting the manager tomorrow.' ➜ *Julia said that they are meeting the manager tomorrow.* (if reported on the same day)
- **we report a past event that happened at a time specified in the sentence.**
  'The company was established in 1908.' ➜ *He said the company was established in 1908.*

We can use the following structures when reporting what someone said:

- *Verb + that: He* ***added that*** *his country was preparing for an economic crisis.*
  add, admit, agree, announce, believe, boast, claim, complain, deny, declare, explain, insist, remind, suggest, warn
- *Verb + to do something: She* ***agreed to sponsor*** *the charity concert.*
  agree, offer, promise, refuse, threaten
- *Verb + somebody + to do something: They* ***advised me to consult*** *a lawyer.*
  advise, beg, forbid, order, promise
- *Verb + doing something: The manager* ***admitted taking*** *company money.*
  admit, deny, suggest
- *Verb + if/whether: The woman* ***inquired if*** *the shop was open on Saturday.*
  ask, inquire, wonder

We can use impersonal report structures to report what people generally believe or say. These sentence structures are mainly used in written English.

- **We can use the subject *It* and the passive of certain verbs (*say, know, believe, report, suppose, expect, think, fear, predict*).**
  It is believed *that unemployment will rise next year.*
  It's known *that small grocery shops are losing customers.*
- **We can also use the structure subject + passive + infinitive.**

  We use an ordinary infinitive if the action reported is present or future at the time of the reporting.
  Organic farms ***are supposed*** ***<u>to produce</u>*** *five percent of all the food sold in Europe.* (It is supposed that organic farms produce five percent of all the food sold in Europe.)
  Teachers' salaries ***are expected*** ***<u>to rise</u>.*** (It is expected that teachers' salaries will rise.)

We use a perfect infinitive if the action happened before the time of reporting.
The businessman ***is supposed*** ***<u>to have run away</u>*.** (It is supposed that the businessman ran away.)
Popular brands ***are known*** ***<u>to have become</u>*** *very expensive.* (It is known that popular brands have become very expensive.)

Infinitives

We can use these infinitives (with or without *to*) in English:

- **the simple infinitive**
  You must ***decide*** *very soon.*
  We met ***to discuss*** *our options.*
- **the passive infinitive**
  I don't want ***to be criticised*** *in public.*
  They will ***be helped*** *by a team of professional event organisers.*
- **the continuous infinitive (to signal that the activity is or was in progress at the time of other events)**
  You must ***be working*** *very hard.*
  It's good ***to be doing*** *nothing for a while.*
- **the perfect infinitive (to signal that the activity happened earlier than other events)**
  They seem ***to have gone out.***
  She may ***have decided*** *to start her own business.*
- **the passive perfect infinitive**
  The bridge is said ***to have been built*** *in the thirteenth century.*
  She might ***have been cheated*** *by a bank.*

MODULE 10: LANGUAGE CHOICE

PRACTICE

59 *could/should* **Use the cues to write the second sentence for each situation.**

1 That desk lamp was cheap and beautiful. I / could / buy it

I could've bought it.

2 This colour looks awful. They / should / paint / the house white

____

3 I visited the Van Gogh museum in Amsterdam. I / could / get / a poster for my room

____

4 We were in London last year. We / could / walk / across the Millennium Bridge

____

5 The arms on this clock are hardly visible. The designer / should / make / them red

____

6 These shoes are too small. I / should / buy / a larger size

____

60 *wish* **Complete the sentences with the correct form of the verbs in brackets.**

1 I know nothing about fashion. I wish my clothes *weren't* (not be) so boring.
2 I saw a beautiful designer clock in a shop in Rome. I wish I________ (have) enough money to buy it.
3 There are a lot ugly objects in my home. I wish my parents ________ (not buy) them when they furnished the house.
4 I love hand-made pottery. I wish I ________ (can) make it myself.
5 I'm a great fan of modern art. I wish my girlfriend ________ (like) visiting galleries, too.
6 I loved my classic iPod. I wish I ________ (not lose) it.

61 Modality **Choose the correct modal verbs or expressions to complete the text.**

My father went to a private school where there were very strict rules. They [1] *had to* be in bed before 10 p.m., otherwise they were punished. They [2]________ get up at 6 a.m. and everybody took part in warm-up exercises in the fresh air. They [3]________ do that even in winter.
My mother, on the other hand, went to an alternative school which was very liberal. They [4]________ wear whatever they wanted and they [5]________ study as long at night as they wished. The only rule was that they [6] ________ come to lessons on time – being late [7]________ and was treated as a sign of disrespect for others. I think all schools [8] ________ be like my mother's school.

	a	b	c
1	a had to (circled)	b could	c didn't have to
2	a couldn't	b were required to	c weren't allowed to
3	a should	b were permitted to	c were forced to
4	a were obliged to	b were permitted to	c couldn't
5	a could	b were forbidden to	c had to
6	a had to	b weren't allowed to	c didn't have to
7	a was permitted	b wasn't allowed	c was obliged
8	a ought to	b are required to	c are forbidden to

REFERENCE

Regrets

To express regrets, we can use the verb *wish*.

- **We use *wish* + past tense to talk about things we regret about the present situation.**
  *I **wish** I **was** taller.* (I regret that I am not taller)
  *I **wish** we **had** more money.* (I don't like the fact that we don't have more money.)
- **After *wish* we can also use *were* instead of *was* for all grammatical persons.**
  *I **wish** I **were** grown-up.*
- **We use *wish* + the Past Perfect to talk about things we regret about the past.**
  *I **wish** I **had studied** harder when I was at school.* (I regret that I didn't study harder.)
  *I **wish** she **had told** me about her problems.* (I regret that she didn't tell me about her problems.)

We can also use modal verbs to talk about the things we regret about the past.

- **We use *could* + perfect infinitive to talk about things that we didn't do in the past and now regret the missed opportunity.**
  *I **could have** (could've) **learned** Spanish.* (I didn't learn Spanish because I was lazy and now I can't communicate with Spanish people.)
  *I **could have** (could've) **gone** with you on that trip.* (I decided not to go and now I regret it because the trip was great.)
- **We use *should* + perfect infinitive to talk about things that didn't happen in the past and we now think there was a mistake.**
  *He **should have** (should've) **won** the competition.* (He didn't win because he was treated unfairly by the judges/other competitors.)
  *I **should have** (should've) **told** her the truth.* (I didn't tell her the truth and the consequences were disastrous.)

Modality

We use modal verbs and expressions to talk about these situations:

- **past obligation or necessity**
  *I **was obliged** to wait for the chief designer.*
  *We **were forced** to study the history of architecture.*
  *I **had to** redecorate my room.*
  *The museum **needed** to be checked before the president's visit.*
  *The students **were required** to use pencils.*
- **permission or possibility in the past**
  *We **were allowed** to enter the museum for free.*
  *The fans **were permitted** to get Marilyn's autograph.*
  *The sofa **could** be used as a bed as well.*
- **prohibition or lack of possibility in the past**
  *I **couldn't** find the switch on my new desk lamp.*
  *We **couldn't** use our notes during the test.*
  *The actors **were forbidden** to use make-up.*
- **lack of obligation in the past**
  *We **didn't need to** put on evening clothes.*
  *The hairdresser **didn't have to** do anything – most of the actors had shaved their heads.*
- **advice**
  *You **should** design your room carefully.*
  *Schools **ought to** teach kids about art and design.*

MODULE 10: LANGUAGE CHOICE

PRACTICE

62 Talking about style Complete the dialogue.

A: What's your favourite object?
B: I think it's my new mobile phone because it [1] _looks_ classy and is very [2]________ -made.
A: Yes, I like it too. [3]________ I don't like is stuff that is [4]________ -fashioned.
B: Me neither. And I hate stuff that doesn't [5]________ properly and that looks tacky. I am very [6]________ -conscious, you know!
A: Me too! I like smart clothes. The clothes that [7]________ me best are stylish jackets and close-[8]________ trousers.

63 Prefixes Complete the words.

1 The bus was over_crowded_ and I had to stand up.
2 I felt in________ when I had to speak in public.
3 My brother is a journalist and got a pre________ of that new science fiction film.
4 I re________ my mobile phone when I got home.
5 That car is ultra-________ and uses very little petrol.

64 *Even* Rewrite the sentences so that they have the same meaning.

1 That motorbike looks really nice but it isn't very safe so I would never ride it.
That motorbike _looks really nice_. Even so, _it isn't very safe so I would never ride it_.
2 She's a really friendly and kind person; she's just a bit arrogant sometimes.
She's ________ even if ________.
3 I was late for the exam but I passed it.
I passed ________ even though ________.
4 That film is very long and a bit slow in parts but I'd recommend you to see it.
That film ________. Even so, ________.
5 My mobile cost a lot of money but it is not very good and there are problems with the battery.
My mobile is not very good and ________ even though ________.

65 *It's time ...* Rewrite the sentences starting with It's time.

1 We should have lunch right now.
It's time to have lunch.
2 They should build a new sports centre.
3 You should have your hair cut soon.
4 We should leave now or we'll miss the bus.
5 They should give sixteen-year-olds the vote.

REFERENCE

Talking about style

I think things should look simple. My favourite object is my watch because it looks stylish. What I don't like is stuff that looks dull and tasteless. I'm very style-conscious and I like clothes that are smart. The clothes that suit me best are close-fitting dark trousers and dark blue jerseys.

Prefixes

auto-: of or by yourself/itself
autobiography, automobile, autopilot, automated
in-: the opposite or lack of something
inability, indecisive, inefficient, insecure
over-: too much
overambitious, overcrowded, overpriced, oversensitive,
pre-: before something or someone
preview, pre-charged, prefix, preschool
re-: again
reinvent, recharge, reorganise, repay
ultra-: extremely
ultra-efficient, ultramodern
un-: negative, lack of or opposite
uncomfortable, unconventional, unemployed, unhelpful,
under-: less of an action or quality than is correct, needed or desired or below
underused, underestimate, underground, underwear

Even

- **We use *even so* to introduce something that is true although it is different from something you have just said.**
  *That car is comfortable. **Even so**, I'd never buy one.*
- **We use even *though* to emphasise the contrast between two pieces of information. It is stronger than *although*.**
  *I'll buy that car **even though** it's expensive.*
- **We use *even if* to emphasise that something will still be true if something else happens.**
  ***Even if** you're careful, that car uses a lot of petrol.*

It's time ...

- **We use *It's time to* ... when we make a suggestion about doing something immediately.**
  ***It's time to** go to class. Our lesson starts soon.*
- **We use *It's time (that)* ... when we state that someone should do something soon.**
  ***It's time that** you did some work for your exams.*
  ***It's time** they improved the roads.*